Sex Roles in Contemporary American Communes

Sex Roles in Contemporary American Communes

Edited by
JON WAGNER

INDIANA UNIVERSITY PRESS
BLOOMINGTON

Manufactured in the United States of America

Library of Congress Cataloging in Publication Data
Main entry under title:

Sex roles in contemporary American communes.

Contents: Sex roles in American communal utopias /
Jon Wagner—Life in a defensive society / Merrill
Singer—Inequality, chastity, and sign endogamy in
the new age brotherhood / Ilse Martin—[etc.]
   1. Communal living—United States—Addresses, essays,
lectures.   2. Sex role—United States—Addresses,
essays, lectures.   I. Wagner, Jon.
HQ971.S48   307.7   81-47571
ISBN 0-253-35187-1   AACR2
1 2 3 4 5 86 85 84 83 82

Contents

Preface

The path to this book began in one of those establishments offering beer, solace, and inspiration to the coming generation of American academicians. Dejected about the value of adding to the endless studies of Indian reservations, I was groping for some less hackneyed subject for a doctoral dissertation in social and cultural anthropology. Communes had captured my imagination, as they had captured many imaginations in 1972, and so I perked up to hear a companion's moaning diatribe about the "patriarchal" commune he had just visited with a former member of the commune. Could I meet the young woman who had introduced him to the community? After an intriguing conversation with her and a surreal visit to "the Patriarch" himself, I found myself asking and receiving permission to study what I still believe is one of the most fascinating communities in America. The "Haran" commune, then only seven years old, had received from its founder a full-blown theology, ethos, and esthetic, all centered on the notion that matriarchy is the source of evil in human history and that the promise of salvation lies in patriarchy.

It seemed somehow incongruous that a commune, which everyone knows is supposed to be egalitarian, should be so attached to patriarchy—especially when all the "expert" testimony seemed to support the notion that communes naturally avoided male dominance. Yet the scant reports from other large, organized communes seemed to point to the possibility that they were also oriented toward charismatic leadership and, in some cases, toward male supremacy. I began to realize that communes are full of surprises; so many surprises as to almost—but not quite—rule out making any sociological sense of them.

Throughout the writing of my dissertation, I longed to contact others who had studied contemporary groups, but such people were rarer than one might expect. It was that same curiosity that prompted a notice in the *Anthropology Newsletter* soliciting contributions from persons involved in the intensive study of particular communes, asking them to describe in detail the attitudes of those communities toward the nature and roles of man and woman. At first the potential contributors included scholars who had studied nineteenth-century groups through historical documents, as well as those who had observed modern groups at first hand. At the suggestion of the publisher, we whittled the project down to the contemporary groups. The result is a compendium of contemporary fieldwork in communes that is truly the first of its kind. Other works on modern groups usually have either reported the communal experience from the participant's point of view or been based on wide-ranging tours of literally dozens of groups which were necessarily limited to brief impressions strongly influenced by the communities' own deliberate image-creating efforts. This volume presents a perspective more detached and broadly comparative than the former and deeper than the latter. One may well debate whether this perspective captures the best of both worlds; one might, as my friend the Patriarch has done, charge us with being too close for minding our own business and too distant to gain any real understanding. Yet despite its shortcomings, the perspective of sociology-anthropology, with its combination of participant-observation and comparative analysis, has its own contribution to make toward the study of utopian communalism.

Communal utopias themselves offer a rare opportunity to view the interaction of human dreams with the "realities" of the human condition. The study of sex roles in these communal utopias is not only a subject of interest in its own right, since the possibility of sex-role change concerns us all, but it is also a convenient way of demarcating a particular subject for study and comparing the way in which traditional and utopian societies have attempted to treat certain perennial issues of social life. Those interested in contemporary trends of sex-role change might see a special relevance in the study of utopias, for throughout American history many utopian societies have expressed dissenting voices against prevailing sex-role ideologies, voices which often struck a chord in our cultural subconscious. These themes are discussed more fully in chapter 1, and the list of references cited in that chapter indicates a number of sources for further reading. The two that deal chiefly with communal sex roles are Muncy (1973) and Kern (1981); each of these concentrates on the nineteenth century and therefore makes a good companion to the present volume.

We do not wish to give the impression that this book represents all recent fieldwork in communal utopias, or even a representative cross section thereof. It is, as any anthology in such a small field must be, partly the "luck of the draw." It happens, for example, that even the most aggressive efforts failed to locate anyone prepared to write about one of the more sexually egalitarian groups, such as Twin Oaks; thus the volume might give the impression that all communes are, like those described here, characterized by some degree of male dominance. That our sample was further biased toward the work of anthropologists and other readers of the *Anthropology Newsletter* may have excluded some other recent work in communes. The first chapter of this volume is therefore aimed at giving a somewhat more balanced comparative framework within which to view the case studies presented here.

JON WAGNER

Sex Roles in Contemporary American Communes

-1- JON WAGNER

Sex Roles in American Communal Utopias

An Overview

WHEN MARK TWAIN UNDERTOOK TO DESCRIBE the character of the Mississippi River, he framed his description not so much in terms of the river's general direction, width, or speed as on the vicissitudes of its currents, transfigurations, contradictions, and turmoils. Similarly, we might stand to learn as much about European civilization and its precocious child, America, from its countercurrents and eddies as from its "mainstream." Most Americans are vaguely aware that their country has provided the setting for several "utopian" and "communal" experiments, but conventional wisdom assures us that they were (and are) of no consequence save as illustrations of the degree to which religious radicals and secular reformers can delude themselves. The one thing most educated Americans "know" about communal utopias is that they invariably "failed" and that this fate was only to be expected in view of their failure to recognize the "facts" of human nature and the inevitability of the institutions—such as private property and conventional marriage—that they sought to abolish. This writer was introduced to the subject of American utopianism by a passage in a history textbook which followed the above argument exactly, offering as evidence the brief debacle of Robert Owen's attempted "commune" at New Harmony, Indiana. The textbook did not mention that the village site of New Harmony had been built by the Harmony Society, a communal group which thrived for a generation before selling out to Owen and which continued in its subsequent location for another three or four generations. Neither did the book mention that the Harmony Society was only one of several communal societies in which thousands of people lived out their lives in an atmosphere of dedicated fellowship and cooperation or that the first such societies existed long before the American Revolution.

The fact is that hundreds of communal utopias have survived long enough to produce coherent lifestyles and social philosophies. With sufficient determination one can manage to define each of these as "failures"—particularly if one is willing to apply different criteria of "success" as the particular case demands. Some societies survived for as many as four or five generations—but this, of course, is less than forever, and one can always argue that they "failed" to provide the things that "make life worth living" or that they achieved their longevity at the cost of "slavery" (Muncy 1973:234). To the extent that definitions of "success" remain ambiguous, so will the question of the viability of communalism.

Regardless of how one estimates the moral worth of communal utopias, however, it should be clear to the dispassionate observer that they are phenomena worthy of attention. The historical and intellectual influence of these communities, all propaganda to the contrary, looms large in proportion to their size and duration. The analysis of such communities holds much promise for understanding what people have found desirable or undesirable, easy or difficult, possible or impossible.

The purpose of the present work is to investigate one issue concerning communal utopias in America: the extent to which they have sought to alter the traditional status, rights, obligations, and character ascribed to each of the sexes. This is a significant issue, since it focuses on the nexus between two major concerns of our time —the possibility of cooperative fellowship and the possibility of sexual liberation. The subject is all the more important because it has, I shall argue, been the subject of confused and sometimes ill-founded generalizations.

"Utopian" and "Communal": The Matter of Definitions

The study of communal societies is plagued by an excess of taxonomies and a dearth of agreement as to their use. In the realm of adjectives alone we have "communal," "communalist," "communist," "communistic," "communitarian," "communitive," "sectarian," "cooperative," "associationist," "utopian," "socialist," and many others that refer to the same or overlapping chunks of reality (cf. Bestor 1950:viii). Even if we restrict ourselves to contemporary sociological usage, the disparity of language is daunting. In her highly successful sociological analysis in *Commitment and Community,* Rosabeth Kanter defines "utopia" as

> the imaginary society in which humankind's deepest yearnings, noblest dreams, and highest aspirations come to fulfillment, where all physical, social, and spiritual forces work together, in harmony, to permit the attainment of everything people find necessary and desirable. [1972:1]

Also inherent in utopia, as Kanter defines it, is the notion that cooperation and harmony are more "natural" to human society than are exploitation and competition, "which arise only in imperfect societies" (ibid.). For this reason, attempts to realize utopian visions usually take the form of communes or utopian communities—that is, voluntary societies withdrawn from the outside world and organized according to the goals of "harmony, brotherhood, mutual support, and value expression" (203). Kanter recognizes implicitly that not all utopias are communes, since some are "imaginary," and she characterizes some modern communes, which lack comprehensive visions of social perfection, as "nonutopian" (166–67). Nevertheless, throughout most of her book Kanter uses the terms "utopia," "community," "utopian community," and "commune" interchangeably; the last three terms are not explicitly distinguished from one another. Kanter's usages stand in contrast to those of Abrams and McCullough (1976), whose definition of "commune" specifically excludes the utopian communities to which Kanter directs most of her attention. Similarly, the American sociologist Ron E. Roberts (1971:19–20) states that "communal societies"—that is, the modern communes with which he is concerned—reject status hierarchies and bureaucratic structures, thus distinguishing themselves from many of the groups treated as "communal" by Kanter and others. Not only are the same terms used to refer to different domains, but different terms are often used for the same—or very similar—categories of phenomena. For example, Nordhoff's "communistic societies" (1965; original 1875), Noyes' "socialisms" (1961; original 1870), Hinds' "communities" (1961; original 1878), Webber's (1959) or Bestor's (1950) "utopias," or Holloway's (1951) "utopian communities" refer to approximately the same group of nineteenth-century communities treated by Kanter.

For the present purposes it is not necessary to complicate the terminological jumble or to attempt to reform it. We shall use "utopia" to mean any comprehensive vision of an ideal society or any community that attempts to model itself on such a vision. As for "commune" and related terms, we shall base our usage on the broadest conception of the societies to which these terms have been applied. Such societies are deliberate alternatives to the existing social order; they attempt consciously to implement social innovations, not through the direct reform of the larger society, but through withdrawal into a small community composed of those who choose to live by the alternative structures. Finally, the communal society strives to improve life through closer fellowship and the renunciation of material competition in favor of a sharing of material resources.

Not all utopias are equally communal, not all communes are equally utopian, and not all communes or utopias are of equal interest in the present study. The focus of this book is American communal utopias; that is, communities modeled on some fairly comprehensive ideal of social perfection based on increased fellowship and material cooperation. Communes of this sort tend to be "corporate" groups; that is, they possess a group identity and a set of purposes somewhat independent of the coming and going of individual members. This focus turns our attention away from "anarchist" and "family" communes oriented toward spontaneity, intimacy, and personal growth more than toward utopian visions, and the applicability of our findings to these latter groups is therefore problematic. Perhaps it is best to think of the definitions of "commune," "utopia," and "corporate" not as boundaries defining discrete phenomena, but as markers denoting regions of interest in a continuous and unbounded territory; in most cases it is probably more useful to describe communities as "more communal" and "less communal" (or utopian) than as "communal" and "not communal." As for the finer distinctions among related terms ("socialistic," "communitarian," "cooperative," and so forth), we shall adopt the practical strategy of allowing the terms to be used more or less interchangeably—a practice already well established in the literature—with such nuances of meaning as are made clear from context. One final note on definitions: "American" refers to any group which existed in the United States during any period of its existence, including not only immigrant groups, but also such groups as the Black Hebrews which emigrated after their founding in the United States.

Sex Roles

By "sex roles" we mean the entire complex of behavioral norms and expectations which a society attaches to a person because of his or her sex, including both sex attributes and sex relationships. "Sex attributes" are the qualities, behavioral patterns, traits of temperament, rights, privileges, obligations, and duties which a society defines as appropriate to each sex. "Sex relationships" are the patterns of erotic, emotional, political, and economic relationships between the sexes, including the allocation of economic and other functions by sex. Not all aspects of sex roles are, however, of equal interest here. The intention is to focus on the extent to which communal societies have tried to liberalize sex roles—that is, to break down the traditional divisions of function and differences of status which have characterized sex roles in the larger society. Although erotic relations and forms of marriage in communal societies have been featured prominently in much of the literature (e.g. Muncy 1973), these subjects will be considered here only insofar as they bear on the problem of the social differentiation or equality of the sexes.

The traditional viewpoint in European and American society has been that, due to immutable differences of temperament and ability (to say nothing of divine will), it is natural that women be subordinate to men. It has been accepted as self-evident that women are less capable than men in all but a narrowly circumscribed range of tasks, many of which are deemed beneath a man's dignity to perform. While women could attain some distinction in the performance of "womanly" tasks, they have had limited access to the ultimately valued positions of status, prestige, recognition, and political influence. Indeed, it has been assumed that women should seek and expect a set of rewards different from and more modest than that for men. Paul made it clear, and most of our ancestors have agreed, that women exist to fill men's needs; this "helpmate" ideology defines women as means to an end, and that end, at least in the most immediate sense, is men. Adherents to this position have not generally seen themselves as oppressors of women, but rather their advocates. After all, they say, obedience to these laws of God and nature can only bring a better and more harmonious earthly life and the promise of ultimate salvation for all.

In some respects the arguments for the subordination of women and the division of function by sex parallel the justifications given for traditional forms of inequality among social classes. It is therefore interesting to pose the question of whether the proponents of equality among men have also championed equality between men and women, and to what extent particular communes have recognized men and women as equals. Has one sex been treated as existing for the sake of the other, or have both been defined equally as ends in themselves (or means to some transcendent end)? Has one sex been held subservient to the other? Has one sex been expected to seek rewards different from or more modest than those sought by the other? Have people been obliged to fit into preconceived notions of temperament and behavior according to their sex? Has the division of labor and other social functions been prescribed on the basis of sex? To what extent are the most highly valued positions or achievements in a society equally accessible to both sexes?

The Egalitarian Hypothesis

It seems eminently logical that those who advocate the equality of men (males) should extend their thinking to embrace the equality of all human beings. In fact, most intellectuals who theorize in print about the relation of communalism to sex-role liberalization conclude, for one reason or another, that the two are inseparable. Their arguments have not been restricted to the apparent incompatibility of sexual inequality with a philosophy of egalitarianism, but they have pursued a variety of refinements and elaborations on this theme. Robert Owen, an influential utopian thinker and experimenter of the early nineteenth century, connected sexual equality with communalism by way of marriage and private property. He argued that "marriage founded on individual property" stemmed from the same selfish possessiveness that spawned economic exploitation and other ills which communalism ought to ameliorate. Thus, he concluded, communalism necessarily entailed the emancipation of women from their position as chattels (Muncy 1973:55–56). Fourier, the French utopian thinker who influenced numerous American experiments, drew a similar connection between female subordination and private property, and considered female equality essential to communalism. It is probably such arguments that Holloway (1951:178) had in mind when he wrote that "the liberal attitude toward women" in some nineteenth-century communes "was a logical consequence of the communistic attitude toward property." John Humphrey Noyes, utopian theorist and founder of the Oneida commune, also saw the "logic" of this connection. In his view sexual exclusiveness was a central feature of "possessive" marriage, and his program for economic equality thus included group marriage. Noyes maintained that there is

> no intrinsic difference between property in persons and property in things; and that the same spirit which abolished exclusiveness in regard to money would abolish, if circumstances allowed full scope to it, exclusiveness in regard to women and children. [Quoted in Nordhoff 1965:272]

True communalism, he argued, could prosper only after sexual monogamy, that bastion of private property, had been abolished. Once this had been accomplished, the happy results would include not only a freeing of women from their status as property, but also the creation of an atmosphere free of sexual jealousy, in which women and men could work easily together at common tasks (Noyes 1961:636).

Frederick Engels, who had read both Owen and Fourier and who praised the latter's "masterly" criticism of bourgeois sex relations, adopted the notion of a connection among monogamy, private property, and the oppression of women in his *Origin of the Family, Private Property, and the State* (1978; original 1884). The influence of Marx and Engels among contemporary radical thinkers probably accounts in part for the continuation of this argument, or variations of it, among modern communal theorists. One contemporary version, influenced by Freud as well as by Engels, maintains not only that the strict regulation of erotic expression is a form of "possessiveness" and "private property," but also that it helps direct psychodynamic energies in directions amenable to an authoritarian, capitalist society (Roberts 1971:5–6, 38–40; cf. Marcuse 1955). Thus the monogamous family may be seen as an instrument of capitalism and as one of the roots of male dominance. Margolies (1972:2) writes:

> The family is much like the state and schools: there tends to be one authority figure, usually the man; the woman, who is docile and loving, takes care of the household; lower still, the children are administrative assistants. A key element of radical community is the liberation of men and women from this kind of mechanical, enfeebling, and narrow definition of how they should relate.

If one accepts the general argument that free erotic expression is the antithesis of "possessive" marriage, that possessive marriage is responsible for inequality of the sexes, and that it is also a mainstay of the system of private property which communalism opposes, it seems to follow that economic communalism entails the abolition of both monogamy and sexual inequality. It also becomes clear why such writers as Conover (1975) and Oats (1972) mention erotic freedom in the context of assessing the progress of communes toward sexual equality.

The logic of connecting free erotic expression, antimonogamy, sexual equality, and communal forms of property can be challenged. The whole line of argument appears to blur an important distinction between the "possessiveness" of sexual jealousy and the "possession" of material property. Must communal ownership of key material resources, or the abolition of economic exploitation, necessarily be accompanied by an abandonment of sexual exclusiveness? For that matter, would the destruction of monogamy lead inexorably to equality of the sexes? It is certainly legitimate to ask whether men could not continue to dominate women even in a situation of sexual promiscuity or group marriage. In any case, there is no ethnographic evidence that rights of authority over persons depend on an economic system of "private property" as we understand it. On the contrary, there is ample evidence that monogamy, rigidly prescribed sex roles, and male dominance can thrive in classless band- and village-level societies whose economic systems involve communal property holding, cooperative production, obligatory sharing, and general economic equality (Harris 1977).

Perhaps the most systematic statement of the egalitarian hypothesis, and the most sophisticated defense of it, is to be found in the works of Rosabeth Kanter. Kanter begins with the proposition that communal societies generally try to deemphasize the importance of the nuclear family, since "familism" and the "dyadic withdrawal" resulting from the mutual attachment of mates threaten to diminish group loyalty and to fragment a community into smaller, self-sufficient units (1972:87-88; cf. Noyes 1961:139 and Mumford 1922:49-50). This "renunciation" of the family can take the form of free love or celibacy, or it can be accomplished more modestly by institutions that are designed to prevent family loyalties from becoming paramount. In any case, the "mechanisms" that counteract familism are said to be correlated with success among nineteenth-century communes and, by implication, modern groups as well. The reduction of familism, Kanter (1973) argues, tends to enhance the status of women in a community. To the extent that "family" prerogatives are redirected toward the community as a whole, women participate more directly in the life of the community and are therefore accorded more status and influence within it. For example, such "domestic" work as childrearing and cooking becomes community work, and as such it is likely to be more highly regarded (and more likely to be performed by both sexes). Likewise, the political and social relationships of women to the larger community take place not through the intermediary of the family (and its male head), but directly—a situation ripe with potential for sex-role liberation. Kanter is connecting many of the same variables that the previously cited theories did, but the relations she draws are sociological rather than moral or psychological. While the supporting arguments vary, it appears that nearly everyone who has written on the subject agrees with the hypothesis that communes tend naturally toward greater equality of the sexes and a breakdown of sex-role differentiation.

The Elusive Egalitarians

It is comforting to see the degree of consensus and the sophistication of sociological argument with which the egalitarian hypothesis is supported. It is less comforting to find that the "facts" in favor of the hypothesis are not as unequivocal as we might have hoped. There is little question that some communes have been in the vanguard of sex-role "liberation" during their time, but it seems that many other successful communes cannot be characterized in this way. Supporters of the egalitarian hypothesis seem remarkably willing to ignore the latter cases, to dismiss them as "exceptions," or to argue (not always convincingly) that they are not what they seem. Holloway, for example, writes that in the nineteenth-century communes "women, in most cases, enjoyed equal rights with men" (1951:223), but elsewhere notes that "in none of these [German immigrant] societies . . . was there any interest in the emancipation of women" and that such communities "made no attempt to alter the conventional relationship of the sexes" (1951:159). Although the German groups made up six of the nine communes Holloway names as the most long-lived (221), he seems to dismiss them as not being among "the most important communities" (159). Clearly, neither longevity nor size is a measure of "importance" for Holloway in this context.

Charles Nordhoff, who visited several communal societies during the early 1870s, remarks in the conclusion of *The Communistic Societies of the United States* that "it is a great point gained for success to give the women equal rights in every respect with the men" (1965:412). Of the six societies Nordhoff described in detail, only the Shakers had attempted this complete equality. Four of the six were among the German groups mentioned above, and Nordhoff offers no evidence that any of these highly successful German communities aimed at sex equality; on the contrary, he felt obliged in some cases to remark on the low status of women, as in the case of Amana, where women were normally allowed "no temporal or spiritual authority" (1965:37).

Kanter concedes that equality of the sexes was neither consciously pursued nor "perfectly achieved" by Amana and the other German groups, but she maintains nevertheless that these groups afforded a more equal role for women than was available in the larger society, and characterizes the manifestations of male supremacy among them as "vestiges" (1973:303–4). We shall return to the question of sexual equality in these communes, but it is sufficient here to point out that Kanter's interpretation remains to be supported by systematic evidence. This is no small matter, for the German groups comprise six of her nine "successful" groups, and except for the Shakers they exceed all other contenders for longevity. Kanter is, to say the least, premature in her conclusion that nineteenth-century communes as a group exhibit "lowered sex role differentiation" (302).

If the evidence from the nineteenth century is equivocal, the record of twentieth-century communes is positively inconvenient for the egalitarian hypothesis. This fact can be gleaned even from an examination of Kanter's own evidence. Of the several varieties of modern communes, she sets aside "hippie" and "rural hippie" communes as exceptions to the "trend" of sex-role equality, and quotes other scholars who clearly affirm the regressive character of sex roles in most such groups (304–5). She concludes, however, that those communes which exploit and oppress women are "unstable" and "neither very communal nor very cohesive" and that the "truly communal family" eschews traditional sex roles in deference to an "egalitarian ethic" (305). There are several important difficulties with Kanter's position. First, she appears to be excluding from consideration all those groups that fail to adopt egalitarian sex roles on the grounds that they are, for that very reason, not "truly communal." Second, as we shall later show, other evidence suggests the existence of groups which are large, cohesive, and "communal" by all other standards, but which are by no stretch of the imagination "egalitarian" in their sex roles. Third, the exclusion of "hippie" and "rural hippie" communes from the "trend" raises the question of exactly where the positive examples of the "trend" are to be found. Kanter offers no explicit statement on this point and names only one example of the "rule" of equality: Twin Oaks; a Virginia community based on B. F. Skinner's utopian novel, *Walden Two*.

Twin Oaks is also the sole example named in support of Patrick Conover's statement that modern communes tend toward sexual equality (1975). Conover further thins the ranks of egalitarian communes by making "exceptions" of the "Eastern" and "Puritanical Christian" groups. For Conover, the communes to which the generalization really applies are those of the "alternate culture" (it is not clear to what extent such communes are among those "hippie" groups disclaimed by Kanter). Even the "alternate culture" communes, however, include an unspecified number of "exceptions," and Stephen Gaskin's "Farm" in Tennessee is mentioned as one. The Farm, it might be noted, was probably the largest commune in the United States even at the time of Conover's writing, its membership numbering about twenty times that of Twin Oaks. Here again we find the examples of the "rule" more elusive, and in some respects less impressive, than the "exceptions." After reading the cited works by Kanter and Conover, one would be in a far better position to locate sexist communes than to locate egalitarian ones, with the one exception of Twin Oaks.

Kanter clarified the positive side of the ledger in a 1975 article, in which she documents the breakdown of sex roles in urban "family" communes. These communal households are relatively small and unstructured groups which conceive their goals in personal and interpersonal terms rather than orienting themselves toward the ideology, structure, or survival of the "commune" as an abstract entity. They are, in other words, communes that are neither utopian nor corporate (in the sense of having an identity and morality transcending the individual members. The reasons for sexual equality in such communes, Kanter argues, are both ideological and structural: the communes are typically composed of educated middle-class persons already committed to the abolition of rigid sex roles and sexual inequality; and the structure of decision making, which involves constant and universal negotiation, prevents the formation of ascribed roles of any sort. There is no reason to question the social importance of the family commune, but it is structurally and ideologically distinct from the corporate commune, and it would be risky to accept Kanter's extension of her findings to "utopian communities" (1975:452).

A glance at the historical record gives cause to doubt whether communes as such tend toward sexual equality. At the same time, there is ample evidence that *some* communes have moved in this direction. Can we say nothing about communal sex roles except that they are unpredictable—that anything goes? I think not. The absence of a simple trend or pattern obvious to the casual observer does not justify the conclusion that there are no patterns whatsoever. If we seek less obvious trends, it is useful first to consider what factors might be expected to influence the patterns of sex roles in a communal utopia.

Patterns in the Formation of Communes

In principle, it would be possible to form a commune by hiring a committee of experts, researching the problems, and placing a newspaper advertisement offering a reasonable salary for participants. Historically, however, most utopian communes have formed as result of the inspired teachings of a visionary leader. The character of such visionaries has been dealt with in the literature on charisma (Weber 1968; Shils 1968; Wagner 1978), sects (Wilson 1975; Lewis 1971), and revitalization movements (Wallace 1956). The charismatic vision is one of the most dramatic manifestations of human creativity in the historical process, and as such it is not subject to neat sociological predictability. On the other hand, there are several ways in which social and historical forces help to pattern charismatic visions in coherent ways. To begin with, charismatic movements arise most frequently in times of sociocultural crisis. Such crisis may be said to exist when significant numbers of people lack a coherent vision of the good life coupled with a workable program for pursuing it. This condition may result from various causes, including political oppression, economic crisis, relative deprivation, disruption of traditional sources of social order and cultural values, or simply the discovery that the "good life," once attained, is unsatisfying. The charismatic "solution," as Weber (1968) has pointed out, rests neither on tradition nor on rational self-interest, but rather on an appeal to the presumed fundamental and transcendent source of human values—what Shils (1968) calls the "order-determining powers." It is, in short, a return to the "basics" of human purpose and value, which is to say, the immutable principles of "rightness" from which all human institutions and motivations are supposed to derive. Such visions are made known through the medium of a charismatic visionary, an individual who speaks not for himself but for an order of reality transcending all particular persons and social arrangements. The charismatic vision is typically a comprehensive view of what is wrong with human affairs and what must be done to remedy the ills of humankind. The "solutions" usually involve not only a radical revolution in human institutions, but substantial sacrifice from individuals as well.

Despite the fact that the charismatic vision is thought by its adherents to transcend society and history, its content is influenced by the conditions in which people find themselves. Thus we observe, in studying the history of such movements, that each age sets the stage for repeated "revelations" of similar diagnoses of human ills and similar prescriptions for human fulfillment. Two general sorts of factors may have important effects on the charismatic vision and the communities growing from such visions: the set of real or perceived conditions responsible for sociocultural crisis and the mode of social criticism current at the time. For the sixteenth- and seventeenth-century German peasant, the perceived sources of crisis had to do with the anachronistic prerogatives of a feudal aristocracy, and the mode of social criticism was predominantly religious, manifested as an injunction to return to "true" apostolic Christianity (Rexroth 1974). The perceived sources of crisis and the prevailing modes of social criticism change with time, and it should come as no surprise that charismatic visionaries of nineteenth-century America and the "hippies" of the twentieth-century Haight-Ashbury movement addressed somewhat different problems with different solutions.

While the charismatic vision is theoretically a comprehensive reform of society-as-it-is, no visionary program attempts to give equal attention to all realms of life. A certain configuration of values, institutions, and kinds of behavior are usually identified as the source of humankind's divergence from the true path of fulfillment, and specific measures are prescribed to set things right. Thus the changes advocated by a visionary will tend to focus on certain aspects of mainstream life and to leave others relatively unaffected. If sex roles are diagnosed as being at or near the root of the "problem," the resulting utopian venture may be expected to depart significantly from mainstream society in these matters. The decision as to whether sex roles are involved in the core problem is partly a matter of charismatic idiosyncrasy, but it is also related to the social setting and to the way both the visionary and his or her followers perceive their lives. It seems, for example, that the founders of German-American communes placed only subsidiary emphasis on sex roles, whereas Americans often used this issue as a centerpiece.

When sex-role innovations are prescribed, we might well expect that the specific form and direction of these innovations are patterned, but not determined, by the particular character of the mainstream society, the perceived conflicts and crises, and the current themes of social criticism. In sum, it is reasonable to expect that the analysis of sex roles by charismatic community founders, and therefore the specific character of communal societies at their onset, could show multiple and perhaps even contradictory trends among "communes" taken as a whole, but that these trends might exhibit patterns relative to particular historical contexts.

Patterns in the Maintenance of Communes

Not all visionary plans become translated into operative social systems, and not all visionary social systems persist long enough to allow for coherent study or description. In order for a utopian commune to persist after its founding, it must provide adequately for (1) provision of food and material necessities, (2) orderly allocation of tasks and responsibility, (3) resolution of disputes, (4) socialization of infants and new members, (5) a viable relationship with the outside, (6) maintenance of discernible boundaries separating it from the larger society, and (7) a means of bringing individual motivation into line with social-systemic requirements.

This last problem, of bringing the motivations of the individual into harmony with the needs of the social system, involves processes which Kanter has discussed at length in *Commitment and Community* (1972) and elsewhere (1968). Kanter states that successful communes employ certain "mechanisms" which, while often requiring sacrifice from individuals, have the ultimate effect of increasing the individual's commitment to the commune and its corporate goals. These "commitment mechanisms" (1968:510) are as follows:

1. *Sacrifice,* including abstinence from sexual or oral gratification, and material austerity.
2. *Investment,* of either the individual's personal property or energy—most effective when the investment is not reversible.
3. *Renunciation* of loyalty to the larger society or to smaller groups within the community, including the family and "special" friends.
4. *Communion;* the placing of loyalty to the group above all other loyalties; engaging in common work and recreational activities.
5. *Mortification;* "the submission of private states of control, the exchanging of a private identity for one provided by the organization, one subject to its control."
6. *Surrender,* whereby "an individual attaches his decision-making prerogative, jurisdiction over even private domains, to a greater power."

The relations between the sexes are such a fundamental aspect of human life that they could scarcely escape being affected in some measure by these "commitment mechanisms." The ways in which commitment mechanisms, and other functional necessities listed above, affect sex roles are not altogether predictable. As concerns commitment mechanisms, for example, it is important to emphasize that no commune need adopt them all. Kanter, in fact, warns of the oppressive atmosphere that can result if all commitment mechanisms are employed. It is necessary only that a commune adopt some combination of commitment mechanisms sufficient to insure the continued participation of members and to meet the functional requisites cited above. Whereas all the functional requisites listed earlier must be satisfied if a commune is to survive, they, like the commitment mechanisms, can be approached in a variety of ways. Particular strategies for dealing with functional requirements and commitment mechanisms will vary with a number of factors, including the character of the mainstream society, the content of the founding ideology, and events unique to the history of a particular group. For example, various aspects of sex roles and sex relationships including free love, celibacy, polygyny, strict subordination of women, and radical liberation could each be used to help demarcate the community from the surrounding society, depending of course on the forms prevalent in society and the ideology specific to the commune. Sex roles could also be used as a convenient way of allocating tasks according to prior training, even when such allocation is unrelated or even contrary to the founding ideology.

Kanter sees renunciation of family and couple loyalties as a particularly important commitment mechanism, and one which has systematic effects on sex roles. Marriage and erotic relationships may be affected by renunciation insofar as renunciation may entail the abolition of monogamy in favor of either free love or celibacy. These strategies, or others that serve to redirect loyalties from the family to the community, may have the incidental effect of equalizing sexual status and undermining sex-role distinctions, according to the argument already cited (Kanter 1973), since they make women direct participants in community life. Kanter's thesis may be correct in some measure, but it must be juxtaposed against certain other considerations. For one, the supposed effects of "de-familization" on sex roles can be counteracted by other, contravening factors. Furthermore, the strategies used to deemphasize familism need not always lead in the direction of sex equality. For example, in the Haran commune, described in this volume, men are discouraged from investing too much in their relationships with their wives, on the grounds that women are ignorant, carnal, and potentially hostile to true brotherhood. According to Haran's ideology, then, communalism can succeed only when men dominate women in patriarchal marriage relationships, while directing their loyalty and their emotional investment toward the "brotherhood" rather than toward the "flesh" relationships of the family (cf. Wagner 1975; 1976).

The details of life in a particular commune are the product of several conjoining factors, including the functional requirements of a viable social system, the sociocultural developments of a particular age, and the imponderables of visionary creativity. These factors lead to a certain degree of similarity among communes in general, a certain similarity within (and divergence among) particular traditions and epochs of communalism, and a certain irreducible uniqueness for each group.

Sex Roles in Nineteenth-Century Communes

It is no easy matter to list a "sample" of the most important nineteenth-century communes. Some groups, particularly the German Pietist communes, made no effort to draw attention to themselves, and their existence became known only when they became unavoidably noticeable. Such groups as New Harmony and Fruitlands, which failed to establish themselves as viable communities even for a short time, attracted widespread attention through their articulate spokesmen; as a result, the fame of these groups equals or exceeds that of many larger and more successful ventures. The first problem in generalizing about these communes, then, is what criteria we shall use in choosing our sample. By choosing the most well-known and well-documented examples we are likely to accord disproportionate attention to certain ephemeral but articulate "intellectual" communes. Kanter (1972) has followed the procedure of distinguishing "successful" from "unsuccessful" communes on the basis of their longevity (twenty-five years being the criterion for "success"), while listing and considering "unsuccessful" communes separately in her analyses. Each community is listed here with its duration and membership as given by Kanter (1972:246–48), although it should be kept in mind that some of these figures are subject to debate. Where Kanter gives population figures for more than one time, the highest is listed here.

Successful

The Shakers (184 years; 6,000 members)
The Harmony Society (100 years; 800 members)
Amana (90 years; 1,800 members)
Zoar (81 years; 500 members)
Snowhill (70 years, but 65 years longer if the "parent" community
    of Ephrata is counted; no population figures given by Kanter)
Saint Nazianz (42 years; 450 members)
Bethel and Aurora (36 years; Kanter gives no population figures,
    but Nordhoff [1965] found 600 in the two communities in 1874)
Oneida (33 years; 104 members)
Jerusalem (33 years; 250 members)

Unsuccessful

Hopedale (15 years; 229 members)
Modern Times (15 years; no population figures given by Kanter)
Bishop Hill (14 years; 1,400 members)
North American Phalynx (13 years; 112 members)

Communia (8 years; 79 members)
Oberlin (8 years; "About 11 families")
Brook Farm (6 years; not exceeding 100 members)
Wisconsin Phalynx (6 years; 180 members)
Northampton (4 years; 180 members)
Utopia (4 years; 12 families)
Kendal (3 years; 150 members)
Nashoba (3 years; 20 members)
Order of Enoch (Mormon communalists) (3 years; no population
   figures given by Kanter)
Skaneateles (3 years; 90 members)
Iowa Pioneer Phalynx (2 years; 50 members)
Jasper Colony (2 years; 10 families)
New Harmony (2 years; 1,000 members)
Preparation (2 years; 50 families)
Blue Spring (1 year; 27 members)
Fruitlands (8 months; 16 members)
Yellow Springs (6 months; 100 families)

Certain adjustments to Kanter's sample are in order: Holloway
(1951:ch. 1) describes two early immigrant communes, the Labadists
of Bohemia Manor (1683–1727) and the Woman in the Wilderness
(1694–1748). He, along with most other writers, also gives attention
to Cabet's "Icaria" (1848–98), a group which is absent from Kanter's
sample. The Hutterites have thrived since their immigration in the
1870s and in 1965 numbered about 16,500 persons in 170 colonies
(Hostetler and Huntington 1967). These groups bring the total of
"successful" nineteenth-century communes to thirteen. Even with
these additions, the list may be incomplete. The "unsuccessful" list
could be expanded almost infinitely, but it seems that Kanter's sample of these groups is adequate and includes the best-documented
cases. We shall use Kanter's list, with the additions mentioned
above, as our sample for analysis.
   A glance at these nineteenth-century communes is enough to reveal considerable variation in the roles and status of the sexes.
While the Amana colonists were instructing their women according
to the Apostle Paul's pronouncements on female subordination, the
communitarian visionaries Fourier, Owen, and Cabet were distinguishing themselves as feminist advocates. If we were to attempt a
division of communes on the basis of women's status, that division

would not correspond to the distinction between "religious" and "secular" communes, for Oneida and the Shaker communities, both religiously based, made notable strides toward sex equality. Nor does the split between native and immigrant groups correspond to differences in sex equality, for the founders of relatively egalitarian groups included native-born John H. Noyes, English-born Robert Owen, and the Shaker founder Ann Lee (also English), as well as the French utopians Charles Fourier and Etienne Cabet. A far neater correspondence may be achieved by distinguishing European Pietist and Anabaptist groups from the others, but neatest of all is to place the Germans and Swedes in one group and all other communalists in the other. For the former it can generally be said that any move toward the equality of the sexes was secondary, if not contrary, to their basic goals; for the latter, the improved status of women was usually part of the design for social improvement.

Why this particular pattern? In order to answer, it is necessary to examine the historical roots of religious communal movements in Europe. The roots of Pietism and Anabaptism are bewilderingly complex. Adequate treatment of the subject is beyond the scope of the present work and would require examination of dozens of sects, "heresies," and intellectual traditions reaching into the radical Reformation from such distant sources as the Essenes, the Greek Gnostics, and the Persian Manichaeans. From this tangled network of heretical theologies and radical social philosophies we can glean certain facts of importance to the present discussion. First, it is apparent that the beliefs held in many nineteenth-century communal sects did not originate suddenly, but had roots in early Christian and pre-Christian sources (cf. Rexroth 1974). Second, the social gospel of these groups contains certain recurrent themes of social criticism: that the privilege, wealth, and authority of the establishment —which included the religious as much as the secular power structure—were illegitimate on theological grounds. Biblical images of Eden, the teachings and personal conduct of Christ, and the supposed communism of Apostolic Christianity were held as models for Christian behavior, and the conclusion that the establishment had gone astray was thus inevitable.

Needless to say, the rebellion of the less privileged segments of society against the most conspicuous agents of their oppression is unlikely to be guided only by theology. While it would be foolhardy to attempt a monadic explanation of such diverse movements as

England's Peasant's Revolt and Bohemia's Hussites, it seems clear
that in peasant social movements the demand for social, political,
and economic reform was based on religious models, given religious
legitimation, and expressed in religious terms. It is not surprising,
in light of this intertwining of religion with radical politics, that
many sects adopted a morality and a theology calculated to make the
establishment appear unchristian—and thus politically illegitimate
—by definition. They abstained from precisely those excesses of
which the elite were most conspicuously guilty: gluttony, ostenta-
tious living, personal grandeur, fornication, and economic exploitation. They flouted the authority of the church—Catholic and later
Protestant—by setting pious living and personal religious devotion
above church ritual, and sometimes by denying the validity of clergy
as intercessors with God or the church's right to baptize unconsent-
ing infants. They adopted a model of Christian behavior which the
privileged classes could scarcely emulate, and which simultaneously
realized on a small scale the reforms which they wished to make
universal: humility, brotherhood, generosity, austerity; a complex of
values sometimes expressed in such extreme forms as obligatory
poverty, celibacy, or communalism.

However radical the social life and morals they proposed, these
sects did not think of themselves as innovating; rather, they fancied
that they were attempting to restore the purity of original Christianity. Speaking of the roots of American communalism, Littell
writes:

> The Anabaptists of the 16th century, the radical Puritans of the
> 17th century, and the Pietist and Evangelical movements of the
> 18th century share a common conviction that religious and social
> salvation are to be found through the restitution or restoration of
> the Christian community as it existed before the Fall of the
> Church. Their view of church history, which they equate with
> universal history, is primitivist. Abandoning the periodization of
> history followed by Augustine and Jerome, and rejecting that
> proposed by Luther and other main-line reformers, they divided
> Church history into three periods: the golden age of the Early
> Church (with the communism of the Church at Jerusalem a
> model), the Fall of the Church (with Constantine and the centuries
> of political privilege and material prosperity), the Restitution of
> the True Church—beginning with their own movement, and in-
> volving the recovery of true Christian community. [1965:xvii, fn.
> deleted]

Littell argues that opposition to private property, along with an extreme commitment to mutual aid, were part of the restitutionist program of the sixteenth-century Anabaptists which emerged as communalism in the Hutterites (xvi). Similarly, such Pietist groups as Amana, Harmony, Zoar, Aurora, and Bethel "stem directly from the 'left wing of the Reformation' and are clearly restitutionist in their purpose and program" (Littell 1965:xvii). This generalization can probably be extended to the Labadists, the Woman in the Wilderness, Ephrata-Snowhill, and the Swedish Pietists at Bishop Hill. In all, seven of our thirteen successful examples (Harmony, Amana, Zoar, Snowhill, Bethel-Aurora, Bohemia Manor, and the Woman in the Wilderness) are German or Bohemian Pietists, and one (the Hutterites) is Anabaptist. Saint Nazianz, a successful Catholic group, is not included among these, but is similar in a great many respects, combining a restitutionist communalism with the traditional Catholic practice of attaching lay people to monastic communities. Bishop Hill, while not a "successful" commune, is among the largest and most long-lived of the "unsuccessful" groups.

The implication of a restitutionist model is that the Bible shall be the principal authority for proper relationships between men and women. The relationship of Adam and Eve is one source of such images; but since the life of the Christian Apostles is the most direct model of Christian life, the writings of Paul on the role of women are of obvious immediacy:

> Let your women keep silence in the churches: for it is not permitted unto them to speak; but they are commanded to be under obedience, as also saith the law. And if they will learn any thing, let them ask their husbands at home: for it is a shame for women to speak in the church. [1 Cor. 14:34–40]

> Let the Woman learn in silence with all subjection. But I suffer not a woman to teach, nor to usurp authority over the man, but to be in silence. For Adam was first formed, then Eve. And Adam was not deceived, but Eve being deceived was in the transgression. [1Tim. 2:8–15]

> For a man ought not to cover his head, forasmuch as he is the image and the glory of God: but woman is the glory of man. Neither was the man created for the woman; but the woman for the man. [1 Cor. 11:7–9]

There is no evidence that the Anabaptist or Pietist German communalists overlooked the significance of such passages or intended to abrogate them. In fact, Nordhoff mentions that the writings of Paul were read during Amana's wedding ceremonies in order to instruct the couple in "the duties of husband and wife" (1965:36). Similarly, the Hutterites' written guidelines for sex roles, as quoted by Hinds (1961:416), shows a clear and systematic awareness of the conservative Scriptural mandate:

> First, we say that as woman was derived from man, and not man from woman (I Moses; I Cor. 11), the man has the sovereignty, and the woman has weakness, suppleness and subjection (I Pet. 3; Rom. 7); wherefore she shall be under the yoke of the man and obey him, as she is commanded of God (I Moses 3), "The man shall be thy lord."
>
> This being so, she shall look up to her husband, provide for him, ask his advice, and do all with and nothing without such advice. If she does otherwise she leaves the order or level wherein she was placed by God, grasps after the sovereignty of the man, loses the favor of her Maker, and therewith the covenants which her husband made to her at their marriage (I Pet. 3; Eph. 5).

This is not meant to give the impression, however, that the "helpmate" and subordinate role of the women and the traditional division of labor were central to the ideologies of these groups. Sex roles were, it would seem, ideologically unimportant. The social conditions to which these movements addressed themselves had relatively little to do with sex roles and much to do with class struggle and economic change. While celibacy, supported by Pauline writings and monastic traditions, was often adopted and had indirect effects on sex roles, the relation of men to women was not usually identified as part of the basic problem to be addressed, nor as a fundamental part of the solution proposed.

The restitutionist European-based communes have been the subject of various contradictory statements by scholars regarding sex roles. Holloway states that among the "heretical sects," including the German Pietists, "The perfect equality of men and women as servants of God was almost always acknowledged" (1951:54), but later makes the statement, quoted earlier, that they generally made no attempt to alter the relationship between the sexes and "showed no interest in the emancipation of women" (159). Kanter presents quite the opposite picture: despite their supposed lack of "explicit concern" for women's roles, these communes are said to have instituted greater sexual equality than was current in mainstream American society (1973:303–4). Nordhoff (1965), on the other hand, mentioned nothing of this equality in connection with the German groups he visited, and gave every reason to believe that sex roles were conservative and Bible-based.

Actually, these statements may not be so contradictory as they seem. As for Holloway's contention about the theological recognition of absolute equality, we might note that Paul also affirmed that "in Christ there is no male or female," but that this theological point did not greatly affect his notions of proper male and female behavior in this world. Holloway may therefore not be contradicting himself. In all probability, the German Pietist and Anabaptist groups did not intend to tamper with sex roles as they found them among the German agrarian and working classes, which was more or less the way they were defined in the Bible. The attitude with regard to sex roles was neither reactionary nor reformist, but merely conservative. When such groups moved into the United States, and into a society where sex roles had come to be identified by some social critics as problematic, these stolid Germans might have seemed, ideologically speaking, rather backward. One might even speculate that "traditional" sex roles could have become, for some such groups, a badge of demarcation from "the world"; but the fact remains that sex-role behavior, conservative or otherwise, was not initially identified by these communalists as an important part of humankind's problems or of the solutions to those problems.

Kanter's argument that these groups tended toward equality for social-structural rather than conscious ideological reasons could still be correct, even though the requisite data for this judgment have not been presented. Kanter cites Hinds' statement that women in Amana managed their own council for "household matters" and that women who were "not represented by male members" could vote, as well as the fact that the "head" of the community was a woman (Hinds 1961:58; quoted in Kanter 1973:303). The leader's role was, however, that of a passive instrument of revelation and was unparalleled in ordinary women's roles. Other examples might better support Kanter's point: Nordhoff notes that at Zoar, a German commune in Ohio, all women were allowed to vote (1965:106), and Holloway credits the celibate communalists of Bohemia Manor with "absolute equality . . . between men and women in all activities, both physical and spiritual" (1951:35), during the late seventeenth century.

The picture of sex roles in these European immigrant communes is thus a complex one. From their own perspective, sex roles seem to have been of little concern. To the outsider, these groups might have seemed ultratraditional in their literal adherence to biblical norms, traditional sex-role demeanor, and orthodox division of labor and domestic roles. On the other hand, the sociological ramifications of communalism, and in many cases of celibacy, may have led to perhaps unintended countertrends which resulted in a more direct participation of women in the community, as Kanter suggests. Thus these groups are in various senses liberal, reactionary, conservative, or simply indifferent to sex roles.

Once the large, numerous, successful, long-lived, and theoretically troublesome German communes (and Bishop Hill) have been dispensed with, nineteenth-century communes do in fact seem to present an impressive trend toward sex equality. Since we have, however, excluded nine of our thirteen successful communes (including the German Catholic commune of St. Nazianz), we shall have to turn for some of our examples to those groups which survived fewer than twenty-five years—in some cases considerably fewer. All four of the groups remaining on the "successful" list (the Shakers, Oneida, Jerusalem, and Icaria) show definite tendencies toward increased sexual equality, as do the majority of the shorter-lived "unsuccessful" groups. Two of the "successful" egalitarian groups were imported from outside America, and the other two were native developments.

The United Society of Believers, better known as the Shaker Society, was founded in England by Ann Lee, but it became a significant social movement and a communitarian society only after its move to America in the 1770s. While still in England, Ann Lee had a vision which revealed to her that the sin in Eden was the sex act in disobedience of God. God was believed to have a dual sexual nature while all other beings, including Christ, were male or female with opposite-sex counterparts. Since these beings included Christ, it followed that the "Second Coming" of Christ would be that of Jesus' female counterpart, who was thought to be none other than Ann Lee herself. It also followed from Shaker theology that the sinless life God's elect would lead after the Second Coming would be communal and celibate. The Shakers lived celibate lives in which they tried to obliterate as much as possible all traces of the repugnant sexual aspects of human social life. Part of the Shakers' program for desexualizing society was expressed in their commitment to political equality of the sexes. Charles Nordhoff, who observed the Shaker communities at first hand, wrote that "they hold strongly to the equality of women with men, and look forward to the day when women shall, in the outer world as in their own societies, hold office with the men" (1965:165–66). The rules of the Shaker Society stated that, at the various levels of the leadership hierarchy, offices would be held by men and by women in equal numbers.

The Shakers' theoretical commitment to sexual equality was to some extent compromised by their commitment to celibacy. It may be true, as Kanter liberating them from their domestic confinement, but in the case of the Shakers the system of defamilization seems to have presented some obstacles to women's freedom as well. In order to safeguard the supreme principle of celibacy, the Shakers went to great lengths to avoid any unnecessary or unsupervised contact between the sexes; men and women even used different doors and stairs. Combined with the characteristic Shaker concern with efficiency, this segregation meant that the various industries and chores of the community were performed according to a sexual division of labor. This division generally fell along the same lines as in the larger society, so that men worked in the fields and at traditionally "masculine" crafts, while women did most of the domestic chores and undertook such "feminine" occupations as spinning and weaving. Furthermore, the women were generally excluded from those positions which involved regular contact with the outside world—presumably from fear of sexual harassment. Despite the fact that the Shaker Society did not completely dispense with sexual biases, the Shakers are to be recognized not only for their radical commitment to the principle of equality, but also for their considerable success in putting the principle into practice. The Shakers might well be called the most successful communal group in American history, having survived more than 150 years as a viable society and having reached a peak population of several thousand persons in eleven different communities.

The Shakers' religious background resembles that of the German Pietist groups, and yet their conceptions of sex roles were apparently quite different from those of the Germans. What accounts for the

Shakers' failure to fit the pattern of these other immigrant religious communes? It is difficult to explain the difference solely as the result of having a female founder, since this fact in itself seems to indicate a different outlook from that of the German groups. Several other factors may be significant. To begin with, the Shakers are the product of a different branch of radical Protestantism, and their most immediate roots lie with radical English Puritanism and the Quakers (Littell 1965:xvii). This difference of religious tradition, combined with differences in the forms of social development and social criticism in England and Germany, may allow for some understanding of the Shakers' uniqueness. Furthermore, the Shakers were the only major English-speaking communal sect to be imported to America, and this difference indicates more than just one of background. Coming to America with only a small cadre of followers, the Shakers were able—in fact obliged—to recruit their followers from among English-speaking Americans. Unlike the women in German communes, who frequently spoke no English and who had few available alternatives to communal life, Shaker women had to be recruited with the prospect of a relatively attractive communal existence. In this connection, Littell states that the Shakers "offered a much better and longer life for young women than they could anticipate in the common social conditions of the society at large" (ibid:xxiii). Since Nordhoff's (1965) population figures indicate a male-female ratio in Shaker communities of about one to two, the sect's attractiveness to women might be considered a significant factor in its recruitment success. The differences that separate the Shakers from other immigrant sects are numerous, and the example of a single commune is too small a base from which to offer confident interpretations. Nevertheless, it is likely that the factors noted here can, if taken together, go far toward explaining the Shakers' departure from the patterns typical of European sectarian groups in America. (Although relatively little has been written about the successful community of Jerusalem, it appears to have paralleled the Shaker Society in certain respects. Contemporary with the early Shakers, Jerusalem was founded in New York by an American woman, Jemima Wilkinson, who was held to be an avatar of Christ. She recognized several female "prophets" among her followers, one of whom eventually succeeded her as leader.)

Another immigrant group, Icaria, is included in the sample of successful groups. Icaria, which was at different times located in

Texas, Illinois, and Iowa, was founded in 1848 by French immigrants under the leadership of Etienne Cabet, whose utopian novel *Voyage en Icarie* had touched off a communalist fervor in France. Cabet's critique of existing social norms and his advocacy of communalism were framed in terms of secular reform rather than of religious salvation, and Cabet's principles included the moral and social equality of the sexes. As Cabet himself put it, "In the Icarian Republic women have the same social rights as men. The Icarians as a whole consider it their first duty and interest to assure the happiness of women" (1917:242). Although women in the family-oriented Icarian commune were wives and mothers before all else and although many vestiges of traditional occupations remained, Icaria did manage to realize in practical terms much of its dedication to sex equality (Snyder 1978).

Most of those remaining from our list of successful and unsuccessful groups are "native" developments, founded in the United States (sometimes from foreign inspiration) and composed primarily of native-born Americans. Oneida was the most successful of this category, which also included numerous shorter-lived ventures. The ideologies of these communes ranged from highly religious to stridently atheistic, but most were profoundly and consciously influenced by the social conditions and social criticism of the time. In mainstream American society of the early nineteenth century, women's role continued to be a clearly subordinate and domestic one, and both the occupational and political emancipation of women in any practical sense was yet to be realized. For most Americans the role of women as obedient helpmates, mothers, and guardians of gentle virtue was no more challenged than was the role of the family as the cornerstone of decent society, of private property as the foundation of rational economy, or of competition as the medium of universal progress. In ordinary social practice and in the values which supported such practice, norms of sex roles, family, and marriage had changed so little that the pronouncements of the Apostles could still be regarded by many as an appropriate guide.

If the degree of practical change in sex roles of the nineteenth century was severely limited, the capacity of social critics for envisioning such change was not. Sex roles and forms of the family were frequently singled out for criticism along with the political and economic arrangements of mainstream society. Radical utopian and communist thinkers including Engels, Fourier, Cabet, and Owen expressed themselves clearly against the oppression of women by conventional family and sex roles, and the nineteenth century saw the rise of what could only be called, even by today's standards, radical feminism. The combination of conservative sex and family patterns with radical social criticism led to the frequent expression of the idea that sex roles are a central problem in human affairs and that the problem can best be solved by means of sex equality. While most immigrant religious communes were relatively disinterested in such intellectual radicalism and seldom recognized sex roles as a problem in need of attention, the more intellectually oriented native communalists showed a general tendency to place sex equality high on their list of necessary social reforms.

Cabet's egalitarianism can be seen as an expression of liberal social criticism, as can the teachings of another Frenchman, Charles Fourier. Unlike Cabet, Fourier never set foot in America or in a communal society, but his writings provided the inspiration for numerous experimental communities in America, including the North American Phalynx, the Wisconsin Phalynx, the Iowa Pioneer Phalynx, and Brook Farm, all included within the sample under consideration here. Fourier envisioned a new age in which humankind would be organized into communes, or "Phalynxes," for the realization of a just and perfect social life. Fourier's criticism of conventional sex roles left no doubt that the perfect society must involve the complete emancipation and equality of women. Some have gone so far as to call Fourier "the first feminist" (Muncy 1973:220). American communes which attempted to follow Fourier's prescriptions seem to have made varying efforts to move in the direction of sexual equality, although there is also evidence that equality was far from perfectly achieved (Muncy 1973:220–21). Brook Farm, which during its six-year career became a Fourierist Phalynx, displayed an active interest in women's rights and included in its social circle the prominent feminist Margaret Fuller.

Another nineteenth-century feminist, Frances Wright, founded the short-lived Tennessee community of Nashoba, which was dedicated to racial as well as sexual emancipation (Webber 1959:116–32). Wright was in turn an associate of one of the foremost utopian thinkers of the nineteenth century, Robert Owen. Owen had already made his reputation as a practical social innovator by establishing a model industrial community at New Lanarck, Scotland, but his liberal environmentalism and visionary sociology could scarcely be contained in that Old World setting, and he turned to America, where he purchased a town from the departing Harmony Society. Owen's venture at New Harmony, Indiana, was a celebrated failure as a communal society, but his influence on nineteenth-century liberal and communalist thinking was substantial. Owen's "Declaration of Mental Independence," delivered at New Harmony on the Fourth of July, 1876, stated that

> man up to this hour has been in all parts of the earth a slave to the trinity of the most monstrous evils that could be combined to inflict mental and physical evil upon the whole race. I refer to private or individual property, absurd and irrational systems of religion, and marriage founded upon individual property.... [Quoted in Muncy 1973:56]

Owen's vision of a perfect society was one in which men and women would have equal rights, equal education, and equal freedom (Muncy 220). In our sample, Yellow Springs, Blue Spring, and Kendal, as well as New Harmony, were based on Owen's ideas.

The Oneida Community, founded in New York in the 1840s by John Humphrey Noyes, combined elements of secular social criticism and religious revivalism. Noyes argued that, since Christ had already returned to earth in A.D. 70, it was possible for people to lead sinless lives if they were provided with the right social environment. The Perfectionists, as they were called, sought to eliminate the sources of evil by combating human possessiveness, conflict, and greed; among their social measures was the abolition of sexual exclusiveness through a system of "group marriage," to which critics referred more bluntly as "free love." In group marriage any consenting adults were able to form sexual liaisons, with the stipulation that certain procedures were followed, that childbirth was regulated through a system of "male continence" (male restraint of ejaculation), and that enduring or "exclusive" relationships not occur.

Oneida's attitudes toward sex-role liberation were, from a modern egalitarian viewpoint, somewhat equivocal. The Oneida *Handbook* makes the following statement about women's role:

> Communism emancipates a woman from the slavery and corroding cares of a mere wife and mother; stimulates her to seek the improvement of mind and heart that will make her worthy of a higher place than ordinary society can give her....

> Gradually, the Community women have risen to a position where, in mind and in heart, they have all and more than all that is claimed by the women who are so loudly asserting their rights. And through it all, they have not ceased to love and honor the truth that "the man is the head of the woman," and that woman's God-given right is to be "the glory of man." [Handbook of the Oneida Community:26]

Even though Noyes did not accept complete sex equality in theory, his thought reflects many of the concerns characteristic of contemporary feminism, and the sex-role practices of the community were egalitarian in many respects as compared with the larger society. Noyes was deeply concerned about the "possession" and exploitation of women in monogamous marriage and the endangering of women's health through childbirth (his system of birth control developed as a way of protecting his own wife, who was unable to give birth without endangering her health). He also argued that sexual jealousy and the domestic confinement of women were contrary to the best interests of either sex and that once freed from such constrictions both sexes could participate fully in community life. He also believed that women as well as men should have personal control over their sex lives. Noyes' interest in sexual technique, together with the Oneida practice of each sex's being "initiated" by experienced elders, seems to indicate a concern for sexual enjoyment and consideration on both sides, at a time when the larger society scarcely recognized that women had legitimate sexual needs at all.

On the practical level there was some expectation that women should perform those tasks traditionally allocated to their sex, but at the same time some women were able to participate in educational programs and in many business and manufacturing functions traditionally reserved for men. Concerning political participation, a descendant of the community told an interviewer:

> Most people have overlooked the fact that Father Noyes delegated a lot more responsibility to the women here than they ever would have received on the outside. Every committee had women on it. It made a difference, too. All the old folks will tell you it made both men and women respect each other. [Kephart 1976:64]

In keeping with their practical participation in community activities and with their liberation from many traditional role expectations, the women of Oneida wore a costume of short skirts and ankle-length pantalettes, and bobbed their hair.

Many communities equaled or surpassed Oneida in their ideological commitment to equality. Hopedale, in Massachusetts, one of the longest-lived "unsuccessful" groups, was described by its founder Adin Ballou as "a sound theoretical and practical woman's rights association" (Hinds 1975:235). The Kaweah Colony in California extended to both sexes the right to vote as well as the right of financial independence (Muncy 1973:222). Equal pay for equal work, a principle which many women are still fighting for, was realized in a number of nineteenth-century groups including not only Kaweah but also the Northampton Association (Massachusetts) and Modern Times (New York). In the latter group, women sometimes earned a higher wage for their work than the men did, and like the Oneida women they sometimes wore a trouser-like costume as a sign of their liberation from traditional norms (Muncy 1973:222–24). Modern Times' founder, Josiah Warren, was also responsible for the Ohio community of Utopia, which like Modern Times was predicated on the inviolability of individual freedom. The women in Utopia could, according to a spokesman, "do about as they please, and they generally please to do about right" (Webber 1959:169). The founder of Iowa's Communia, William Weitling, although wary of women's supposed anticommunal tendencies, was nevertheless an advocate of increased rights for women. Hinds (1961:435–41) recorded an example of a phenomenon often thought of as radical even today: a women's commune. Few if any of the nineteenth-century groups achieved the complete abolition of traditional sex roles, but, while the information is largely anecdotal and difficult to assess, it seems that most communities except for the German and Swedish religious groups moved deliberately toward sex equality.

To summarize the argument concerning nineteenth-century communes: an examination of the German immigrant and Swedish immigrant communes, which made up the majority of larger and longer-lived groups, would lead to the conclusion that communalists had little interest in sex-role changes, that their ideology regarding sex roles was conservative, that their sex-role behavior was also predominantly conservative, and that such changes as they did introduce were incidental to other concerns. If, on the other hand, one considers only the *other* communes—typically composed of Americans acting under the inspiration of American, English, or French visionaries—the impression gained would be quite different: these societies were often predicated on the notion that sex roles were problematic and that some measure of sex equality and liberation from traditional roles was necessary. The difference is not surprising in view of the fact that the German and Swedish groups grew out of Pietist tradition which saw social problems as rooted in religious apostasy and which prescribed solutions in terms of a restitution of "true" religion on a Scriptural model. These groups could in a sense be regarded as remnants of a form of radicalism that flourished in the transition from a feudal to a capitalist social order and whose image of the good life was deeply influenced by an idealized model of traditional village life. The remaining communes tended more to be products of early-nineteenth-century social criticism, with or without supporting religious interpretations. Religious justification, when it did occur, was based on more radical and imaginative notions than those of the Pietists and appears in many cases to have been influenced by secular social criticism; the theology of John H. Noyes serves as an example. The rise of rational, radical critiques of human inequality coupled with the essential conservatism of sex-role behavior in the early nineteenth century led to a frequent voicing of demands for sex-role reform, which was taken to mean something more closely approaching sex equality.[1]

Although I have proposed historical generalizations and causal relationships, I do not intend that such generalities should substitute for the complexities of history. It would be foolish, for example, to suggest that *all* American-based communes of the nineteenth century were egalitarian; the Order of Enoch was a Mormon communalist group which adopted the thoroughly patriarchal Mormon perspective (cf. Muncy 1973:218) on sex roles. It is virtually certain that the categories will overlap and that explanations offered for a gen-

---

[1]Louis J. Kern, in *An Ordered Love: Sex Roles and Sexuality in Victorian Utopias —the Shakers, the Mormons, and the Oneida Community* (Chapel Hill: Univ. of North Carolina Pr., 1981), which appeared during the final stages of preparation of this book, offers a treatment of nineteenth-century utopian sex-role ideologies that is unprecedented in its sophistication and thoroughness. According to Kern's argument, even the Oneida, Shaker, and perhaps other "egalitarian" utopian concepts of the last century may be in some respects more "regressive" than I have portrayed them here, since they sought in an indirect way to restore the "time-honored traditions of the patriarchally organized extended family" as against the "domestic feminism" and romantic sexual ideologies of the nineteenth century (which in turn offered women a new sort of "power" even at the same time that they were being used to justify women's continuing domestic dependency [286–87 and *passim*]). While Kern's ideas are too complex and subtle to lend themselves easily to paraphrasing here, his volume is well worth the attention of anyone interested in pursuing the subject.

eral pattern may apply poorly to the marginal cases. What I propose to suggest, nonetheless, is that the apparently contradictory forms of sex roles in nineteenth-century communes are distributed not randomly, but in a broad pattern of differentiation which is intelligible in terms of historical and social conditions.

Sex Roles in Contemporary Communes

Jerome (1974:14–18) estimated that as many as three-quarters of a million Americans were living in more than fifty thousand urban and rural communes in America. Such figures must remain conjectural, partly because the majority of communes do not publicize their existence and partly because any generalizations depend on how one chooses to define what is or is not a commune. There is continuous gradation from the nuclear family household with a more or less permanent expense-sharing house guest to the formally structured religious communes with many hundreds of members. Communes vary not only in size but also in organizational principles and ultimate purposes; Jerome (1974) suggests numerous axes along which important distinctions can be made. For our purposes, it is useful to draw a general distinction which has not explicitly been made in the existing literature on communes: that of corporate versus noncorporate communal societies. Jerome has noted that, while most communes tend to limit their membership to between six and fifteen, those which pass the critical number of twenty "are likely to grow into the hundreds (almost always under charismatic leadership)" (ibid.: 13). While the smaller communes tend toward informal social structures and ideologies, the larger ones often manifest very clearly defined group purposes as conceived in comprehensive charismatic ideologies. A commune of this latter sort has an identity and a set of purposes to which the newcomer must adapt and which can survive independently of the comings and goings of particular members. Such a commune has a "corpus" which transcends its individual parts (members), hence the term "corporate." Corporate communes stand in contrast to the small "family" communes. In the latter, all ideologies and structures are negotiable and held answerable to the felt needs of individual members, whose participation defines the group rather than vice versa. A considerable literature surrounds the small, relatively unstructured family commune (e.g.

Kanter 1975; Jerome 1974; Veysey 1973; Abrams and McCullough 1976; Weiss 1974), and rightly so in view of their apparent potential as innovative living arrangements. However, the philosophical and organizational differences between family and corporate communes are so great as to suggest extreme caution in lumping the two together in sociological generalizations, as so many writers have tried to do. Since this volume deals with corporate communes, generalizations about small "family" groups have limited applicability.

It has already been noted that virtually everyone who has addressed the subject of sex roles in contemporary communes sees a general trend toward sex equality and dismisses the many nonconforming cases as "exceptions" to this trend. Such generalizations do not sufficiently recognize the major differences between corporate and noncorporate communes. While it may be true that family communes tend toward equality, the evidence for equality in contemporary corporate communes is extremely weak.

When I encountered the strongly patriarchal ideology of the "Haran" commune, described in chapter 7 of this volume, I concluded at first that the commune, which was founded prior to and independently of the "Sixties," was an anachronistic "exception." This conclusion was abandoned quickly in the face of contrary evidence. Not only are the leaders of modern corporate communes usually male, but also the communes frequently manifest strict sex-role divisions which in many respects parallel those of Haran. In Christ Commune women are blamed for men's sexual desires and are expected to "learn their place," which is, in their own words, "one of submission to the men, just as the men are in submission to the Lord" (Harder et al. 1972:46). According to Harder, "No woman is in a position of authority over a man within the group, a practice justified by biblical practices" (1973:16). Although Christ Commune is a modern West Coast group, its sex-role concepts appear no less conservative than those of Amana or of the Hutterites. The Bruderhof, a modern group akin to the Hutterites, affirms that women ought to stick with their traditional tasks and to seek neither community leadership nor authority equal with men (Zablocki 1971:120–21). At Stelle, a middle-class commune in Illinois, the author was told that clothing and hair styles, as well as work activities, ought to reflect the different (and apparently rather traditional) social roles of men and women. Fort Hill's leader, Mel Lyman, has stated that "if a woman is really a woman . . . then everything she does is for her man and her only satisfaction is in making her man a greater man." Continuing with an argument almost identical to that used in Haran, Lyman states that

> a woman who seeks to satisfy herself is the loneliest being in God's creation. A woman who seeks to surpass her man is only leaving herself behind. A man can only look ahead, he must have somewhere to *look* from. A woman can only look at her man ... I have stated the law purely and simply. *Don't break it.* [Quoted in Felton 1973:218]

Just as Conover (1974) dismisses such religious communes from the "trend" of sex equality, Kanter (1973) exempts those "rural" and "hippie" communes for which she quotes the following generalizations:

> The women's liberation movement would probably not approve of the position of women in most communes.... Women tend to do traditional women's work: most of the cooking and cleaning (they are more concerned with tidiness than most men), and in the rural communes much of the traditional female farm roles in addition ... they are ideologically less forceful than men and express themselves with generally less authority (Berger et al. 1971:18).

> Although communal living appears to be a step in the right direction, the hip commune uses women in a group way the same as the fathers did in a one-to-one way. The communes are too fluid to create any sense of security for a woman. Her stability is lost and her isolation complete ... kicking the men out is haid because they own the land and are the breadwinners.... The hip style of life encourages a pernicous form of bourgeois individualism (Estellachild 1971:41).

Even the most ardent advocates of the new communalism sometimes express disappointment over the continuation of sharply defined sex roles in many contemporary communities (e.g. Veysey 1973:435). Gardner's (1978) survey of thirteen contemporary communes does not attempt a systematic treatment of sex roles, but male-female relations are usually mentioned only in contexts which confirm the image evoked by Berger et al. (1971). At Morning Star East and the Reality Construction Company, "the only participation of women was in traditional housekeeping roles" (Gardner 1978:115); the "3HO" sect of American Sikhs has formed a "Grace of God Movement of the Women of America" in opposition to the women's liberationists who have criticized the inferior status of women within the sect (132); and work roles at Saddle Ridge Farm "were generally assumed along traditional lines of sexual differentiation" (207). Fairfield's tour of communes reveals some tension over the issue of male chauvinism. The following comment, elicited in an interview with a (male) communal leader, will probably win no prizes for human liberation:

> It's really unbelievable what those chicks have learned to do over a fire that's nothing more than a hole in the ground. I think we're really lucky and I've been in a lot of communes before this, three of them before we got together. If the chicks aren't making it, if the chicks don't have any energy and don't want to do anything, like be chicks, you know, wash dishes, cook, then you're in for trouble because there's nothing worse than not getting your food, having all the dishes stacked up. [Quoted in Fairfield 1971:107]

Of the contemporary communes presented in this volume, all show a clear-cut distinction between male and female roles, and all possess, in some measure, an explicit ideology of female subordination. It should be pointed out that the articles included here were solicited through the *Anthropology Newsletter* and various other professional channels and that no respondents proposed articles on groups more egalitarian than those described herein. Numerous inquiries to communal-studies scholars, organizations, communes, and communalists failed to turn up any author interested in writing a first-hand account of a contemporary egalitarian commune.

Let there be no mistake: communes with egalitarian sex roles do exist. Among the prominent examples are the closely related communes of Twin Oaks and East Wind. These communes and others like them deserve attention for a variety of reasons. Although they are generally smaller than the charismatic religious communes, they present a clear and viable alternative to the latter. They have deliberately eschewed charismatic leaders and monolithic ideologies in favor of a pluralistic ethos, rational social planning, and participatory democracy. Unlike many religious communes, which see outsiders as doomed Philistines, Twin Oaks and East Wind are articulate in their attempts to communicate their ideals. The Twin Oaks publications *Leaves* and *Communities* are excellent sources of information, not only on Twin Oaks, but also on modern communalism in general. In these respects, and in their inspiration from the rational utopianism of Skinner's *Walden Two* (1962), these communities are the true analogues of the liberal Fourierist and Owenist communes of the nineteenth century. As in those earlier communities, the aspirations and intellectual influence of Twin Oaks and East Wind are great in proportion to their size (about 85 and 60 persons, respectively).

Much has been written on sex roles in the Virginia commune of Twin Oaks and its Missouri offshoot, East Wind, for sex roles have been identified in these communities as a problem central to human growth. I am particularly grateful to Kathleen "Kat" Kinkade, one of the founders of Twin Oaks now living in East Wind, for her recent, detailed communication to me regarding sex roles in these communities. In describing the "theoretically nonsexist" organization of these groups, she states that

> these two communities make a strong point of absolute sexual equality and ... attempt to do away entirely with roles based arbitrarily on sex. This idea is fundamental to our idea of "equality," and equality is fundamental to our approach to changing society. There is no platform of our ideology that is more central.

Sex differences are not recognized as an appropriate basis for allocating jobs, and Kinkade reports having seen no instances of such allocation in her twelve years in these communities. Both men and women perform even such commonly sex-allotted jobs as heavy-equipment operation and kitchen work. Equality in management roles is apparent not only from Kinkade's own general comments, but also from the current list of managerships at East Wind, which she has kindly provided. Thirty men and twenty-six women occupied managerships at the time of her communication, but the composition naturally fluctuates in such a way that the managerial structure has at times been perceived by outsiders as a "matriarchy." Differences in male and female clothing are also breaking down, and some men have adopted the long skirt as everyday apparel. Women and men are held equal in matters of courtship and the initiation of sexual relations. Extraordinary measures, including the use of the "co" as a sex-neutral third-person pronoun and the replacement of "man" by "person" in such words as "workpersonship," have been taken to eliminate sex-biased usages from written and spoken language. "Sometimes," Kinkade writes, "people forget and use the old form, but they are quickly and vociferously 'corrected' by other members. No other norm in the community is so vigorously enforced."

Kinkade acknowledges that the achievement of sex equality is by no means complete. There are still, for example, more women than men volunteering for kitchen duty, and the managerships of various activities reflect comparable biases. Similarly, sex-typed clothing is still favored by many persons. All in all, however, Kinkade's portrayal of these communities is in keeping with other accounts of Twin Oaks, including Conover's statistical study of deference behavior (1974; 1975), Oats' report to *Women: A Journal of Liberation* (1972), and personal communications from David Ruth, former Twin Oaks member and *Communities* editor. Each confirms the impression that, while the battle for sex equality is not entirely won, the goal of equality ranks highly in the community's ideals, and major strides have been made toward achieving it. These communities may be among the most nonsexist social systems in human history.

Twin Oaks and East Wind are not unique. The Federation of Egalitarian Communes includes not only these two communities, but also Aloe, Dandelion, and North Mountain. The Federation explicitly disavows discrimination on the basis of religion, race, or sex. These particular communities are small enough (five, nine, and five adults, respectively) to resemble family communes, but their self-descriptions generally indicate a sense of corporate identity and a desire for expansion (Federation of Egalitarian Communes, n.d.), and they might thus be considered as corporate communes or at least as borderline examples. Other communes, too, have striven to abolish male dominance. Some are women's collectives, and one—Blue Mountain Ranch—is composed of equal numbers (ten and ten) of men and women, but is sufficiently female-directed to be characterized approvingly by one female member as a "matriarchy" (Singer 1975:36). Some urban communes show parallel developments. Boston's Life Center communal house, affiliated with the Movement for a New Society, (MNS), has a strong feminist orientation, as do other MNS groups in Durango, Colorado, and Ann Arbor, Michigan (Mallory 1978; MacLeod and Bedard 1977). These reports and others (see also the special women's issue of *Communities* 1978, no. 33; and Judith 1974) tell a story similar to that of Twin Oaks: strong commitment and substantial victory against male dominance and arbitrary sex roles.

Paradoxically, then, modern communes offer examples both of radical sex equality and of sex-role systems so rigid and hierarchical that they can fairly be called reactionary. While the moral and sociological importance of the egalitarian communes cannot be denied, there is no factual justification for characterizing them as a trend and for dismissing the more conservative groups as exceptions. The total combined population of all the nonsexist corporate communes mentioned above is apparently smaller than that of, for example, the Farm. Furthermore, the evidence from these large, charismatically based communes lends no support to Kanter's claim that "exploitation and oppression of women ... seem to occur in communes that are neither very communal nor very cohesive" (1973:305).

Generalization from the examples of modern communes mentioned above is risky. Assessment of sexism and equality is a difficult matter even for someone intimately involved in a community. Self-images cannot always be taken at face value; the patriarchal Haran commune views itself as nonsexist despite its belief that "no woman can hear or tell the truth." Furthermore, it could conceivably be the case that great numbers of large, cohesive egalitarian communes have somehow escaped notice. It could even be that the apparently successful male-dominated communes will soon become extinct, giving way to a new age of nonsexist communalism. But if we restrict our observations to the available evidence, it does not appear that either rigid behavioral differentiation on the basis of sex or the domination of females by males is inimical to communal success. On the contrary, it seems that many of today's "successful" communes have adopted more, not less, rigidity and inequality than is present in the mainstream society. Those communes moving toward sexual liberation deserve all the more credit for bucking the current rather than riding with it, and they could still be taken as models for those committed to the abolition of sexually ascribed roles and servitude.

Why should so many of the contemporary communes manifest ultraconservative sex roles when the American-based communes of the last century showed an overwhelming trend in the other direction? In the twentieth century, sex roles are widely acknowledged as problematic, not only as an intellectual matter, but also as one impinging on practical behavior. Conflicts over sex-role behavior are widespread. We are hard put to reconcile, for example, the attitude that dishwashing is "women's work" with the fact that many women are employed outside the home, or the still-cherished ideal of the demure, obedient, supportive woman with increasing demands for political and economic equality. No one, conservative or liberal, is in a position to escape the widespread effects of these conflicts, and therefore few visionary reformers are likely to ignore the problem of sex roles. But while *recognition of the problem* is virtually determined by today's social conditions, the *diagnosis* is not. American society has moved sufficiently far from the traditional, Bible-mandated ideals of sex roles that it is possible to attribute sex-role-related problems *either to excessive social change or to excessive social conservatism.* Each of these options of interpretation has been followed, in various ways, by certain communal societies. Communalism based on biblical models, Eastern religions, or images of the "old-timey" rural life may often favor conservative or even reactionary sex roles, while secular, liberal intellectualism often leads the other way.

The various demands of commune maintenance may also bear on sex roles in modern groups. For example, it appears that communes with rigid authority structures and ideologies are among the largest and most affluent communes, and, as Singer argues in this volume, patriarchy can serve as one of the structuring principles in an authoritarian social order. A commune or other intentional community needs to demarcate its boundaries from the larger society, and this can be accomplished either by the deliberate nonsexist behaviors of a commune such as Twin Oaks (as in the use of the sex-neutral pronoun "co") or in the extreme patriarchy of Haran. Haran sees itself as different from the rest of the world in being patriarchal rather than matriarchal; informants at Haran made statements almost identical to the following comment by a Fort Hill woman:

> The men here on the Hill are real men; the men out there are faggots, with their long hair and everything. If they weren't, they wouldn't let their women get away with the things they do. [Quoted in Felton 1973:217]

Another factor that may favor some adherence to traditional sex roles is the need to allocate tasks according to people's aptitudes, which in turn reflect socialization in mainstream society. If a commune's ideology endorses traditional task allocation, it need not compromise on this practical issue; if it is egalitarian it must struggle daily with matching tasks to skill levels in a nonsexist way, as Twin Oaks is obliged to do.

However compelling the connection between sex equality and communalism may appear to some thinkers (myself included), it is universal neither in communalist theory nor in practice. For many communalists of both the past and the present, the ideal of equality refers to the abolition of aristocracies and social classes and the establishment of economic cooperation, but does not rule out the existence of rather traditional sex-role distinctions. Such a view of the "egalitarian" Eden is aptly summarized in the words of the fourteenth-century radical John Ball:

> When Adam delved and Eve span,
> Who was then the Gentleman?

ACKNOWLEDGMENTS

I wish to thank Helen Irwin for her comments on this introductory article, and Kat Kinkade for her helpful correspondence. Let me also take this opportunity to thank all those who have offered their help, encouragement, and suggestions as this volume took shape, including Ruth Shonle Cavan, Raymond Lee Muncy, Carolyn Anderson Wilson, Jonathan G. Andelson, David Ruth, William M. Kephart, Robert Fogarty, Lillian M. Snyder, and Carlos C. Drake. Special thanks to the contributors of this volume, and especially to Bryan Pfaffenberger for his incisive comments and his indispensable help in turning a "pipe dream" into a finished work.

REFERENCES CITED

Abrams, Philip, and Andrew McCulloch
    1976   Communes, Sociology and Society. New York and Cambridge: Cambridge Univ. Pr.
Armytage, W. G. H.
    1961   Heavens Below: Utopian Experiments in England, 1560–1680. London: Routledge and Kegan Paul.
Berger, Bennett M., Bruce M. Hackett, and R. Mervyn Millar
    1971   Child-Rearing Practices of the Communal Family. Progress Report to NIMH.
Bestor, Arthur Eugene, Jr.
    1950   Backwoods Utopias: The Sectarian and Owenite Phases of Communitarian Socialism in America, 1663–1829. Philadelphia: Univ. of Pennsylvania Pr.

Cabet, Etienne
1917 History and Constitution of the Icarian Community. Trans. Thomas Teakle. New York: AMS.
Conover, Patrick W.
1974 Socialization to Changed Genderal Roles in a Contemporary Commune. Paper given at the American Anthropological Association.
1975 An Analysis of Communes and Intentional Communities with Particular Attention to Sexual and Genderal Relations. The Family Coordinator, October, pp. 453-63.
Engels, Friedrick
1978 The Marx-Engels Reader. 2d ed. New York: Norton.
Estellachild, Vivian
1971 Hippie Communes. Women: A Journal of Liberation 2:40-43.
Federation of Egalitarian Communes
n.d. Federation of Egalitarian Communes [photocopied pamphlet ca. 1978].
Felton, David
1973 The Dangers of Charisma: Mel Lyman and Fort Hill. *In* Communes: Creating and Managing the Collective Life, ed. R. M. Kanter. New York: Harper and Row.
Gardner, Hugh
1978 The Children of Prosperity: Thirteen Modern American Communes. New York: St. Martin's. Ph.D. diss., Univ. of Nevada.
Handbook of the Oneida Community
1875 Oneida, NY: Office of the Oneida Circular.
Harder, Mary White
1973 The Children of the Christ Commune: A Study of a Fundamentalist Communal Sect. Ph.D. diss., Univ. of Nevada.
Harder, Mary White, James T. Richardson, and Robert B. Simmons
1972 Jesus People. Psychology Today 6 (7): 45-50, 110-13.
Harris, Marvin
1977 Cannibals and Kings: The Origins of Cultures. New York: Random House.
Hinds, William Alfred
1878 American Communities and Cooperative Colonies. Reprint 1961. New York: Corinth.
Holloway, Mark
1951 Heavens on Earth: Utopian Communities in America, 1680-1880. New York: Library Publishers.
Hostetler, John, and G. E. Huntington
1967 The Hutterites in North America. New York: Holt.
Jerome, Judson
1974 Families of Eden: Communes and the New Anarchism. New York: Seabury.
Judith
1974 Some Views on Women in Communes. Communities: Journal of Cooperative Living 7:11-13.
Kanter, Rosabeth Moss
1968 Commitment and Social Organization: A Study of Commitment Mechanisms in Utopian Communities. American Sociological Review 33:499-517.

1972 Commitment and Community: Communes and Utopias in Sociological Perspective. Cambridge, MA: Harvard Univ. Pr.

1973 Family Organization and Sex Roles in American Communes. *In* Communes: Creating and Managing the Collective Life, ed. R. M. Kanter. New York: Harper and Row.

Kanter, Rosabeth Moss, Dennis Jaffe, and D. Kelly Weisburg

1975 Coupling, Parenting, and the Presence of Others: Intimate Relationships in Communal Households. The Family Coordinator, October, pp. 433–63.

Kephart, William M.

1976 Extraordinary Societies: The Sociology of Unconventional Life-Styles. New York: St. Martin's.

Lewis, I. M.

1971 Ecstatic Religion: An Anthropological Study of Spirit Possession and Shamanism. Harmondsworth, Middlesex (Eng.): Penguin.

Littell, Franklin H.

1965 Prefatory Essay. *To* The Communistic Societies of the United States, by Charles Nordhoff. New York: Schocken.

MacLeod, Diana, and Rachel Bedard

1977 Women in Community. Communities: Journal of Cooperative Living 23:8–15.

Mallory, Cynthia

1978 Feminism in MNS. Communities: Journal of Cooperative Living 33:15–17.

Marcuse, Herbert

1955 Eros and Civilization: A Philosophical Inquiry into Freud. Boston: Beacon.

Margolies, Rick

1972 Building Communes. Alternatives 3:2–6.

Mumford, Lewis

1922 The Story of Utopias. New York: Boni and Liveright.

Muncy, Raymond Lee

1973 Sex and Marriage in Utopian Communities: 19th-Century America. Bloomington: Indiana Univ. Pr.

Nordhoff, Charles

1875 The Communistic Societies of the United States. Reprint 1965. New York: Shocken.

Noyes, John Humphrey

1870 History of American Socialisms. Reprint 1961. New York: Hillary House.

Oats, Marnie

1972 Twin Oaks. Women: A Journal of Liberation 2:28–30.

Rexroth, Kenneth

1974 Communalism: From Its Origins to the Twentieth Century. New York: Seabury.

Roberts, Ron E.

1971 The New Communes: Coming Together in America. Englewood Cliffs, NJ: Prentice-Hall.

Shils, Edward

1968 Charisma. International Encyclopedia of the Social Sciences 2: 386–90. New York: Macmillan.

Singer, Morningstar
    1975   Developing a Matriarchy. Communities: Journal of Cooperative
            Living 17:36–37.
Skinner, Burris F.
    1948   Walden Two. Reprint 1962. New York: Macmillan.
Snyder, Lillian M.
    1978   The Role of Women in the Icarian Colony. Paper given at meeting
            of the Illinois Sociological Association.
Veysey, Lawrence
    1973   The Communal Experience: Anarchist and Mystical Counter-Cul-
            tures in America. New York: Harper and Row.
Wagner, Jon
    1975   Haran: Charisma and Ideology in a Contemporary American Com-
            mune. Ph.D. diss. Indiana Univ.
    1976   Male Supremacy: Its Role in a Contemporary Commune and Its
            Structural Alternatives. International Review of Modern Sociology
            6:173–80.
    1978   Utopian Societies and the Charismatic Individual. In Essays in
            Humanistic Anthropology, ed. B. T. Grindal and D. W. Warren.
            Washington: Univ. Pr. of America.
Wallace, Anthony F. C.
    1956   Revitalization Movements. American Anthropologist 58:264–81.
Webber, Everett
    1959   Escape to Utopia: The Communal Movement in America. New
            York: Hastings House.
Weber, Max
    1968   On Charisma and Institution Building. Selected Papers, ed. S. N.
            Eisenstadt. Chicago and London: Univ. of Chicago Pr.
Weiss, Michael
    1974   Living Together: A Year in the Life of a City Commune. New York:
            McGraw-Hill.
Wilson, Bryan
    1975   The Noble Savages: The Primitive Origins of Charisma and Its
            Contemporary Survival. Berkeley and Los Angeles: Univ. of Cali-
            fornia Pr.
Zablocki, Benjamin
    1971   The Joyful Community. Baltimore: Penguin.

-2- MERRILL SINGER

Life in a Defensive Society

The Black Hebrew Israelites

RECENT RESEARCH BY WAGNER (1976) at the midwestern commune of "Haran" has shown that the supposed link between sexual egalitarianism and communal solidarity (Kanter 1973) is illusory. According to Wagner, male supremacy "is not only compatible with the survival and growth of a commune, it may indeed ... contribute to group cohesion" (1976:180). At Haran the belief that the female influence is potentially dangerous discourages males of the community from forming intimate love bonds with female members. By functioning as a technique for "dyadic renunciation," this type of male supremacy can be grouped among the organizational patterns and beliefs which Kanter (1972) labels "commitment-building mechanisms." Only by developing various methods for the enhancement of group loyalty and devotion can communes overcome the numerous internal and external forces which threaten communal life.

This paper reports another way in which male supremacy may contribute to communal cohesion. In their effort to combat outside opposition and internal dissension, members of the Black Hebrew Israelite community have adopted a rigidly hierarchical structure which includes the complete subordination of women to men. The Black Hebrew woman looks to her husband as her personal godhead and to every adult male of the community as a direct superior. What Kanter (1972) terms "dyadic withdrawal," the investment of one's commitment in a spouse or a lover, is avoided through an elaborate system which blocks the formation of intimate pair bonds and which diffuses affective ties throughout the community.

Because it is a highly insulative system which emerged during a period of perceived external opposition, the organizational pattern developed by the Black Hebrews is described as a "defensive structure" (Siegal 1970). This organizational arrangement also proved extremely successful in solving problems of internal disunion, and as a result the Black Hebrews now have a highly ordered and cohesive community.

Besides contributing to our understanding of communal sex roles, the Black Hebrews, or, as they now call themselves, the Original Hebrew Israelite Nation, are of special interest in the study of American communal utopias for two reasons. First, their migrations are a reversal of the general flow of Atlantic sectarian traffic. From the colonial period onward, North America has provided the richest soil for the transplanting of utopian and communitarian aspirations generated in other lands. In 1967 the Black Hebrews became an exception to the pattern when the founders of this millenarian sect left their homes in the American Midwest and journeyed first to Liberia and then to Israel. Rejecting traditional Black American involvement in orthodox Christianity, members of this group claimed lineal descent from the biblical Hebrews and viewed their inspired trek as a return to their never-forgotten homeland. Second, the Black Hebrews are important to understand because of the paucity of published information on Black communalism. Although not well reported, communalism has been one of a number of important religio-political strategies adopted by Black Americans for surviving in a land marked by individual and institutional racism and class oppression (Baer and Singer 1981).

In order to show how male supremacist patterning contributes to group cohesion, this paper analyzes the origin, development, and current organization of the Black Hebrew community. Although formalization of male supremacy developed in response to internal and external problems, the following section places Black Hebrew attitudes toward sex roles in their historical context.

The data presented here were gathered between August 1977 and June 1978 during a participant-observation study of the Black Hebrew community in Israel. During most of this period, my wife and I resided in the apartment complex which houses most of the Black Hebrews living in the Israeli development town of Dimona. I also visited branch settlements of the Black Hebrew community in the towns of Arad and Mitzpe Ramon. In addition to being participants in many aspects of community life, my wife and I conducted formal and informal interviews with both male and female group members. All quotations without bibliographic citation are from informants in this field study.

Origin and Significance of Black Judaism

The emergence of values supporting male dominance in the Black Hebrew community can be attributed partly to a reaction among group members to conditions which they experienced as Black citizens in America. The Black Hebrew community in Israel today has its roots in the fragmented messianic-nationalistic tradition in Black America. This tradition, which at various times and in various groups has borrowed elements of Christianity, Islam, and Judaism, can be traced to the migration of southern Blacks to ghettoized northern cities following the mechanization of southern agriculture. Migration marked an alteration in the geography of Black poverty and suffering but did not lead to an end to these conditions.

In the North, many Blacks were drawn to a diverse assortment of storefront churches and sectarian movements which sprang up in the inner cities and catered to the dissatisfaction and longings of the migrant. Although the majority of these religious groupings were moderate in tone, others developed as nationalist sects combining radical interpretations of Black history and destiny with a rejection of traditional "Negro" identity. Black-nationalist sectarians viewed Negro identity as a White invention which kept Blacks from feeling they had a worthwhile heritage of their own. These sectarians sought to rectify the situation by creating a new Black identity founded on a belief in the unique spiritual importance of Black people.

The rejection of Black life in the United States by Black nationalists included a condemnation of the high rates of "divorces and separation, female-headed households- ... shifting-unions" (Hannerz 1969:71) and resultant "feminine domination" and "masculine marginality" (Schulz 1969:67, 107) now common among lower-class urban Blacks. For example, the Black Muslims, the best known of the Black nationalist groups, "claim to have restored the woman to a place of dignity and respect, while restoring to the man his traditional responsibilities as head of the family" (Lincoln 1961:22). Such values are shared by the Black Hebrews, as is evident from this statement by an informant in the Dimona community:

> In America, because of slavery, the structure of the family was torn apart; the man wasn't allowed to be the head of the family and so families became matriarchal. The man is the head in an ideal marriage; there is so much love, the woman wants whatever the man wants and so there is complete harmony. He is the head and makes all the decisions.

The exact date when Black-nationalist ideas turned to an identification with Judaism is not known, but with northern migration the proximity and harmony which initially developed between Blacks and migrant Eastern European Jews provided an environment for the growth of Black Judaism. This identification was no doubt founded on an older Black empathy with the hopes and sufferings of the biblical Hebrews. Eventually the idea was forged that the forefathers of the Jewish people were Black men whose descendants were taken as slaves to America. Following the creation of the earliest organized Black Jewish groups in Harlem during the post-World War I period, similar groups emerged in a number of eastern and midwestern cities. A recent comparative study (Shapiro 1970) disclosed a great deal of variation among the various Black Jewish sects, including some, like the Black Hebrews, who accept the New Testament as one of their holy books.

Since the appearance of the first Black Jewish sects, there has been a great deal of fragmentation, reorganization, and dissolution of the various independent factions. During the 1960s the radically increased expression of Black dissatisfaction, heightened expectation, and associated search for a respectable identity for the Black person in America led to the emergence of a more activist form of Black Judaism. Patterned on the Zionist model of rejection of assimilation and a return to the homeland, this more rebellious impulse found its ultimate expression in the exodus of the Black Hebrew Israelites from America's shores.

Exodus of the Black Hebrew Israelites

One of the many small Black Jewish congregations in America, formed during the early 1960s, was called the Abeta Hebrew Israel Cultural Center. Meeting in a rented apartment on the south side of Chicago, the Abeta congregation was under the leadership of a number of *Morim Tzaddakim* (Hebrew for "Righteous Teachers") who preached that American Blacks were God's chosen people and that the time of their redemption was near. Among the teachers at the Abeta center was a young foundry worker by the name of Ben Carter, who was to become the charismatic leader of the Black Hebrew Israelite movement.

Carter began his prophetic career with a "vision from God," which he professes to have received in 1966:

> The reason that the Father blessed me was my sincere love for the Father and my sincere love for my people. Other than that I was like many of our people in the ghettos of America.... The plan came to me by a vision. One day as I was meditating on the Father the entire plan from the going out, the exodus from the land of captivity—America—on up until the Kingdom of God would be in its glory was revealed.

After receiving this vision, Carter, who had adopted the Hebrew name Ben Ami ("Son of My People"), began to preach that the time for the exodus from America, the land of enslavement and oppression of Black people, had arrived. In time, Ben Ami and the other Abeta leaders were able to gather around them several hundred enthusiastic young followers who shared a rejection of American life.

In line with the Back-to-Africa dreams of previous Black-nationalist groups, the Abeta members looked to Africa as the awaiting homeland. In early 1967 the group secured several hundred acres of thickly forested land about 100 miles from the Liberian capital of Monrovia, and by August 1967 the first settlement groups were ready to depart. Over the next two and a half years, approximately 200 men, women, and children left their homes, friends, and families to join the Black colony planted on the African continent.

The Black Hebrews erected tents and structures of plaited bamboo on the land they came to call "The Camp." They cut back the forest, planted the seeds they brought from America, and dug wells for water. Despite these efforts, their communal agricultural endeavor was a failure. Group members squandered available funds on expensive, imported American foodstuffs and on taxi trips to the city. When their funds ran out, the Black Hebrews were forced to subsist on an unwholesome diet of rice and flour gravy. Further complicating their situation, many fell victim to malaria and other disabling diseases, and seven members of the Camp died. At this point group commitment began to waiver, and internal dissension mounted. As a result, several of the leaders dropped out, as did about fifty of the rank and file.

During this low ebb in community fortunes, Ben Ami turned to the

Liberian government for assistance. With the aid of Liberian president William V. S. Tubman, the Black Hebrews were able to secure
a three-month government subsidy as well as employment for a
number of individuals at mines and factories around the country.
This infusion of new capital enabled the Black Hebrews to open
several ice cream parlors and to organize a successful jazz band.

Even with these various new sources of income, the Black Hebrews never achieved financial stability in Liberia. The colony per-
sisted, but did not thrive, and finally Ben Ami announced to his
followers that the time had arrived to move to Israel. The Black
Hebrews now maintain that they always intended to go to Israel
after a "cleansing period" in the African wilderness. Ex-members
deny this claim, and thus it is difficult now to know at what point
Israel became the object of their utopian dreams. At any rate, in the
spring of 1968, the Black Hebrews began to make preparations for
another migration.

Even prior to this second migration, a male supremacist pattern
was already evident in the Black Hebrew settlement. It was the
men's job to clear the heavy jungle growth, to construct housing, and
to dig wells while the women were busy with domestic chores, including cooking and the care of small children. Decision making was in
the hands of the males, and the women were expected to be obedient
to their husbands. Yet, like much else in the community at this
point, sexual relations did not conform to a rigidly prescribed pattern, nor were they supported by an elaborate rationale. Several
women were employed in Monrovia and another opened a small
restaurant near the Camp. Only with the second migration, as the
group began to confront the problem of commitment, did masculine
domination emerge as a highly formalized system of beliefs and
behaviors.

The Black Hebrews and the State of Israel

At two o'clock on the morning of December 12, 1969, 39 Black
men, women, and children landed at Lod Airport near Tel Aviv and
claimed the right to enter Israel as Hebrew Israelites returning to
their homeland. This unusual group of would-be immigrants attracted a great deal of media and public attention. A smaller contingent, which had arrived a few months earlier and which was already
settled in the town of Arad, had gone largely unnoticed by the mass

media. But this larger group of Blacks, their worldly possessions in hand, attracted the attention of even the international press.

According to the Israeli Law of Return (sec. 1), "Every Jew has the right to come to [Israel] as an immigrant." Because of the law, airport officials are accustomed to the arrival of Jewish immigrants from all parts of the world. But the appearance of the Black Americans, speaking broken Hebrew and wearing skull caps, astonished the immigration personnel. Finally, with the approval of the deputy prime minister, the new arrivals were given temporary status, assigned apartments in the Negev development town of Dimona, and extended other privileges usually accorded new immigrants. The permanent status of the Black Hebrews was left open, because initial questioning suggested to Israeli officials that the Blacks, though sincere in their desire to settle in Israel, did not appear to be a community with a long-standing Jewish tradition or identification. The determination of the Black Hebrews' claims to Israeli citizenship was left for the Ministry of the Interior to decide.

It appears that the Black Hebrews were initially well received in Dimona, a spartan but successful development town founded in 1955 as part of a dual effort to populate the Negev and to provide for a wave of North African immigrants to Israel. Sect members were housed in furnished, low-rent apartments in an integrated neighborhood, employment was provided at local factories, and children were admitted into Dimona's schools. Not long after settling in Dimona, a leader of the Black Hebrews stated, "It is wonderful to be in a free country and be among one's brothers who have behaved so kindly to you" (quoted in Cheatham 1972:8).

Upon their arrival, the chief rabbi of Dimona set out to welcome the Black Hebrews to their new home. After lengthy discussions, the rabbi concluded that the Black Hebrews did not qualify as Jews under Jewish law and therefore did not meet the requirements for entrance into Israel under the Law of Return. The rabbi offered to begin conversion procedures so that the new arrivals might qualify for citizenship and be fully integrated into the Israeli state. After considering the conversion idea for some time, the Black Hebrews eventually rejected the offer and instead made a counterproposal: they would be happy, they said, to convert the rabbi into a true Hebrew. The bitterness evoked on both sides by this incident set the stage for potential conflict between the Black Hebrews and their Israeli hosts.

The event which appears to have triggered the rejection of the conversion offer was the arrival in Israel in March 1970 of Ben Ami Carter and his remaining seventy followers from Liberia. The new-comers were admitted into the country as tourists on the basis of their American passports, but, because of the determination that the Black Hebrews did not qualify under the Law of Return, they were not given jobs or other immigrant benefits. Rather than return to Liberia, Ben Ami and his followers crowded into the existing apart-ments held by the group in Arad and Dimona. Several groups of Black Hebrews who subsequently arrived in Israel directly from the United States were also denied housing and other privileges. The Blacks protested this action, moved their cohorts into their already overflowing apartments, and withdrew their children from Israeli public schools. Herein began a conflict-strewn trail of accusations, threats, demonstrations, arrests, and deportations—a spiral of con-frontation between sect members and the Israeli government which still continues.

The position of the Israeli government has been that Israel was founded as a refuge for Jewish exiles the world over and as such cannot be thrown open to settlement by every quasi-Jewish sect which might seek to settle there. Already struggling with a multi-tude of internal problems created by the arrival of Jews from diverse backgrounds, Israeli officials have become hesitant to admit commu-nities such as the Black Hebrews which do not seek to integrate with the Israeli population. Contributing to the ill feeling on the part of Israelis have been Black Hebrew statements to the effect that Jews are usurpers and that only Black Hebrews have a biblical claim to Israel. As a leader of the Black Hebrews stated:

> We did not go into Israel to integrate into the European-Jewish economy there. We did not go there to be Black Jews. We did not go there to get a job per se and become part of that structure. We went there to make it clear that Black people in America are the descendants of the Biblical Israelites and that the appointed time has come for us to stand up and claim our land, our language and our culture, and that's what we went for. [Quoted in Fuller 1975:71]

This leader, the chief recruiting officer of the Black Hebrew group, went on to say that soon the "illegal government" in Israel will fall and that Israel "will be in the hands of Black people from America, with the authority in the Original Hebrew Israelite Nation" (Fuller 1975:76).

As relations between the Black Hebrews and the Israeli government degenerated, the government began to block the entrance of new Black Hebrew recruits into the country and to deport those already in Israel whose tourist visas had expired. The deportations continued until 1973, when Israel's attention was diverted by the October War with her Arab neighbors. In the confusion during the aftermath of the war, the Black Hebrews were able to rebuild their depleted ranks through a rapid influx of several hundred new members. To avoid further antagonization of Israeli officials, the Black Hebrews also began to tone down their public statements and demonstrations.

Today the Black Hebrew population in Israel stands at approximately 900 individuals living in three development towns in the Negev Desert. Members of the community are allowed to work in factories and mines in the surrounding area, and in 1978 Black Hebrew workers won membership in the Histadrut, the major Israeli trade union. Although the Israeli government does not provide low-cost housing to the Black Hebrews, sect members are free to rent apartments on the open market. Black Hebrew children have never returned to Israeli public schools; instead, the community began its own school called the Kingdom School in Holiness. Overall relations between the Israeli government and the group have remained unsettled. In 1978, in response to growing citizen demands that a resolution to the problem be reached, the Interior Ministry established a special committee under parliamentarian David Glass to study the group and make recommendations to the Israeli Knesset. After two years of deliberations, the Glass committee concluded that the Black Hebrews should be given resident status, citizenship benefits and obligations, and a plot of land to establish an agricultural community, in exchange for an agreement from group members to end their active recruitment of new adherents in the United States and Africa. Claiming a basic incompatibility between Israel's efforts to maintain and nurture the Jewish character of the country and the Black Hebrew lifestyle and alleged anti-Semitism, government officials have either ignored or openly spurned the recommendations of the Glass committee. Recent media reports of extensive illegal activity by Black Hebrew members still in the United States (Fish and Tofani 1981) have bolstered the rejection of the committee's findings.

Consequently, tension continues to mount and no just solution seems in sight.

Black Hebrew Communal Organization

Bernard Siegal (1970:11) has argued that societies "whose members attempt to establish and preserve a cultural identity in the face of what they feel are external threats to that identity" develop a particular organizational arrangement which he labels "defensive adaptation." Members of such defensive societies "see the surrounding environment as hostile and the people in it as preparing to engage in destructive or depriving actions" (ibid.). The current social organization of the Black Hebrew community evolved in response to what group members feel are (perhaps not unwelcome) threats to their identity by the Israeli state. This social organization conforms to the structural arrangement which Siegal claims is typical of defensive societies. Interestingly, the characteristics of defensive societies described by Siegal are quite similar to the "commitment-building mechanisms" which Kanter (1972) has shown are necessary for the forging of successful communities. In response to outside opposition, which community statements and actions apparently helped to generate, the Black Hebrews have been able to develop the commitment mechanisms they lacked in Liberia. As a result, the Black Hebrews have been able to build a stable communal society characterized by tight organization and high morale (Singer 1980). The remainder of this paper will focus on the current organization of the Black Hebrew community, including their handling of sex roles, in light of the arguments of Siegal and Kanter.

In contrasting the Black Hebrew community of today with what it was in Liberia, one of the Black Hebrew leaders stated:

> In Liberia, we wasn't a nation of people. . . . At that point we were just a group of people. We had no structure. On entering the land [Israel] we had to get some kind of governmental structure and become a nation of people.

Nomenclature changes adopted by the Black Hebrews since going to Israel graphically portray this transition: today the Black Hebrews refer to their community as "The Nation" or "The Kingdom" and to group members as "Saints." The structural modifications associated with this transformation conform to the following features of defensive societies described by Siegal (1970):

1. Strong centralized authority, including stress laid on subordination of the individual to the group.
2. Emphasis on solidarity, in-group harmony, and cooperative effort.
3. Clearly defined group boundaries marked by distinctive badges of membership.
4. Rigid patriarchal family patterns and general female subordination.

Each of these features will be discussed as it is manifested in the Black Hebrew community.

Centralized Authority

A striking aspect of the Black Hebrew community is its highly centralized organization resembling a pyramid in structure. At the pinnacle of this pyramid is Ben Ami. Though he was but one of several leaders in the beginning of the movement, Ben Ami survived the "trials" of Liberia to become the undisputed head of the Black Hebrew community. It appears that as the other leaders dropped out and as morale plummeted, Ben Ami was elevated to a position of near deification, which gave ultimate legitimation to his pronouncements. Today, Ben Ami is viewed by his devoted followers as the Son of God and heralded messiah. The Black Hebrews hold that following World War III Ben Ami will reign over a worldwide Kingdom of God; a kingdom which will "establish peace, justice, truth, mercy, and love throughout all of the earth." This charismatic leader, his three wives, and eleven children constitute the "royal family" of the Black Hebrew kingdom. Like many communal leaders (Kanter 1972:119), Ben Ami is known to his followers as "Father" (*Aba* in Hebrew). His other titles include *Adonenu Rabenu* ("Our Lord and Master") and *Nasi Hashalom* ("The Prince of Peace"). Ben Ami explains his transformation from manhood to near godhood in the following terms:

> I belong to the Father. I am His vehicle which He is using. I have no mind of my own whatsoever. It all belongs to Him. Whichever way He uses it I don't have no question to raise. I don't have any doubt. I have no mind which belongs to Ben Carter, the old body. . . . That's dead and that's all past.

With regard to his mission, Ben Ami stated:

Moses taught the natural law and he gave the law written upon the stone unto the people. Jesus taught the spirit of the law. I feel that the mission now is the fulfilling of Moses and Jesus and bringing all righteousness into one ... Moses and Jesus are being made to live again through me.

Ben Ami is treated with utmost reverence by his followers, and his picture adorns at least one wall in every Nation apartment. When he enters a room everyone immediately stands, and, should he pass by a group of Saints, the men bow and the women curtsy. One member summed up his first meeting with Ben Ami by saying that he was so awestruck "words could not describe the experience." Like many charismatic leaders, Ben Ami is allowed privileges not enjoyed by the average member. Despite overcrowding in the apartments rented by the Nation, the group maintains two private homes, one in Jerusalem and the other in Arad, largely for Ben Ami's private use.

Beneath Ben Ami in the leadership hierarchy are twelve *nesim* ("princes"; singular: *nasi*), who together with the leader constitute the Holy Council, the unelected, unquestioned ruling body in the Black Hebrew community. Pronouncements from the Council are seen as divinely inspired, hence not subject to debate. For the highly committed member, this unquestioning attitude can be carried to great lengths, as evidenced in a comment by a young man: "If one of our leaders told me to jump out of the window, I would, because I know he would have a good reason to do it. Perhaps it is because now we can fly." The nesim are believed to be the reincarnations of Christ's twelve apostles, and each nasi is seen as personifying one of the "divine attributes" of God. Titles of the various nesim which reflect these attributes include "Prince of Mercy," "Prince of Zeal," "Prince of Love," and "Prince of War." The Black Hebrews always provide elaborate definitions for the different roles in their communal structure. The following definition of a nasi was given in the Black Hebrew School:

A nasi is one who sits at the right hand of God, around the throne of God. He is the closest being to God in the flesh. God in the flesh is in the body of Adonenu [Ben Ami]. A nasi is the next step down from God, an elevated one, elevated beyond all beings on earth.

Given their lofty position, the nesim are accorded great respect by the Saints. In an address to a Black Hebrew gathering, the Prince

of Mercy summed up the attitude Kingdom members should take
toward the nesim:

> The thing you've got to learn is to do what you are told without
> questioning it.... If you're told to run up those stairs and stand
> there for two days, then you better run up those stairs and stand
> there for two days. Don't get to the top of the stairs and start to
> questioning, why am I up here.... Just do what you're told.

Although violations of their leader's instructions still occur, on the
whole the Black Hebrews seem to be a fairly obedient following.

The wives of the nesim are also shown great respect. They are
titled *nesiot* ("princesses") and are expected to set a "divine example" for the other women of the Nation. The nesiot tend to be the
leaders of women's activities.

Subordinate to the Holy Council are ten *sarim* ("ministers"; singular: *sar*) who serve as the heads of various government-style ministries. These ministries function to meet the basic needs of the
community such as food, clothing, shelter, transportation, education, and entertainment. Like many aspects of the community, the
names given to these ministries, such as "Divine Distribution," "Divine Education," and "Divine Sanitation," are imbued with the
spiritual power believed by the Black Hebrews to be incorporated
into their Nation.

Together, the nesim and sarim make up what the Black Hebrews
call their "Divine Government." As Kanter (1972:117) suggests, the
authority hierarchy in communal societies like the Black Hebrews
seems to limit "members' access to the ultimate wielder of power in
the community and thus enhance the sense of awe surrounding the
demands and dictums of the system." By forming a protective buffer
between Ben Ami and the members, the nesim and sarim support
the leader's aura of infallibility. The individuals holding the positions in the Divine Government are appointed by Ben Ami for life,
barring some major transgression of group rules. Only one sar has
been deposed from office, and he has since left the group and returned to America.

All the top leaders of the Nation are male, for it is not believed
proper for a woman to have such a calling. However, both the Deputy Minister of Education and the community's "doctor" are women.
The former assumed her office when her husband's illness began to
interfere with his effective functioning as Minister of Education, and
the latter gained her position while the group was still in Liberia

(Singer 1981). Both these women are married to members of the Divine Government.

The remaining members of the adult population of the community are organized into the Brotherhood and the Sisterhood. Members of these groups fill the numerous slots within the bureaucratically structured ministries. Almost all the brothers and sisters hold one or more positions within the hierarchy of the Nation.

Entrance into the Brotherhood or the Sisterhood occurs at about age seventeen, but can vary depending on the leaders' evaluation of an individual's spiritual progress. Before this time an individual is not allowed to marry or engage in courtship. When it is decided that a group of youths is ready for the transition from the asexual world of adolescence to the sexual world of adulthood, a rite of passage entitled "Coming Out" is held. This is a festive occasion marked by celebration held in honor of the initiates. Another important ritual associated with these sodalities is called "International Sisterhood Day." This holiday functions as a rite of reversal in Black Hebrew society. On this day, women gather together for picnics, fashion shows, volleyball games, and craft displays, while men are responsible for the housework.

Even within the Brotherhood and the Sisterhood there exists a stratification system which differentiates members on the basis of spiritual progress. The more advanced are called "Senior Brothers and Sisters" and are looked upon with deference by junior members. Kanter (1972:108–9) has shown that in nineteenth-century communes similar stratification enhanced group commitment by creating a desire for spiritual mobility among the less committed, hence lower-status, members.

As the description above suggests, the individual within the Black Hebrew community is fitted into an all-embracing structure, or total institution. Each member has a designated place in the group and a set of associated responsibilities. As is characteristic of defensive societies (Siegal 1970:12), the individual is subordinate to the group. Consequently, all assertions of individualism are criticized as being "of the devil." Deindividuating mechanisms, such as multiple-couple wedding ceremonies, undifferentiated burial, and collective graduation into adult status, serve to substitute "a group-based identity for one based on individual differences" (Kanter 1972:110). Individuals who continue to disobey the "Guidelines of the Kingdom" are subject to various sanctions including hair shaving, beatings with a rubber paddle, and temporary or permanent expulsion. A fifteen-year-old boy caught shoplifting during the author's field study, for example, had all his hair shaved off and was not allowed to wear the usual male head covering for over a month. The Ministry of Divine Sentinel handles erring members and acts as an internal police force.

All the Black Hebrew communities—Dimona, Arad, and Mitzpe Ramon—conform to the same structure. Both branch settlements are under the immediate direction of a nasi and a sar who reside in the community. But Dimona, which the Black Hebrews call "The Spiritual Capital of the World," is the headquarters of the Nation, and all important instructions are issued from there. Dimona also has the largest Black Hebrew population, approximately 500 individuals, with Arad and Mitzpe Ramon averaging about 200 members each. Travel and telephone contact among the three towns is constant, and individuals are shuffled back and forth among settlements, as jobs or apartments become available. The geographic separation of the Black Hebrew communities provides several unintended benefits for the Saints: greater intimacy is possible in the smaller groups, while a sense of "nationhood" is provided by having a number of settlements.

In sum, the Black Hebrews have created a highly ordered, centrally controlled community structure. This pattern, which grew up in response to the perception of outside opposition, provides certainty and security for its members. However centralized decision making may be in the community, most Black Hebrews, males and females, enjoy a great sense of participation in group life.

Communion

A second characteristic of defensive societies which closely coincides with life in the Black Hebrew community is an emphasis on solidarity, in-group harmony, and cooperative effort. Among the Black Hebrews, group unity is a topic of constant concern, as seen in the common expression by the Saints that theirs is a community which has achieved "perfect love" among all its members. Speakers during Nation gatherings often express their love for the assemblage, and, like the Shakers, Black Hebrews passing on the street exchange embraces and expressions of love. The Saints have even instituted a holiday called *Yom Mokeerim* ("Day of Appreciation"), which focuses on group solidarity. As a man of the community explained:

> It is a day on which we express our love for the other Saints,
> especially for the Prince of Peace [Ben Ami].... It is geared to
> express love to those in the Nation outside your immediate family,
> a day on which we give gifts and send cards ... I'm sending cards
> to people who haven't been in the Nation a long time, to make
> them feel welcome and a part of things. Also to brothers who
> might be stumbling a little bit or having a hard time. I'd send it
> to them just to let them know that someone loves them.

Another member of the Nation described the Saints as forming
"the only personal community in the world." This sentiment reflects
the effort to create a *Gemeinschaft,* or face-to-face community. Like
many communal utopias, the Black Hebrews express the *Gemeinschaft* ideal by describing their group as "one big family" and by
referring to community members as brothers and sisters. This
familial model is further emphasized through the establishment of
fictive kinship ties called "spiritual relatives." Members of the community, most of whom left their consanguineal relatives behind in
the United States, are urged to seek out spiritual mothers, fathers,
sisters, and brothers within the community. Because the nesim are
looked to as the elders of the Nation and are generally somewhat
older than others in the community, they are usually chosen as the
spiritual fathers, and their wives as the spiritual mothers, of group
members. Consequently, even the chain of authority is incorporated
into the familial pattern. As Kanter (1972:131) has suggested, "Cen-
tralization in a face-to-face group need not ... be coercive, but may
merely be the organizational fact that lends the group coherence and
unity."

Fictive kinship ties among the Saints create numerous, crosscut-
ting lines of sentimental connection which unify the community.
Yet these ties may also reflect how the rapid growth of the Nation
in the last five years is straining the *Gemeinschaft* experience of
group members. Some spiritual families have begun to have their
own private celebrations, and a certain degree of interfamily rivalry
has developed. The emergence of spiritual relatives may well be an
attempt to adapt the familial model to an ever-expanding community.

Another aspect of the emphasis on solidarity in the Nation is a
condemnation of all in-group fighting and arguing. For example,
during the fieldwork, a woman who quarreled with another over

food preparation was severly chastised by one of the men. When she tearfully defended her actions, the woman was told as follows:

> You shouldn't have argued. The *yeledim* ["children"] are never supposed to see that kind of thing. Instead or arguing, you should have gone to her husband and said "You better get control of your wife," or you should have gone to the nasi.

In another case, this time involving a domestic quarrel, the erring couple was placed in separate living quarters until they could get along more peacefully. As these examples show, interpersonal conflicts are ultimately referred to individuals of higher authority, usually the nesim or sarim, for resolution. Even among the children, when arguing breaks out someone usually runs off to get an adult. Given the size of the community and the cramped living situation, the amount of openly expressed in-group hostility is suprisingly low. Apparently, shared perception of outside opposition functions effectively to suppress or redirect internal dissension.

The Black Hebrews employ several additional techniques which enhance group solidarity. One such technique is the arranging of regularized group contact. Kanter (1972:99) has proposed that

> frequent group meetings and member attendance at a large number of community events ... serve a communion function ... because they bring together the entire collectivity and reinforce its existence and meaning, regardless of the purpose of the gathering.

Black Hebrew gatherings are numerous and varied. Some of the regular gatherings include weekly Sabbath services, Saturday talks by Ben Ami, group concerts, game nights, Brother- and Sisterhood meetings, sports events, dance performances, plays, parties, food sales, holiday gatherings, craft displays, weddings, and classes in group ideology. Two types of these gatherings—concerts and sports events—are especially important because they bring together members from all three towns. Concerts, featuring various of the many musical groups in the Nation, are held about once a month. Often the community center in Dimona is rented for this purpose, and Black Hebrews attend clothed in their finest garments. A handful of Israelis also usually attends. Concerts almost always end with most of the audience up on their feet singing and excitedly dancing to the music of the group's main band, the Soul Messengers. Often at these events several women enter into altered states of consciousness and fall writhing to the floor or "speak in tongues." The group explains such occurrences as "possession by the Holy Spirit." These trance states do not seem to be especially encouraged or discouraged by the Black Hebrews, but are casually accepted as proof of the spiritual importance of the Nation.

The other type of group gathering which regularly brings together Saints from all three settlements is sports events. The Black Hebrews maintain a busy year-round calendar which emphasizes team sports such as baseball, basketball, and volleyball. For each activity the Nation has organized teams dressed in special uniforms made by the community's seamstresses. Not surprisingly, more attention is focused on the male sports league than on the women's league. For both males and females, however, great emphasis is placed on staying in top physical condition. Included within the ideology of the group is the belief that, by staying physically fit and by abstaining from such "harmful foods" as meat, sugar, and dairy products, it is possible to live forever.

Other solidarity-building mechanisms found in the Black Hebrew community include the presence of group ritual and the growth of a group tradition. Following the biblical injunction, the Black Hebrew Sabbath runs from sunset on Friday until sunset on Saturday. No work ought to be done during this period, but, unlike Orthodox Jews, the Black Hebrews turn on electric devices such as tape recorders or sound amplifiers during the Sabbath. This is but one example of the many ways in which the religious system created by the Black Hebrews differs from those of mainstream Judaism.

On Friday evenings a worship service is held in the group's *beyt knesset* ("House of Assembly"). In Dimona, the beyt knesset is located in a bombshelter lent to the Saints by the municipal government. The Sabbath service usually consists of an opening prayer, followed by a sermon on group values and beliefs, gospel music, and a closing prayer. Sermons are delivered by one of the priests or aspiring priests of the Nation and are accompanied by a lively responsory from the audience. Other services, which are either based on the holidays listed in Leviticus or are inventions of the group, also follow this pattern. Jewish holidays not listed in Leviticus, such as Channukah or Rosh Hashana, are not celebrated. Instead, the Black Hebrews commemorate a number of important dates in their own community's history, such as the exodus from America (called the

"New World Passover") or the inauguration in October 1971 of the Divine Government (Guidelines of the Kingdom of God Revealed). The Black Hebrews issue their own printed calendar, citing the holy days of the group, which is found in all Nation apartments. The annual cycle of Black Hebrew holidays functions to separate the group from its Jewish neighbors, while simultaneously reifying group existence. The new recruit finds he is invited to participate in an active community with its own ritual cycle and group traditions, factors which undoubtedly aid the individual in making the break with his American past.

The Black Hebrews have not limited their community-building efforts to techniques which facilitate solidarity and harmony. Despite difficult circumstances, the group has evolved a truly communal society. In contrast with the majority of successful communes, the Black Hebrews are situated in an urban setting, and, unlike the few successful urban communes, such as Synanon, the Saints are not physically isolated from the outside world in a private building. In Dimona, for example, the community rents twenty-four two- and three-bedroom apartments. Sixteen of these dwellings are in a residential area called Victory neighborhood, a complex of four courtyards situated around a central commercial plaza. The courtyard in the northeast corner of the complex is the center of the Black Hebrew community in Dimona and in Israel generally. The Nation rents thirteen of the sixty apartments in this courtyard. Ben Ami and three nesim, including the man who is second in charge of the community, live here. Also located in this building, either in apartments or in basement bombshelters, are many of the major institutions and facilities of the community. These include a leathershop, sewing shop, vegetable store, band rehearsal room, meeting room, appliance repair room, infirmary, guest house, and the central office of the Nation. Members of the community can always be found in this courtyard, standing around talking, sunning themselves, or conducting classes. Israelis passing through the courtyard may nod politely to the assembled Black Hebrews, but contact is usually kept to a minimum. Both the psychic defense and the sense of self-importance among the Saints are sufficiently strong to enable them to ignore the stares of nonmembers. Three Black families, who either quit or who were expelled from the Nation, also live in the community's central courtyard. These "rebel" families are completely shunned by the Saints.

In each Black Hebrew apartment resides an average of eighteen individuals. This number commonly includes two or three married couples, a number of unmarried adults, and a group of children. By Western standards the apartments of the Black Hebrews are extremely overcrowded. Yet this situation may be quite conducive to successful communal life; perhaps for this reason many utopias develop residential patterns which limit private space. Supporting this interpretation is the fact that despite crowding in the apartments the Black Hebrews rent two houses which often stand empty. These houses serve as retreats for Ben Ami, rest areas for overwrought Saints, and honeymoon quarters. In 1980 the Dimona city government allowed the Saints to move into a number of duplex apartments in an abandoned immigrant absorption center. Consequently, the level of crowding in the Black Hebrew community is now somewhat lower than during the period of research.

Each married man and his wife (or wives) are given their own bedroom, while children and unmarried adults sleep dormitory-style in the living room. Curtains are strung across the front room every night to separate the unmarried males and females. If a man has more than one wife, co-wives rotate sharing their husband's bedroom. On days when they are not sleeping with their husbands, women will sleep in another room or in a sectioned-off portion of the living room. During the day, the curtains are drawn back and the foam mattresses used as beds are piled up to serve as sofas and chairs. Private property in the household is limited to clothing and such small items as books or paintings; all other household articles are collectively owned.

The principle underlying communal sharing is called "Divine Economics." In explaining this concept, the minister in charge stated:

> Divine Economics is an economic program that is geared to providing the needs of every inhabitant of our nation. . . . Divine Economics is not representing any of the commercial models that you find in the world. It is more of a humane, more of a personal program that serves a man and his family. The underlying principle of Divine Economics is that it is a program that is blessed to God, an economic program in which all men love their brother as themselves and all things are shared in common.

In Liberia the Black Hebrews used a tithe system to meet community needs, but today all production and distribution follows the communistic ideal of "from each according to his abilities, to each according to his needs." On payday all the men bring their checks to the Minister of Divine Economics, who in turn distributes the money on a preestablished plan according to need. The minister explained:

> If a man has a family with five children and another has a family with ten children, then based upon what we have to distribute, the man with the largest family would receive the most because his need is greater.

The economics minister and his staff calculate the amount needed by each family to pay for food and clothing, and allocate funds accordingly. The minister holds back money to pay the rent and utility bills for all the apartments rented by the community. In addition, money from the *kupa* ("central fund") is used to meet "national needs" such as maintenance of the community's four vehicles and the salaries of the teachers in the Kingdom School in Holiness.

The funds furnished to each of the families or individuals living together in an apartment are pooled to provide for the entire household. One man, who is "well vested and thoroughly knowledgeable" of the guidelines of the Nation, is appointed the "senior brother" in each apartment. He oversees the functioning of the dwelling and meets with the other adult male residents to make household decisions. Should difficulties arise, a ready procedure exists for handling them. Individuals who are in disagreement call in a third person to listen to the problem. Should a settlement not be reached in this way, the quarreling individuals are expected to take their conflict to the sarim for resolution. Housework is shared by the women of the apartment, usually on a rotational basis. A "senior sister" watches over the performance of women's tasks in each household; she in turn is directly responsible to the senior brother of the apartment. Each apartment sets its own schedules and procedures, but all dwellings must abide by the dictates of the Divine Government.

Most of the food for the household is purchased at the "Nation Store," a distribution center located in a basement bombshelter. Several times a week members of the Ministry of Divine Distribution drive to the wholesale vegetable market in the West Bank Arab city of Hebron to restock the Nation Store. There is considerable savings in collective purchasing, allowing prices in the Nation Store to be somewhat lower than in commercial outlets nearby. Only Saints may shop in the Nation Store, but a health-food store run by the Nation in Dimona's downtown area is open to the public. If a desired item is not available in the Nation Store, women will go to the local markets and greengrocers to make purchases.

In addition to its basic allowances, each family is provided a "discretionary fund" to be used for entertainment or snacks. Often the Nation's school or various of the ministries sponsor fund-raising bake sales or parties, insuring that most of the discretionary funds stay within the community. The Black Hebrews have found that using money within the Nation facilitates equal distribution of goods and services. Each family must budget its consumption to fit its allotted capital. In this fashion the Black Hebrews have successfully integrated a communitarian society into the surrounding market economy.

Community Boundaries

Kanter (1972:83) has shown that "most successful [utopian] communities of the past developed sets of insulating boundaries—rules and structural arrangements that minimized contact with the outside." These boundaries simultaneously limit the appeal the outside world might hold for the sect members, while protecting members from negative evaluation from outside the community. A variety of insulating devices are available to communitarian societies, and the number which a group adopts undoubtedly suggests the degree of distance the group feels from the surrounding social world. Judged by the numerous devices the Black Hebrews employ, they can be described as feeling almost totally at odds with the world.

An obvious boundary-maintaining aspect of the Black Hebrew community is geographic isolation from the familiar and alluring sights and sounds of the Black neighborhoods of America. Geographic isolation frees the Saints from the presence of old "bad habits" and from the appeals of rival Black sects, while at the same time insulating members from criticism from old friends and relatives regarding their putative Hebrew identity. Migration to Israel also makes withdrawal from the community physically difficult. Since members are not allowed to accumulate private wealth, returning to America is contingent upon securing aid from outside the community. The Black Hebrews' desire for isolation is not limited to separation from America. As their request for land for agricultural settlement suggests, separation from Israelis is also desired.

A second strategy of insulation is through the renunciation of affective ties outside the community. Maintenance of relationships not shared by other group members is disruptive to the familial ideal. A young man of the community, when asked if he missed his family in the United States, responded "No" and then, pointing to several other community members, said, "These are my brothers." In the Black Hebrew community, almost all primary relationships are with other group members, and for good reason: a number of individuals who have left the community had developed friendships with one or more Israelis prior to their disaffection. Black Hebrews are allowed to maintain contacts with their families in the United States and are even encouraged to proselytize in their letters home. Despite this encouragment many Saints stop writing home when confronted with the problem explained by a Minister of Distribution: "I stopped writing to my family because they're in a different world and just can't relate to what I'm talking about."

Associated with renunciation is endogamy. Since coming to Israel, only one Black Hebrew has taken an Israeli spouse, and he has since left the community and returned to the United States. Ethnic homogeneity undoubtedly serves the same function for the Black Hebrew community that physical isolation serves for other communes. Though many of the Indian and North African Jews of Israel are as dark or darker than the Black Hebrews, the Saints share a common background which separates them from nonmembers.

"Institutional Completeness" (Stinchcombe 1965) is a third means of securing group boundaries. Except for outside employment, and some shopping, members of the Nation do not have to go outside the community to satisfy their basic needs. The Black Hebrews even tend to hold community parties on dates coinciding with Israeli holidays, thereby insuring that the Saints will not be attracted to the celebrations of their Israeli neighbors.

Yet another insulating device is the development of a negative conception of nonmembers. To a large degree such a conception is inherent in the initial rejection of society which gives rise to the separatist urge. But in groups like the Black Hebrews, rejection of nonmembers may be greatly embellished over time as a protective measure. The Black Hebrew "response to the world" is of a type which Wilson (1973:23) labels "revolutionist." Groups of this kind believe that "only the destruction of the world, of the natural, but more specifically of the social order, will suffice to save men" (ibid.). This attitude was expressed by a Black Hebrew leader in the following way:

> There's too much wickedness going on in the world. It's too much hate, it's too much selfishness and too much greediness. God Almighty is going to bring disasters down upon the world that's going to destroy all wickedness. After this happens ... the righteous people, those who have been raised up by God, will begin to take the bits and pieces and put them back together and teach the world about the love of God.

An aspect of this defensive ideology is the Black Hebrew doctrine that there exists an evil conspiracy to hide the true identity of the Saints from the people of the world. Products of this "grand conspiracy" include the digging of the Suez Canal (so that people no longer realize that Israel is part of the African continent), the transplanting of Europeans to the Middle East under the guise of the Crusades (so as to replace the Black Arabs who once dominated the region), the adoption of the Jewish religion by White Europeans (so that the world would forget that the original Hebrews were Black), and the "big lie" that six million Jews were killed by the Nazis (so that Jews would gain the sympathy of the world and be given the State of Israel by the United Nations). The Black Hebrews maintain that the ultimate organizer of this far-reaching conspiracy is the devil himself, who acts in the world to frustrate the establishment of God's kingdom on earth. The devil functions as a very useful symbolic enemy for religious groups because he can be seen as wielding almost unlimited power, and his presence can be deduced wherever it is convenient. Even individuals who leave the Nation are called "devils," thereby insulating the Saints from interaction with those who have rejected the community.

Included in the Nation's negative conception of the outside world is a tenet similar to a belief of the communitarian Separatists of Zoar, who held that their native Germany was Babylon. The Black Hebrews believe that America is the latter-day Babylon and is soon to be destroyed. In fact, the term "America" is rarely used in Black Hebrew conversation, being almost wholly replaced by "Babylon" or "the other side." The message communicated to the Saints is that only a fool would drop out of the community and return to a country soon to be a "wasteland covered by howling jackals."

Terminology has also emerged to apply to the Israeli neighbors of the Saints. Nonmembers are referred to as either "gentiles," "strangers," or occasionally "heathens." The seriousness of terminological boundary building was brought home to the author when he was asked by a three-year-old Black Hebrew boy, "Are you a man or a stranger?"

A final boundary-maintaining device employed by the Black Hebrew community is the adoption of distinctive badges or markers of membership. Colorful homemade garments, consisting of crocheted headcoverings, long robes or dashikis, wooden staffs for the men, and large multicolored turbans and long dresses for the women, easily set the Black Hebrews off from the Israeli population. Also, the use of English in a Hebrew-speaking country provides the Saints with a private language for closed communication. Though they assert that as Israelites Hebrew is their true language, after eight years in Israel English is still generally used in community interaction. Like the German of the Hutterites or the Russian of the Doukhobors, the English of the Black Hebrews is a boundary device which was unplanned, but useful nonetheless.

Family Organization and Sex Roles

Choosing neither the path of sexual egalitarianism which Kanter (1973:305) argues is characteristic of cohesive communities nor the completely misogynous road taken by the Ohio River Valley commune of Haran described by Wagner (1976), the Black Hebrews have created a unified society of some duration. Building on a set of attitudes toward sexual relations generated in a rejection of Black life in America, the Black Hebrews have incorporated sex roles into a highly structured system of community organization.

The "Divine Order" of the Black Hebrew community is based on an authority hierarchy in which women are subordinate to men, and both are in turn subordinate to the charismatic leader and his appointed assistants. This chain of authority is replicated in family organization, with children being subordinate to their parents, and wives being subordinate to their husbands. The family model is used to characterize this triadic system of authority relations even with reference to God: "We say that man is the wife of God and is to please God, and women is the wife of man and is to please him."

It is the Black Hebrew belief that God created man and woman to fill different functions in the world. Man's task is to maintain dominion over the world and to be obedient to the will of God, while woman was created to serve man and to be his helpmate. Flowing from this underlying principle, the Black Hebrews have developed a set of community standards which regulates sex roles, sexual relations, and the sexual division of labor from infancy through adulthood. The following discussion examines the Nation's handling of gender differences throughout the life cycle of group members.

The Black Hebrews maintain that the primary reason for marriage is to have children, and the more children the better. Couples attempt conception immediately after marriage. The basis for this belief is said by informants to be divine prescription:

> Sometimes women [in the world] don't want to get married. But how can a women not want to get married? This is natural, to get married and raise a family. . . . God said to be fruitful and multiply, He ain't never said to decrease.

That there may in part be a political motivation behind the high birthrate in the Nation is suggested by a comment of one of the sarim: "We believe in being fruitful and multiplying. We mean to fill up this land." The Black Hebrews are very aware that, as more and more children are born in Israel and as the group expands, it becomes increasingly difficult for the Israeli government to deport the group without incurring international condemnation and accusations of racism.

So far the largest number of children born to a woman in the Black Hebrew community has been ten, but most members are in their early or middle twenties and are well within their childbearing years. The Nation does not fear overpopulation and chides world concern with this issue. In an address to his followers attended by the author, Ben Ami declared: 1

> There is no such thing as overpopulation of the earth. . . . All of a sudden it's going to be too many people and no food. If that could be, rabbits when they have a litter have hundreds of babies, then the world would be overpopulated by rabbits in two or three years. Do it look like it's getting overpopulated with rabbits? Overpopulation, it's a lie. . . . If you needed some family planning, don't you think God would have planned your family?

Childbirth in the Nation is done without the assistance of sedation. In line with the community's condemnation of modern medicine (Singer 1981), babies are born in the "House of Life," an apartment converted by the group into a clinic of natural medicine. The expectant mother is attended by midwives and a Nation priest. Should problems develop, however, the Saints are prepared to overlook ideology and call in a medical doctor.

Based on the twelfth chapter of Leviticus, a mother is considered unclean for forty days after the birth of a boy and for eighty days after the birth of a girl. During this period the mother is freed of all household responsibilities. (The burnt offering, which accompanied this purification rite in biblical days, is not practiced by the Black Hebrews.) A similar seven-day "separation" period is adhered to during menstruation. During these periods of ritual pollution a woman tends to isolate herself somewhat. A red cord is affixed to the door of the woman's apartment to notify others that the dwelling is unclean. At Nation gatherings, new mothers and menstruating women sit apart from the rest of the assemblage. These women usually sit on wash towels so as not to pollute the benches on which they are seated. Male attitudes toward menstruation are reflected in a remark of a new member of the Nation made in the author's presence: "You know, I'm on my separation and I brushed against a brother and he said to me, you're *lo tov* ['no good']. They act like you've got T.B. over here when you're on your separation." The rest period associated with childbirth and menstruation is welcomed by the women, who normally carry a very heavy work load. Despite the longer rest period involved with delivering a girl, expectant mothers showed a definite preference for male children. Of the ten pregnant women queried by the author, nine were hoping for boys, and only one said the sex of her baby did not matter.

Children undergo several rituals soon after birth. At eight days, all male children are circumcised; this brief ceremony is performed by the priest in the House of Life. No parallel rite is performed for girls. The names given to both boys and girls must be approved by Ben Ami. The Deputy Minister of Divine Education is responsible for preparing a list of potential names from which the leader selects the one he feels is most spiritually fitting for the child.

Children are breast-fed for two years, although they begin receiving solid foods at the fifth month. During nursing, children tend to sleep with their mothers, and consequently mother-child contact is initially very close. By contrast, fathers are rarely seen holding young children. The closeness of the mother-child bond starts to loosen at age three when the child begins kindergarten. Mothers admit that this is at first a difficult time. In fact, one of the few problems which the community acknowledged is a certain degree of overprotectiveness in new mothers.

As in other defensive societies (Siegal 1970), nurturance of self-discipline begins early in the Black Hebrew community. From infancy children are taught to be on guard against violation of group rules. A special school class, *Yeledim Tsadikim* ("Righteous Children"), focuses on imparting community standards and is mandatory for all children. As suggested in the following remark by a man of the community, self-control and submission to group leaders are stressed in Black Hebrew socialization:

> We teach discipline and control of ourselves. We learn to discipline ourselves, our actions, our activities, speech and emotions. It's all about submitting ourselves to Ben Ami. . . .

Further, since adults are considered mothers and fathers of all the children in the Nation, anyone is free to punish physically a misbehaving child. Outside observers, including local Israeli officials, marvel jealously at the obedience of Black Hebrew children, although storekeepers complain of shoplifting by Nation youth. Children perceive their parents' hostility toward the surrounding society and are probably inclined more toward rule violation across group boundaries than toward offenses within the community. Peer pressure also plays an important part in obedience. Adults, for example, encourage the children to hold special youth courts to judge their rebellious age-mates. Temporary ostracism by the peer group is a common punishment handed down by these courts.

Sexually differentiated socialization begins early for the Black Hebrew child. An emphasis of the education program developed by the Saints is that girls learn "divine womanly virtues," while boys learn "masculine behaviors." Classes are given to teach the girls cooking and sewing, and the boys auto mechanics and sports skills. As is evident in the following remarks of a Nation teacher, emphasis is placed on teaching status relations and sex-role identification:

> Girls are taught at an early age to respect the brotherhood and that the brothers always come first. Then they can adjust their lives at an early age and are ready to fall into their roles as sisters. . . . Girls are taught to cook, the arts, the handicrafts at an

early age. And they spend a large portion of their day after school
... with their mothers. A boy should be like his father, or the
masculine image, any masculine image in the Kingdom.... But he
should never be found trying to imitate his mother.... Boys
should be interested in sports and in learning many trades or
many things that the brothers know how to do.

Even outside school, boys and girls do not spend much time together.
Children's peer groups are segregated by sex and activity: girls
spend their free time playing jump rope or with homemade dolls;
boys prefer marbles and baseball. After age twelve boys begin trying
to find part-time jobs washing windows or delivering groceries, but
girls never work outside the Nation.

Boys and girls begin to interact more as they enter their middle
teens, but active interest in the opposite sex must be contained until
after the Coming Out ceremony. Following their debut, Saints are
free to engage in "Divine Pursuit." This courtship period, as described by a newlywed man, is structured so that males are able to
maintain the dominant position:

In the Nation, the pursuit is the opposite of the Western World.
In the world, whereas it is the man that pursues, here it is the
woman that pursues the man. If a brother sees a sister he likes,
he can approach her and talk to her. He may even want to take
her for a walk. But he is restricted to the point where he would
not be able to approach her in a serious manner in relation to
marriage.... It is a form of humility for the woman to choose to
come to the man, rather than for the man to come and humble
himself to her.

Men evaluate a potential spouse in terms of the woman's ability to
"humble herself." While engaged in courting a particular young
woman, a Black Hebrew man told the author, "I'm still testing her,
seeing how she serves me, humbles herself to me in a certain kind
of way. She is to be my servant ... so I'm testing her virtues."
Developing the proper submissive attitude is sometimes difficult,
however, for Black Hebrew women. Feeling that her fiance was
being too demanding, one woman commented, "I'd like to hit him
over the head with something. No, I shouldn't say things like that.
The brothers run everything. What I said was unkingdomlike."

Although there are about fifty percent more females than males
among the Black Hebrews, the practice of polygamy has led to what

the community sees as a shortage of women. A number of adult males have been unable to find wives even though they have been in the community for a number of years. One man in this situation became the brunt of derisive gossip among the women when he asked one of the nesiot to help him find a wife, rather than patiently waiting for a wife to find him.

Despite the availability problems, all members of the Nation, including the few elderly members, are expected to marry. When a couple decide that they are ready for marriage, they go see a priest of the Nation. One of the functions of the priest is to serve as a marriage counselor. After conferring with the couple, if the priest decides that they are serious in their desire to be wed, he announces to the Nation that the couple has entered *Mikodeshit* ("Sanctification"), a period of engagement lasting a minimum of seventy days. At this point the names of the couple are removed from the posted list of Saints available for Divine Pursuit, and the engaged individuals are expected to limit their courtship activities to their intended. During the period of Mikodeshit, the couple may go for walks together or hold hands, but all other sexual activity is prohibited. Also during this period, the woman begins to do some of her fiance's laundry and cooks for him occasionally.

The priest sets up ten counseling sessions during Mikodeshit, at which time he teaches the couple about "Divine Marriage." If at any point the priest decides that the couple is not ready for marriage or that they are incompatible, he can extend the engagement period or break it off altogether. The couple also have this prerogative. Marriage is taken seriously in the Nation, because divorce is not permitted.

After they are wed, the couple are provided a room in one of the Nation's apartments, and the husband and wife begin functioning in their respective roles as adult members of the community. For the man this means either working at a paying job outside the Nation or working at a position within the community, such as a schoolteacher. The new bride joins the other women of the household in taking care of the apartment. Because labor-saving devices such as washing machines are prohibited by the group, women are kept quite busy with household chores. Additionally, both men and women are also very involved in numerous Nation activities and responsibilities. This structured "busyness" no doubt serves to limit introspection and questioning, while reinforcing involvement through constant participation. As a woman in the community explained to the author:

> We have so many sisters in each *beyt* ["home"] but still we can't get all the work done. Personally, I feel it was made that way so that we don't get off to thinking about wrong kinds of things. We're too busy for that.

Only after one year of marriage may the man take a second wife. The practice of polygyny is explained as part of God's intended plan. Saints point to biblical figures such as Abraham and Jacob, who had more than one wife, as justification for plural marriage. At present the Black Hebrews believe that a man is allowed four wives, at most, although this figure, based on an original interpretation of Isaiah 4:1, will eventually be raised by God to seven. The current distribution of wives is decidedly in favor of the leaders. Only two men, both leaders, presently have four wives, and only five men, also leaders, have three wives. Of the twenty-three Nesim and Sarim, sixteen have entered plural marriage, compared with about twenty percent of the rank and file. In a society like the Nation, which favors polygyny, plural wives are both a status marker and a reward of leadership.

Although the Black Hebrews may have been practicing polygyny to a limited extent even prior to leaving the United States, it was not until the group was settled in Israel that the system was formally instituted. When the practice was first adopted, there was resistance on the part of some of the women, and several left the community as a result. A woman who overcame her initial objections remarked:

> In accepting the Kingdom, and in accepting our God, and the way of life He has set before us, we can't be accepting in portions. It has to be all or nothing.... So I began to make myself more cooperative and to really look into the advantages of it. And once it's looked at like that it becomes easier to adjust to it. It's only when you're being rebellious that things are hard.

Women who remain in the group come to defend both polygyny and women's subordinate status in Black Hebrew society. In discussing the feminist movement and its attempts to raise women's status, one female informant stated:

> The women's liberation movement to me is a very backwards movement. . . . I wish I could have a chance to talk to some of these women and tell them about the Kingdom and about what women need to be or have got to be. . . . It's certainly not about being liberated in the sense that they speak of in women's liberation.

Although women resist aspects of their assigned role through such acts as going for walks about town without the required male escort and complaining about their difficulties with their Nation sisters, most women accept female subordination as a divine virtue. As Kanter (1972) notes, successful communes tend to require sacrifices of their members. The greater the cost to the individual of a communal practice, the stronger it will be defended in order to maintain psychological consistency.

Despite the verbal and ideological emphasis given to the family unit and to the familial model of organization in the Nation, the Black Hebrew family performs few traditional functions, nor is it a center of emotional intensity or intimacy. As in most communes, the community as a whole has assumed many of the activities commonly associated with the family, including childrearing. Many children in the Nation do not live in the same apartment or even in the same town as their parents. The Saints explain that this is done to teach the children independence. The outside observer is, in fact, struck by how rarely a man is seen together with his wife (or wives) and children. Additionally, there is a great deal of physical contact between all males and females in the community. Women greet males in the Nation with a kiss on the cheek, and dancing with partners other than one's spouse is very common at parties. Fairly intimate physical contact occurs at a Nation function called "Utopia Night," at which women wash and massage the feet, comb and braid the hair, and manicure the fingernails of the men, irrespective of marriage ties. Polygyny can also be added to the list of factors which limit family intimacy or extend intimacy beyond the family unit. All these behaviors support Kanter's (1972:86) assertion that dyadic or family intimacy poses a threat to group cohesiveness that must be controlled or regulated by the community. The Black Hebrews have developed a number of mechanisms for spreading affective ties throughout the community while limiting the strength of any particular set of ties. It appears that it is still important for the Saints, as part of their rejection of the Black American experience, to maintain statements supportive of the nuclear family in official rhetoric. Group organization, however, has long since reduced the functional importance of the family in the course of enhancing group interconnectedness and commitment.

Summary and Conclusions

The foregoing discussion has attempted to view sex-role patterning in the Black Hebrew community from a dynamic perspective. It has been shown that sex roles developed in the community in response to a variety of factors. Some of these influences were purely historical; the founders of the Nation were reacting against a set of experiences they associated with the oppression of Black people in America. Consequently, the dominant position of the woman in many lower-class Black American families was rejected by the Nation, and the male was firmly established as the household head. Beyond this initial reorganization of the family, the Black Hebrews eventually instituted a fairly rigid subordination of female members. This development was part of the overall defensive adaptation which emerged in the Black Hebrew community in response to post-migration disunity and to the perception of outside opposition. This paper has focused on the defensive pattern and the circumstances which led to its formation within the Black Hebrew Nation.

It has been shown that while living in Liberia the Black Hebrews lacked many of the commitment-building mechanisms which characterize successful communes. As a result, the community was plagued by dissatisfaction, dispute, leadership changes, and defections. Beset by overwhelming difficulties, the Saints resorted to migration to Israel as an attempted solution to their problems. Given their identification with the biblical Hebrews, the ease of entrance into Israel for holders of American passports, and the availability of government aid to new immigrants, Israel seemed a likely site for relocating the community. Initially the Black Hebrews were well received in Israel, and, had group members undergone a simple religious-conversion procedure, they might have been integrated into Israeli society (as have other Black Americans who have converted to Judaism). But assimilation was not a desired goal of the Saints in Israel any more than it had been in Liberia, and conversion was rejected.

In time the Black Hebrews discovered that migration had not solved their problems of internal disunion. In 1971 the community was rocked by a major split resulting in the death of one individual and the disaffection of about forty others. A political scientist (Lounds 1976) who studied the community a year later described the Nation as relatively unorganized. It is at this point, it would seem, that the Black Hebrews discovered that the best force for internal unity is a shared outside threat. The Black Hebrews began to make claims to being the only true Hebrews and stated publicly that the Jews would soon be forced out of the land. Having heard the latter decree for some time from various Arab spokesmen, the Israeli government began to stiffen its policy with regard to the Black Hebrews. Saints who violated Israeli law were deported as illegal aliens, and there were even veiled threats that the whole Nation would be deported en masse. Under these conditions of outside opposition, the Black Hebrews were able to forge a unified and highly organized community, and to overcome the commitment problems which almost destroyed the group in Liberia and during the first years in Israel.

Defensive structuring provided the Black Hebrews with a centralized command, a chain of authority, and a unified and ordered membership ready to deal with internal and external threats. Age and gender offered convenient and easily justified axes upon which to extend this structuring through all levels of the community. The pattern of defensive structuring which developed is reflected in the organization of authority in the Nation as shown here:

Ben Ami⟶Nesim⟶Sarim⟶Brotherhood⟶Sisterhood⟶
Children

Every individual in the Black Hebrew community knows his or her place in this hierarchical scheme, thereby facilitating the rapid flow of instructions and increasing the likelihood of compliance. The sex-role patterning which emerged in the process of defensive adjustment emphasizes the subordination of women. In the sense that this subordination directly contributes to effective organization by assigning women a clearly defined position, it can be termed adaptive. The need of group members to reject their experience of Black life in America—including male marginality—in part explains why women's position is at the lower end of the authority hierarchy. Both male and female members of the Nation view lower-class family patterns in the ghetto as an aberration and seek, in the words of one informant, "to return man back to his natural place as the head of woman." Further, to a limited degree, the "deliberate cultivations of ignorance among women" (Siegal 1970:19), common among other defensive societies, is also found among the Black Hebrews. Siegal (1970) explains this tendency in terms of the important role played by women in early socialization. Individuals who possess partial knowledge of valued information often exhibit greater commitment than do those who are fully informed (Festinger 1957). Consequently, the younger generation in the Black Hebrew community acquires a firm psychological attachment to the central values of the Nation through their mothers and mother surrogates even prior to their introduction to substantive information about the community.

Contrary, then, to Kanter's (1973:302) hypothesis, communalism among the Black Hebrews has not been associated with lowered sex-role differentiation. This has been the case because rigid sex-role differentiation has contributed to both psychological adjustment and social adaptation. On the other hand, the extreme patriarchal ideology of the Haran commune also has not developed in the Black Hebrew Nation. The Black Hebrew woman, though at times polluting, is viewed as neither sinister nor disruptive. In fact, Black Hebrew males often praise the sacrifice and devotion of the women of the community. The Black Hebrew case seems to represent another alternative in the range of possible ways for successfully handling sex roles in communal life.

The Black Hebrews also developed alternative approaches for the discouragement of dyadic love bonds and nuclear families. Choosing neither the celibacy of the Shakers, the "free love" of Oneida, nor the misogyny of Haran, the Black Hebrews combined polygynous marriage with a high degree of tactile involvement between all males and females to block exclusive attachments.

The question now becomes, how wide a range is possible for communal organization of sex roles and sexual relations? Kanter's work on the necessity of commitment mechanisms and Siegal's contribution to the understanding of defensive adaptation suggest that structural constraints do exist in communal patterning. The exact nature of these constraints merits further research.

ACKNOWLEDGMENTS

Support for the research reported in this paper was generously provided
by the Graduate Research Fellowship of the University of Utah and the
Jerusalem Center for Anthropological Study. I would like to thank Cheryl
Gorn, Linda Zaleski, Lois Beck, and Kristen Hawkes for reading and commenting on earlier drafts of this paper.

REFERENCES CITED

Baer, Hans, and Merrill Singer
    1981 Toward a Typology of Black Sectarianism as a Response to Racial
          Stratification. Anthropological Quarterly 54:1–14.
Cheatham, Thomas
    1972 Blacks Cite Racism in Israel. Chicago Defender, 2 August, 8.
Festinger, Leon
    1957 Cognitive Dissonance. Stanford: Stanford Univ. Pr.
Fish, H. Bradford, and Loretta Tofani
    1981 Papers Seized at Home of Sect Member. The Washington Post, 12
          June, B3.
Fuller, Hoyt W.
    1975 The Original Hebrew Israelite Nation: An Interview. Black World
          24:62–85.
Hannerz, Ulf
    1969 Soulside Soulside: Inquiries into Ghetto Culture and Community.
          New York: Columbia Univ. Pr.
Kanter, Rosabeth Moss
    1972 Commitment and Community: Communes and Utopias in Sociolog-
          ical Perspective. Cambridge, MA: Harvard Univ. Pr.
    1973 Family Organization and Sex Roles in American Communes. In
          Communes: Creating and Managing the Collective Life, ed. R. M.
          Kanter. New York: Harper and Row.
Lincoln, C. Eric
    1961 The Black Muslims of America. Boston: Beacon.
Lounds, Morris
    1976 Hebrew Israelite/Black Jews: A Case Study in Formation of Group
          Identity. Ph.D. diss., M.I.T.
Schulz, David A.
    1969 Coming Up Black: Patterns of Ghetto Socialization. Englewood
          Cliffs, NJ: Prentice-Hall.
Shapiro, Deanne Ruth
    1970 Double Damnation, Double Salvation: The Sources and Varieties of
          Black Judaism in the United States. M.A. thesis, Columbia Univ.
Siegal, Bernard
    1970 Defensive Structuring and Environmental Stress. American Jour-
          nal of Sociology 76:11–32.

Singer, Merrill
  1980 The Function of Sobriety Among the Black Hebrews. The Journal
        of Operational Psychiatry 22:162–68.
  1981 The Social Meaning of Medicine in a Religious Sect. Medical An-
        thropology.
Stinchcombe, Arthur L.
  1965 Rebellion in a High School. Chicago: Quadrangle.
Wagner, Jon
  1976 Male Supremacy: Its Role in a Contemporary Commune and Its
        Structural Alternatives. International Review of Modern Sociology
        6:173–80.
Wilson, Bryan
  1973 Magic and the Millennium. New York: Harper and Row.

-3- ILSE MARTIN

Inequality, Chastity, and Sign Endogamy in the New Age Brotherhood

THREE CONCEPTUAL SYSTEMS, WITH THEIR concomitant explicit and implicit rules, structure the relationship between men and women in the California commune treated here: inequality, chastity, and sign endogamy. This article describes these conceptual systems, or ideal structures, and analyzes how they function and how members use them, resent them, and are affected and constrained by them even when they try to ignore them.

The data for this study were gathered during a five-month stay in the community as a quasi-member between July and December 1974, as well as during visits to the community in 1973 and 1975. Leading members agreed to permit my study because they also regarded me as a potential long-term member. Discussions with ex-members were also helpful, because members were usually guarded and did not always express their true feelings within the community, whereas ex-members spoke more candidly.

The commune—referred to here by the pseudonym "New Age Brotherhood," or simply "Brotherhood"[1]—was founded in 1970 when a group of about fifteen young people gathered around a man in his early forties who had been a disciple of Paramahansa Yogananda, founder of the Self-Realization Fellowship. At the time of my fieldwork, nearly 200 members lived in four branches located within a few hours' driving distance of each other. The various landholdings amounted to 554 acres, of which 234 acres were leased but have since been purchased. Parts of the latter acreage are fruit orchards. Much of the land is mountainous, and other parts are arid and are mostly

---

[1]"Brotherhood" actually appeared in connection with several other words in the name the community used for self-identification.

dry-farmed because of lack of water. None of the branches was able to support itself completely with farming or horticulture, but since the period of my fieldwork a large tract of coastal land, which is more suitable for agricultural self-sufficiency, was acquired.[2]

Members supported themselves at first by holding jobs in the nearby town, but soon they began to establish a number of businesses. In 1974 there were four community-owned retail markets, a wholesale market operated from a large warehouse, a juice factory, a bakery, and a restaurant. A bus takes members each morning from the branch closest to town to the various enterprises. By June 1975 a financial statement cited $2,000,000 in sales for the preceding twelve months. As early as April 30, 1974, an accounting firm prepared an unaudited financial statement in which a net worth of $2,396,104 was cited. Donations from members, some of them quite wealthy, have been an important additional income source and have aided in rapid expansion. All property is held in common, and members contribute their labor without remuneration. Through hard work they strive to show their dedication to God and their commitment to the community.

Members come from all areas of the United States and Canada. Some have college degrees, whereas others have not completed high school. Many had worked intermittently at low-paying jobs such as janitor, busboy, house painter, or waitress. Many of the early members had previously been involved with drugs, some in smuggling and selling. They had traveled and had in many instances led lives rife with anxiety, insecurity, and confusion. When they happened to come across the Brotherhood, often quite accidentally in their travels, they knew that they had been looking for a place like it, a place that provided structure and answers to their questions.

Many of the "brothers" and "sisters," as members refer to themselves, are in their early twenties when they join, others are still in their teens, and only a few are over thirty. A membership list for August 1974 showed 184 members, of which 16 were children. Of the adults, 90 were male and 79 were female. All children are kept at one branch where those of school age are taught by three adults in a one-room structure. The younger children attend kindergarten, which is taught by two adults in a smaller one-room building. In 1974 there were also two toddlers (one born in the community), who

[2]A rumor (1981) is that this tract of land is being sold at an enormous profit.

were looked after by one adult during the day. The older children sleep in several tepees in the company of one or two adults, whereas the kindergarten children sleep with a parent or with a male or female "sponsor" in individual huts. One toddler lived with his parents most of the time, the other with a female sponsor. For a few months, from late 1974 to early 1975, there existed a children's house, in which seven or eight kindergarten children lived under the supervision of several adults. Most members share a small hut or a trailer with one or several others, but a few live by themselves. All meals are taken in a common dining room.

During the first years few who wanted to join were turned down, but in 1974 some applicants were told to visit a few times in order to be sure that the Brotherhood was really what they wanted. About once a month new members go through an initiation involving collective instruction in the use of a meditation technique. Before the initiation takes place, a leading brother holds for new members one or two orientation sessions, in which he talks about the community's rules and beliefs.

Except for visitors and new members who have not yet been initiated, there are two types of members in the community: council and noncouncil members, in a ratio of approximately two to one. Usually a member is invited to the council after a period of seven months to a year. There are exceptions, though; several members were asked to be on the council after only two months; others had lived in the community for several years and were still noncouncil members. New council members make a collective vow of chastity, poverty, and lifetime membership in the community. The council meets once a week for discussion of problems and new plans, and for affirmation of commitment. Important economic decisions are made by Mel (a pseudonym), the charismatic leader, with the help of some leading brothers, and not by the council. Items of general interest discussed by the council are announced to the general membership in a weekly general meeting.

Branch leaders and certain other brothers form an elite which has decision-making authority over other members in many areas of daily life, as well as other privileges, including greater access to Mel, greater freedom, and greater access to money. A few of the sisters share in some of these privileges, either as wives of leading brothers or because they work in an area, that is, as office secretary or kitchen manager, that affords them some degree of authority.

At each of the branches, members attend morning and evening meditations, and now and then the whole community gathers at one of the branches for a harvest bee, a wedding, a holiday celebration, or one of Mel's periodic speeches. Mel lives in town in a small frame house which also serves as an office. Mel's ideas expressed in his speeches to the whole community and in private talks with leading members are the authoritative sources for Brotherhood doctrine. Many of his ideas derive from his former teacher, Paramahansa Yogananda, who introduced him to Hindu lore and practice. Books by James Churchward, *The Lost Continent of Mu* (1931) and others, also supply Mel with ideas for Brotherhood cosmology. In the beginning there was a strong emphasis on Eastern religion, but, about two and a half years after the founding of the community, Mel imposed a "Christian" identity on the community. The Bible replaced "guru books" as approved reading material, and, whereas the goal was expressed during my early visits as "God realization," members later talked more about preparing for the Second Coming of Christ. They see themselves as the vanguard of the "new age," as the elect who will survive the coming destruction of the present civilization and who will return to the "garden."

Inequality

The ideas for the conceptual system I have called "inequality" derive from Mel's traditional attitude and his strict adherence to the Bible. The main elements in the system are male superiority and female inferiority, or male dominance and female submission. Meaningful terms the community uses to describe these concepts are "head," representing the male, and "heart," representing the female, with the "head" ruling the "heart"; "positive" (male) and "negative" (female), with "positive" standing for the first act of God, the creation of the "Eternal Light," or His Son, and "negative" standing for the creation of "Mother Earth," the female principle of the universe, which God projected out of the "Light."

In order for brothers and sisters to "meet the Father face to face" and to regain their birthrights as sons and daughters of God, they must "go through the Son," the Eternal Light, a male. Only by going through the Son can one come to the Father. So far only Mel has achieved this goal, although some of the leading brothers have come close to it, but eventually everybody in the Brotherhood can achieve the same through meditation, virtuous living, and God's grace.

In meditation one brings the Light mentally down through the crown of one's head, directs it through the body, and then releases it in the center of the earth. One then returns it upward through the body again, thereby trying to unite the positive force from above and the negative force from below, the groom and the bride, in the mystical marriage. The negative and the positive forces are equally necessary in this process, and the greater importance of the male, or positive force, seems thereby contradicted. Mel himself, however, invalidated the importance of the negative force by telling members that it was no longer important to bring the Light back up; it was sufficient to bring it down and then to release it in the center of the earth. This modification of the meditation technique occurred at the time when he imposed Christian beliefs on the community and discarded Yogananda's teachings as no longer relevant to the "new age." He also cited Jesus' words: "When you have received me, the Light, the Life and the Truth, you shall be as new creatures." In other words, the positive force is preeminent and the negative force is only a reflection. That members also understand it in this way is illustrated by a sister's prayer: "Let us feel your presence. Let us pass on your Light to the Mother so that she may also glow in Light."

The conceptual system is expressed in Mel's actions. His marriage to one of his young followers manifests it and serves as an example for members. He chose a quiet, subservient young woman, and the relationship between them seems to be one of dominance and submission. Theirs is regarded as the perfect marriage. A brother said that Mel had once told the members that all marriages should be like his. The brother also expressed the ideal by saying that the wife should be meek and follow her lord. This has always been so in the past and will be so in the future, he added.

Mel's young wife, about twenty years his junior, stays in the background at membership gatherings. When Mel gives a speech, she is there to fetch him water; she cooks and shops for him and protects his privacy. Many brothers regard her as very special. One devoted early follower wrote a poem about her which illustrates the subordinate role she plays. The poem is titled "Angel of the Northwind," Mel representing the northwind. The lines are as follows:

Where the northwind does blow
The gentle handmaiden goeth also.

Long golden tresses flow from her crown,
Plentiful as the love that from her heart abounds.

Graceful as a doe, her humble eyes
reflect the charity that flows from deep inside.

Loyal she stands in the task she's been shown.
To care for the wind from the north as he's blown.

Watching over his needs, she leaveth him free
to carry away the spirit of iniquity.

And as he cometh to remove all sin,
She goeth with him, the angel of the northwind.

The choice of the name "Brotherhood"[3] also reflects the greater importance of men in the commune, at a time of "consciousness raising" and demands for equality by women in the larger society. The charter members included not only brothers, but a number of sisters as well. Sisters who objected that the name did not include them were advised that "male" stands for "head," and "female" for "heart," and that the head rules the heart. Paradoxically, members are often told to listen not to the mind but to the spirit, the terms "spirit" and "heart" sometimes being used synonymously.

After about a year of living communally, Mel created the council, originally consisting of twelve brothers, which was to help him make decisions and plans for the future. Only after a sister's complaint, which resulted in a long discussion between Mel and the brothers, were some sisters also put on the council. Admitting women to the council seems to have been done in a mood of compromise in order not to make the sisters feel unwelcome in the community. Mel is usually careful in his speeches to the general membership not to offend sisters by excluding them. For example, he makes statements such as "Within man, as well as woman, these two principles are confined today" and "God treats each son and daughter differently." In a speech about creation, however, his apparent feelings were revealed. He said, "The Father decided, and desired a Son. Now every son wants to be a father. We are no different as men than our Heavenly Father. What man does not want a son?"

According to an ex-member, who complained to Mel about the community's male dominance, Mel explained to him that the posi-

[3]See footnote 1, above.

tive and negative energies are out of balance on earth, and more positive energy is needed; therefore, man needs to be in charge. This private remark reveals his dissatisfaction with contemporary sex roles and shows his commitment to tradition.

In the realm of authority and the division of labor, the conceptual system is also a model for reality. All leaders such as heads of the branches, store managers, treasurer, council chairmen, those in public-relations jobs, and so on, are brothers. The only enterprise started and run exclusively by sisters during the first nine months was a small restaurant, but even that was eventually managed by a brother. Cooking, serving, and washing dishes, the main tasks at the restaurant still performed by women, are of course traditionally female activities.

Occasionally, when a manager of a store left, an inexperienced brother was appointed as the new manager instead of a sister who had been working in the store and who knew all the facets of running it. I am not sure how often such a decision caused resentment, but in one case it contributed to the departure of a sister who had long been troubled by the unequal treatment of women.

Sisters were also excluded from the decision-making process concerning the protection of the community. Whenever the protection of property was discussed and the acquisition of weapons was rationalized, it was done by saying that women and children had to be protected. During my stay, there took place several "brothers' meetings" in which the brothers discussed security matters and retaliatory measures against some obscenity-shouting youths. Sisters were not permitted to travel alone or with another sister from one branch to another. A rule in the guidelines handed out to prospective members states, "A sister must always be accompanied by a brother when traveling or hiking in remote areas. The simple presence of a brother is usually enough to turn away someone who would cause her harm."

In daily living the traditional division of labor is followed to a large extent. Cooking and most other kitchen work is done more frequently by sisters, whereas carpentry and mechanical work is performed almost exclusively by brothers. When a sister who had experience in carpentry offered to help with the work involved in the expansion of the restaurant, she was turned down. She could not understand why Mel had denied her request and told herself to have faith in order to deal with the disappointment.

One exception to the traditional allocation of tasks is in childcare. Small children have adult male and female sponsors who help the children to get dressed in the morning, who assist at mealtimes, and who are willing to listen to the children's problems or occasionally play with them.

My impression was that the direction of services rendered by members to each other is consistent with the ideal. For example, females massage males more often than vice versa, and brothers usually ask sisters for a massage rather than the other way around. Hairbrushing and braiding is another service almost exclusively rendered to males by females.

Many of the sisters seem satisfied with their subordinate status. In the opinion of two ex-members, many welcomed the rule that a brother must always accompany a sister. On the other hand, there are those who are bothered by the great gap in influence between themselves and the brothers. One of the most important sisters— important because she was assertive and managed the domestic affairs at one of the branches—mentioned to another, who had recently joined and who was energetic and eager to contribute in an important way, that she felt more of a balance than had existed in the past was going to be established. The reason for her optimism was a warm and, as she put it, "mutually supportive discussion" she had the night before with some of the brothers. They had mentioned her friend, the new sister, commendably. Her hope for change was not warranted, however: no real change occurred in the position of sisters in the succeeding months.

An ex-sister phrased her criticism in a typical Brotherhood manner, speaking of three levels: the spiritual, the physical, and the mental. The superiority of brothers operates on all these levels, she said: spiritually because only through Christ, a male, can a person get to the Father; physically because sisters are not allowed to go anywhere on their own; and intellectually because men hold nearly all the positions of responsibility.

Those who agitate for change are not popular. An unusually assertive ex-member recollected that she had been termed "self-willed" and told that her vanity was showing. A brother sympathetic to women's liberation suggested carefully to one of the leaders, who often asked brothers to volunteer for heavy tasks, to ask simply for strong volunteers in order not to single out sisters as weak and unable to perform hard work. He was taken to task afterward for making this suggestion in an open meeting. In the opinion of some members, this brother was using his mind too much. After he had left the Brotherhood, a young sister who occasionally had disagreements with him said, "He was never really here anyway. He was very much into women's lib." Then she added, "We are all natural men and women, and it doesn't matter whether a woman works in the kitchen or not, as long as she serves." It does seem to matter to many brothers, though, where they work, for those who constitute the leadership or who think they belong to it are never seen working in the kitchen.

Despite the traditional role of women in the Brotherhood, there is one aspect in the relationship between the sexes that differs in the eyes of the sisters from the traditional one; that is, the sisters feel that the brothers do not regard them as sex objects. The sisters have commented on their feelings of relief at not having "to play the game" anymore. One sister observed that her husband, who had previously had an intense dislike for fat women, was seen hugging a rather fat sister after his first week in the community. It is true that the warm and affectionate hugs which are often exchanged, seem relatively free of sexual connotations. The fact that sisters often mentioned the new relationship they enjoy with brothers in the context of chastity, suggests that they perceive that the chastity rule makes it possible. It is plausible, though, that the third system, "sign endogamy," also contributes to making such a relationship possible. Despite the brotherly and sisterly exchanges of hugs, relationships are not always free of sexual interest on the part of either sex, as will be shown in the following section.

Chastity

The concept of chastity with its related elements is embedded in a larger conceptual system, a kind of master symbol devised by Mel with the help of members. It prescribes how members must live in order to reach their goals in becoming God's children again. This master symbol has twelve petals around a circle. The petals represent twelve virtues which must be lived; each virtue is opposed by a temptation symbolized by a second ring of petals. These temptations must be overcome "in order to enter the gates of heaven." In this scheme the virtue "chastity" is opposed by the temptation "lust." This pair is accorded more importance than are all the other pairs. Not only do council members make vows of chastity, but it is often said that living the virtues means above all to control the "life force" and not to waste it by "spilling the seed." When Mel explained the master symbol to members, he said this about chastity:

> Chastity: to preserve the Life that God gave you. Not to misuse it for the gratification of sense pleasures, not to throw it away upon the earth, but to use it as the fire, the force of Life, to really create and do things for God and for His children; to use it to bring forth in the womb another vehicle for one of God's children to inhabit when told by God to do so, that's chastity.

Only when God tells a couple to conceive a child is intercourse permitted. Because of lust, contact with God was lost, and in order to regain it men and women must not "indulge in the senses."

Mel demonstrated a great concern for chastity by talking about it repeatedly. One time he quoted God's words: "Neither shall ye eat nor shall ye touch, for on that day ye shall surely die." He explained, "It means that by our selfishness to entertain sensual desires and fulfill sensual pleasures, we waste or misdirect God's life through our bodies. We become completely out of tune, dissipated, lost in our outer-going energies and we die spiritually."

Perhaps most significantly, Mel told members during my stay that God revealed to him four years earlier that he could never enter another womb again and have physical relations. I interpreted this at first as a symbolic description of impotence, but after discussions with ex-members who provided me with conflicting bits of gossip, I am inclined to think that if impotence was an affliction at all, it was only a temporary one. It is possible that some of Mel's sexual ambiguity stems from his early association with Yogananda, who required celibacy from his disciples, a sacrifice which Mel was not willing to make then, according to his own testimony to early members.

The chastity system has a concomitant rule that is explicitly expressed. In 1973 questionnaires were introduced with the question "How do you feel about living a life of celibacy until you meet the Father face to face?" The term "celibacy" was used interchangeably with "chastity." In 1974 the question was phrased as "Do you feel able and willing to live a life of chastity? Chastity is a requirement for all brothers and sisters, including married couples." Members spoke of "celibate marriage," and it did not seem a contradiction to them that married council members made vows of celibacy. In the history of Christianity, celibacy and marriage were regarded as two possible vocations; if one was chosen, the other was thereby automatically excluded. It is possible that somebody pointed out the contradiction in the use of the term "celibacy," which led to a revision of the questionnaire.

Mel had begun encouraging members to lead celibate lives soon after the Brotherhood was founded. However, he himself lived with the woman he later married, and other couples also shared rooms or beds. An ex-member explained that at this early stage only promiscuity was frowned upon, by which she meant a frequent change in partners. According to her, there was also a brief flirtation with the idea of using the sexual act as a mystical technique, as in Tantrism; sexual union with a steady partner was sanctioned as long as the male did not ejaculate. I did not, however, verify this in interviews with other early members.

Mel was exposed to ideas of celibacy, and probably also to the Hindu belief in the sacred quality of semen (Yalman 1963), while living in the monastery of the Self-Realization Fellowship from age seventeen to twenty-one as a "renunciant," as one who makes the initial vow is called. Yogananda, the Fellowship's founder, cited from 1 Corinthians in his autobiography (1972): "He that is unmarried careth for the things that belong to the Lord, how he may please the Lord; but he that is married careth for the things of the world, how he may please his wife." Ex-members reported that Mel told them he refused to take the celibacy oath when Yogananda wanted to initiate him and a number of others to a higher level. Mel later left the Fellowship in order to marry a woman he had met there. According to old friends, he married twice more before he founded the Brotherhood. "He attracted women like flies," commented one person who knew him well.

Although Mel himself married about a year after the community was founded, he began to discourage marriage for other members. In 1973 he urged those who had been living together to get married or to separate. By August of that year five marriages had been performed since the founding of the Brotherhood, including Mel's. When other brothers and sisters subsequently asked to get married, they were told "to go once around the sun together" in order to be really sure that they had made the right decision. In addition to requiring a one-year engagement period, Mel introduced at about that time a questionnaire which included the question "Can you be content to serve the Father and wait for your helpmate to come?" Mel also admonished members not to look for a helpmate, but to seek God first: then everything else will fall into place. "God will send a helpmate when He sees fit, for He created male and female to be helpmates for each other," he said. He added that he himself had waited a long time before God sent him his helpmate, a remark which had led me to believe that the marriage to his young follower was his first. The initiation of "sign endogamy" also served to discourage relationships that might have led to marriage.

As his own behavior indicates, Mel was not in principle against marriage. Furthermore, he regarded ideological conversion alone as insufficient for the community's growth, and marriage therefore a necessity. This can be inferred from a paragraph he added to Ginsburg's (1955) description of the life of the Essenes. Ginsburg's account is reproduced verbatim in the Brotherhood's communion book (containing mainly Mel's speeches, of which every member has a copy), with the exception of the following added paragraph (and a few added lines pertaining to another subject):

> Although some orders of Essenes did not marry, many others did because they believed that those who refrained from marriage cut off the principal part of human life, that is, succession—because if all were of the same opinion, the whole race would soon be extinguished. They, however, tried their spouses for three years, and after giving evidence, by three natural purgations, that they were fit to bear children, they married them. They had no connubial intercourse with them when with child, to show that they did not marry to gratify lusts, but only to have children.

Some of the information in this passage agrees with what Allegro writes about the Essenes in *The Dead Sea Scrolls* (1961:161), and it is possible that Mel read that book before he added the passage.

To strengthen the chastity rule, Mel suggested to his environmentally concerned followers that chastity can be a solution to the world's population problem. Because man did not practice chastity and control of life force in the past, "millions of spirits that didn't ask to be born are forced into a birth to die from lack of food through lust and ignorance." He often talked about the time when "the command comes to go and conceive and bring forth." This command from God would of course come through Mel, for he is the mediator between God and members. The present was the time for preparation, the time for purgation. He said:

> We still have disease in the midst of us; impurities, uncleanliness, disorderliness. We have a ways to go before we have any right to invite spirits into this life. Our houses need to be cleaner and our clothes a brighter white. We need to scrub things down; to be orderly and mindful to take care of the things that God has given us. We need to be concerned for each other; we need to improve our lives. When we have done this, and we have clean clothes and no disease or pestilence, then we are fit to bring forth.

That a number of members were ill with staphylococcus infections at this time provided a convenient reason for postponing children.

It was, of course, advantageous for the community to establish itself on a sound economic basis before having children. Pregnancies and the care of young children take women away from the work force, and more money has to be earned by others in order to feed and clothe mothers and children. Many communes in the past have postponed having children in the beginning of their history. Oneida, for example, permitted few offspring during the first twenty years of its existence. In the *kibbutzim* of Israel fertility was also low during the pioneer stage of development (Talmon 1972).

Confirming the view that Mel did not want to burden the community with children is the fact that he counseled several sisters to have abortions when they became pregnant during the first few years of the commune's existence. Two of them (both unmarried) agreed, but a married sister gave birth to a baby in May 1972. Another child was born to a short-term member about this time. Earlier, a pregnant sister had been made unwelcome and was asked to leave just a few days before her child was born. An ex-brother recalled, "Mel didn't feel that she belonged in the Brotherhood because that Brotherhood was not equipped to have a child born." The brother himself had strongly opposed Mel on this point. By 1974 the community was doing quite well economically, but even then Mel preferred that members remain childless, even though parents and single mothers with small children were made welcome. In the summer of 1974 there were also in the community four children whose parents lived on the outside.

Questions that arise are, How is the ideal of chastity perceived and accepted by members? and How does it influence their behavior?

During the first two years it was taken only as a suggestion by Mel and not regarded too seriously. Members still had their own cars, and those who had been used to an active sex life before joining were able to drive to the nearby town and visit old and new friends. An ex-member, who did this frequently, said that Mel once saw him come home long after midnight. Mel did not say a word about it, but woke him up at five o'clock that morning to ask whether he could help with an important task. At the isolated branch many of the brothers and sisters lived with each other, but gradually they pressured each other to refrain from sexual relations. One early member recalled that Mel had told a Black brother not to sleep with a White sister, whereupon the former began watching over others so that they would not sleep together.

When Mel became more demanding of members and asked them in questionnaires how willing they were to live a life of celibacy, many answers showed hesitance and ambivalence. Others reflected the ideas Mel had presented to them, as in, for example, "I am glad to offer my seed of life to God that I may know him." Several members filled in only names and date of birth. One sister told Mel she did not believe in getting married without having had sexual relations with her partner; he told her that chastity was just a rule necessary for living in a group, and left it at that. A brother's answer touches on the question of consequences for the mental health of members. He wrote:

> Celibacy: I don't feel that I am ready to lead a celibate life. I already tried it once for a period of six months and psychologically the results were disastrous. Instead of sublimating I was merely repressing my sex drive, and the subconscious frustration that resulted created more psychological problems than I have yet been able to solve.

According to Murdock (1949:261), "... a society must permit sufficient sexual gratification to maintain the mental health and efficiency of its members." Perhaps this dictum does not apply to alternative societies. In the absence of contradictory data, we must assume that many of them managed quite well in maintaining the mental health and efficiency of their members despite the institution of celibacy. The Shakers, for example, had instituted ecstatic nightly rituals with "singing, shouting, stomping, embracing, and dancing in a group with waving hands," which brought "great physical release, with members perspiring profusely in the process"

(Kanter 1972:102). In the Brotherhood such release is much rarer. Only on special occasions such as a wedding or a harvest bee do members get together for folk or square dancing. Occasionally during the evening communion there is frenzied clapping of hands, swaying back and forth, and sometimes dancing. My impression is that a number of members suffer from strong mood swings; depressive episodes, or "heavies," are fairly common. Many long-term members seem rather tense and are rarely seen laughing. However, sexual frustration is only one of a number of possible explanations.

There is no provision for keeping the sexes apart, as was done among the Shakers, who employed a number of devices for this purpose (Hayden 1976). Only at the main branch, where visitors are welcome, are there separate bathrooms for brothers and sisters. At two other branches the outhouses are used by both sexes. One has two adjacent seats, divided by a wall, but without doors; another has doors, but there is a window in the wall that separates the two seats. Although it has a curtain, a number of sisters, myself included, avoided the latter outhouse whenever possible. I am not sure whether the building of these outhouses was guided by a conscious motivation to deemphasize physical shame.

Unlike women in the *kibbutzim* described by Talmon (1972), Brotherhood women as a group have not abandoned beauty care and adornment. Many of the sisters are fond of wearing white blouses and dresses with colorful embroidery from Mexico. One of the sisters washed her long blond hair every morning. Except for a few who have put on too much weight, many sisters are attractive and feminine. A male visitor with whom I discussed the subject of chastity commented that he sensed an "undercurrent of sensuality." It should not come as a surprise that temptations are frequent and that deep commitment to the chastity rule is lacking. It is not only that the women are attractive; brothers and sisters work side by side in the fields, orchard, and stores, and often hike together across a mountain range from one branch to another.

If members are overcome by feelings of lust, they can try to transmute these feelings by means of a special meditation technique. During my stay one of the brothers instructed members from time to time in its use. According to the brother, it is especially easy to succumb to feelings of lust between August 23 and September 22, when Virgo rules. The temptation is greater during the second half of this period because it is negative. Everybody experiences this temptation, although not with the same intensity. The brother mentioned that Jesus had wished that all men were eunuchs. Then he talked about his own past, of the time when he had lived "in the house of lust" and had experienced strong temptations. He referred to a medical exam (a brother and a sister had examined members a few days earlier) and commented on the healthy vesicles on the brothers' testicles, which he attributed to the conserving of life force. The energy saved can be used instead for serving God, he said. Then he explained the meditation method. It involves bringing the Light down through one side of the brain and transferring it to the opposite side of the body at the throat. From there it is directed into the ovaries or testicles on that side. One can learn to tense one side of the ovaries or of the testicles; it should be done three times during each circulation (a circulation consists of bringing the Light down and then back up again). Then the Light is brought down to the Mother and returned with exhaling. With the next inhalation the Light is brought down on the opposite brain side. The positive side and the negative side must thereby be neutralized. He drew an analogy to one of Mel's visions in order to illustrate "crosscurrents," as the technique is called. In this vision one side of Jupiter's brain was black, the other side white. He held the reins of eight horses; four black ones on the side of the white brain side, and four white ones on the side of the black brain side. Out of his head came fire. The brother continued, "We must keep our lusts and temptations in check and center them like Jupiter did with the horses, so that we can observe and control everything from the third eye or observer's seat." About a month later the same brother said that it is necessary for "the spirit" to tell a brother when to enter a sister. The same evening he sang a song about chastity.

A week after the lesson on "crosscurrents," the branch leader explained at a council meeting how negative thought-forms can be transmuted and sent away through circulation of the Light. Another leading brother admonished members to "sexually chastise" themselves. He said that having ideas of lust is disobedient; one must constantly work on being obedient in all things. This repeated concern with chastity and lust suggests the presence of sexual frustration. Some brothers indicated in conversations with me that the "celibacy rule" was sometimes difficult for them. One said that sisters become nervous when brothers approach them. Another called celibacy "a constant battle."

The experience of a young sister, who had fallen in love for the first time, suggests that some brothers were uneasy when sisters showed them unusual attention. She said critically one day, "Many things are suppressed in this community, as, for example, passion. I miss it." She knew what she felt was "truth," yet she had to be miserable: the brother she was in love with was afraid to hug her. Early in their relationship she had hugged him often, but he must have interpreted it as an attempt to seduce him, she thought, for he avoided her now.

Although the chastity rule caused resentment in some members and was the reason for others' leaving, some welcomed the rule as a relief from unsatisfactory and exploitive sexual relationships on the outside. A few brothers and sisters said that they had decided to be celibate even before coming to the Brotherhood. A sister explained that she was glad to give up sex in order to relate to people on a different level. Another said similarly that she had been looking for such a life of celibacy because she did not like the type of relationships based on sex one has on the outside. She added, though, that she misses the intimacy associated with sex, and she admitted to loneliness. She hopes that getting to know the Father really well will take the place of intimacy with people. Most of these members were sincere, I believe. However, in one case a formerly married sister told me that it was easy to obey the chastity rule once one had made up one's mind; later, when I talked to her as an ex-member, she admitted having had sexual relations with several brothers.

When I asked what sacrifices had been made in joining the community, several members spontaneously answered, "Giving up sex." One brother, who first answered, "Smoking," added, "Sex was really the hardest to give up, but I knew I had to do it." Some seemed to perceive chastity as a temporary sacrifice. Apparently they did not plan to remain in the community for long, or they expected the rule not to remain important once the time for having children would come. Some speculated in the summer of 1974 that they would be ready for children in about two years.

Toward the beginning of my stay, I first became aware that visiting between members of the opposite sex occurred when a young, flirtatious sister, who had recently joined, announced to me and another sister that she would be having a visitor for the night. A few months later I learned that commerce between the sexes was quite frequent. In November 1974 a wedding took place, the first such event since August 1973. I was surprised when the announcement was made because the couple had not been engaged. I learned that they had liked each other for a long time. At this wedding Mel gave an emotional speech in which he mentioned the couple only briefly at the very end, but in which he reversed his stand on children taken only three months earlier. He talked of "hordes of angels that are waiting to come" and said that the time had come to have children, if God gives a couple a sign. What he knew, and what members learned only later, was that the bride was pregnant. This fact made it expedient for him to say that children could be conceived now.

The emphasis on chastity did not change; the chastity rule was reinforced by the couple's transgression, which was not taken lightly. They were severely chastised. The brother had to resign from his position as branch leader and had to make a public confession during communion. He said that the child would be born in the spring, which meant that they had not been patient and waited for the will of the Lord. But they had suffered for it and been properly chastised. He continued that he himself knew especially well what chastisement is and that he also knew that he had brought much suffering onto Mel. If it were to happen again, it would kill Mel. This incident, he added, should serve as a stepping stone and not as a stumbling block, and in the future all would have to try even harder to live the virtues.

About a month after this marriage, a sister was found one morning in the tent of a guard (each night a number of brothers take turns in guarding the community), and Mel was apparently informed about it, for it was said that the spirit had told him to call a meeting of council members for a confession. The council meeting was "closed" (sometimes noncouncil members are permitted to attend council meetings), and noncouncil members were not informed about the extent of disobedience to the rule. The rumor spread, however, that there had been quite a few who confessed to infractions of the chastity rule. A day after this confession a brother gave a brief report during communion (meditation service), beginning with the words "The Father has come down on us and pride was sent out the window." Ex-members who had participated in the confession later described it as "awful." They reported that the council meeting had opened with a leading brother announcing, "The house of the tent of David is defiled and we have to cleanse it." Members were also admonished to be completely honest and open with each other from then on. An Aries brother, the first in the round of zodiacal signs, began with a tearful admission that he had sinned. The brother next to him followed suit. Those who had not had intercourse admitted to dreams, masturbation, and thoughts about sex. An ex-member later said, "There was so much guilt and fear!" One brother was even reported as having prayed to God to be killed after having had sex.

A day or two after the confession (the only such confession reported), a leading brother said that Mel had wanted to speak to everyone who had confessed, but there had been too many. A brother who seemed to me to be the most fanatical said that Mel had known what was going on; the devil had come to him and said, "Your followers are not keeping their vow to your God." Mel had offered to pay for it, and his subsequent ill health was the payment for members' sins. The brother then threatened that Mel should never again have to pay for others' transgressions or he would personally deal with the culprit. He added that the devil had promised to provide Mel with the names of those who would have sexual relations in the future.

A while later, within a two-week period, Mel gave two speeches in which he dwelled on chastity. He said:

> And you, brothers and sisters, I warn you, that you seek each other not out for the house of lust, but to be true mates in this power, and to use these God-given bodies to make more bodies. . . . Meditate deeply and be with God. If He shows truly that He is talking to you from him or her, these pairs of people the infinite, almighty God is going to use to bring forth from the womb the power of heaven.

He told members that, if he had not kept that vow he made four years before, it would have "broken the back of this Brotherhood." He also said that God will call some members to be forever virgins. Several times it seemed as if he had ended the speech, but then he began talking again. He repeatedly returned to the subject of chastity. Finally, he said that he wanted to talk in private to all married couples.

The insistence on chastity and the elaborate effort expended by Mel and the leading brothers in the form of exhortations and intimidations in order to achieve compliance indicate a desire for control over members. Making a martyr out of Mel and enlisting the help of the devil to make the names of offenders known are designed to instill fear and guilt. The testimony of an ex-member, who had sexual relations a while after the confession, shows that this was accomplished. She said, "I went through hell because of guilt. What could have been a beautiful experience was a nightmare." However, such guilt feelings were not shared by all who had sexual relations. My conversations with two other ex-members, whom I also knew as members, suggests that those who internalized Brotherhood doctrine and who were emotionally dependent on Mel were more likely to feel guilty than those (apparently a minority) who remained relatively critical and detached.

Various sanctions were employed when the chastity rule was broken. The offense was more serious for a council member, for he or she has made a vow of chastity and is supposed to be an example for others. Sometimes a member was removed from the council for a while. As already mentioned, a leading brother was relieved from his job as branch leader. Others were sent to another branch. Only in more serious cases was a member expelled. In one case a brother upset a fifteen-year-old sister by his sexual advances. A second sister incriminated him further, and it was also said that he had bothered his wife with pleas for sex. She had complained about him, and they had lived at separate branches before his expulsion. A sister who had seduced a number of brothers was also expelled. Usually, though, the measures taken against an offender seemed limited to a talk by one of the leading brothers or to a transfer to another branch, especially when noncouncil members were concerned. The leading brothers were always watchful for signs of a sexual relationship. They were also informed by others when there might have been a need for a special talk. One of the brothers in charge of a branch had told a new flirtatious sister that in the old days monasteries and nunneries were separated by a mountain range; he presumably was trying to tell her that the closeness of males and females in the Brotherhood demanded that they try very hard to live the virtues.

Sign Endogamy

The conceptual system I have called "sign endogamy" states that ideal helpmates, or "soulmates," are born under the same astrological sign of the zodiac; that is, an Aries brother should marry an Aries sister, and so forth. In contrast to the hierarchical model of inequality, this belief puts brothers and sisters in a relationship of equality.

It is said that helpmates "from the same sign" can see each other's faults better and can help each other to overcome them. Another saying is "People from the same sign gravitate toward each other." This belief, like most others, originates with Mel. One of his earliest female followers was born on the same day as he, February 3. As a strong believer in astrology, he must have been fascinated by the coincidence; he married her on February 3, 1972.

Sign endogamy is embedded in a larger astrological belief system, most elements of which are shared by other contemporary communes and by many sectors of the larger society. The Brotherhood's version of astrology is distinguished by the designation of a specific virtue and a specific temptation for each of the twelve signs of the zodiac. As indicated in the previous section, the virtue and the temptation for Virgo are chastity and lust. Other signs of the zodiac, with their virtues and temptations, are as follows:

Aries	=	loyalty: treachery
Taurus	=	patience: anger
Gemini	=	honesty: deceit
Cancer	=	perseverence: surrender
Leo	=	compassion: vanity
Libra	=	equanimity: prejudice
Scorpio	=	courage: fear
Sagittarius	=	humility: pride
Capricorn	=	temperance: debauchery
Aquarius	=	charity: greed
Pisces	=	faith: doubt

Members say that a person is strong either in the virtue or in the temptation of his or her sign. If one is strong in the virtue, one must help others to become stronger in it as well; if one is bothered by the temptation, one must work to overcome it. By knowing a member's sign, one is provided with information by which to judge that member. An example of how this works is the following: a sister taking care of the animals complained one day that a sentry she had asked to wake her up had not done so. She added, "No wonder, he is Aries." When I asked her why she said that, she explained, "Aries are not responsible." A person might say "You must be Cancer because you are so sensitive" or "You must be Capricorn because you are so temperate." If a member guesses wrong, there is yet the possibility that the person's "rising sign" is more significant. If that does not fit either, astrology is not thereby invalidated, however.

In addition to providing information which can be used as a standard by which to judge others, the question "What's your sign?" which is unfailingly put to new members, also functions to inform the questioner as to who the other members born under the same sign are. When the question is put to a member of the opposite sex, the answer indicates whether the person is of one's marriageable class. As I learned about marriages in the community, I found that sign endogamy is practiced. Although it is nowhere explicitly stated, each new couple from the same sign confirmed for me and others that the belief stated as "Helpmates from one's own sign are best" had the force of a prescriptive rule. Those who rejected the dictum were pressured into compliance. Some budding romances were terminated when the couples were told, "You should not be together." Other couples kept a low profile. On one level sign endogamy functions as the incest taboo in that it regulates access to the opposite sex. It divides members of the opposite sex into two groups: a small group from which it is permitted to choose a partner and a large group that is prohibited. The injunction "You should not be together" to a couple from different signs is similar to "You should not marry your parallel cousin." In a small community, where only a few people from each sign are present, the distribution may be skewed, and for some members even fewer than twelve may be available as partners. In 1973, when I first visited the Brotherhood, there were only about sixty members. An ex-member from the early period, whom I asked whether he knew which of the sisters were from his sign, recalled, "Yes, there was Alice, who was married to Gregg; Maureen was going with Bill; and Bridget I did not like, so I remained celibate." Another former brother put it similarly.

At least some members were aware that sign endogamy functioned to limit relationships; they mentioned it spontaneously in conversations with me. I feel, however, that Mel did not consciously intend it for that purpose, for after his own wedding he actually encouraged members to look for same-sign partners. He talked about creating a "master vortex for the coming of Christ" by having twelve same-sign couples, representing each sign, assemble and "receive the Light." Three same-sign marriages had taken place by August 1973. Previous to Mel's marriage only one couple, of different signs, had married since the community was founded. One must recall that by the summer of 1973 Mel demanded that members live a life of chastity, and he asked those members who lived together either to marry or to separate. Afterward he discouraged marriage by requiring a one-year engagement period. There were two engaged couples in the summer of 1974; both were same-sign couples. If Mel was not aware in 1972, of the effect of his fascination with soulmates born under the same sign, he certainly must have realized by 1973 that such a rule limited the opportunity for close relationships.

Not only did sign endogamy regulate new relationships, but also it had an effect on existing ones. The number of separations of married couples suggests the hypothesis that the belief acted to spawn or to increase doubt about one's partner's compatibility. The chastity rule also might have caused tensions, especially if one partner accepted it while the other was less committed to it and was therefore relatively free from guilt feelings. The opportunity for close and affectionate relationships further helped to undermine the strength of marriage relationships. "The Brotherhood is hard on marriages" was the verdict of an ex-member, and this view was supported by the testimony of a woman who had separated from her husband.

Mel was concerned with the community's outside image of respectability. A brother once announced, after having talked to Mel, that Mel did not want the community to become known as a place where one can get rid of wife and children. Mel wanted marriage to be a strong and solid institution, even though, paradoxically, his fascination with same-sign marriages undermined it. Of ten married couples who arrived at the Brotherhood, six had separated by the summer of 1974. Another wife left the community a little later, as did one of the separated husbands. Another husband, already mentioned, was expelled. Of the three mariages still intact, two were having difficulties. One wife went to another branch for a while, leaving her small child with her husband. When I asked a sister why the wife had left, the answer was, "They [the couple] could not feel each other." Another wife was rumored to be quite frigid, to the extent of not even cuddling with her husband. She frequently worked at another branch, but returned when she learned that her husband had a very friendly relationship with another sister. The tenth couple, whose relationship appeared to me to be the healthiest, worked closely together, belonged to the elite, and kept somewhat separate from the rest of the community. As a result, the pressures on them were probably minimized. None of these couples was a same-sign couple. Interestingly, one of the separated couples (the husband was for a time engaged to a sister from his sign) later left, and they are happily reunited on the outside.

When I asked one of the formerly married members whether the sign endogamy rule had anything to do with the breakup of her marriage, she denied it at first, but then admitted that "the vibration 'You should not be together' was very strong." Ex-members who knew the couple before the breakup and who had considered them a well-matched couple, were convinced that the rule was the cause for the separation. Other breakups followed theirs. The wife of the couple who are still together asserted that a great deal of pressure was put on them to split up also. In one case Mel pointed out to the husband, who had married before the rule was adopted, that the husband's soulmate was another sister born on the same day as he. Afterward, the husband frequently sought out the other sister, but she did not feel attracted to him. His wife became upset and accused Mel of ruining her marriage. Ex-members said that she hated the other sister. The wife was eventually expelled, with the stipulation that she could return after a year, and she did. The marriage did not continue, so far as I know. Even one of the same-sign marriages has been dissolved, and another was in trouble, even though these marriages had been strongly encouraged by Mel. Obviously, being from the same sign is not enough for a solid marriage, but, interestingly, in the case of the broken same-sign marriage, each partner has since the time of my fieldwork remarried somebody else also from the same sign.

By the fall of 1974 members were saying self-consciously, "We excessively limited our relationships to people from the same sign" (individuals had often sought friends of the same sex from their own sign) and "The Brotherhood tripped out on it and overdid it." It was suggested at a council meeting that the rule was limiting and that it should be possible to transcend differences. This change was prompted by the couple who were married and chastised because the woman was pregnant. Mel had told them that it did not matter whether they were from the same sign as long as they could help each other. "He [Mel] had changed his feelings" on the subject, a sister explained.

Following that couple's marriage, two other couples decided to take the step; only one couple was of the same sign. The same-sign couple had been going together, but the announcement by the couple of unlike signs came as a surprise. The brother, however, reassured the other members with the report that he had asked God to show him a rainbow if the marriage was in the spirit and that God had complied. Another double wedding occurred two months later, and at least six more weddings took place in the succeeding two years. Of these eight, five are same-sign marriages. The rule has become a preferential one. After several marriages by couples from different signs had occurred, a formerly married brother said that he was considering for the first time marriage with someone from another sign. This also suggests that his earlier breakup might have been influenced by his acceptance of the belief that helpmates from the same sign are best.

The increase in the number of marriages after the relaxation of the sign-endogamy rule and after the announcement that children can be conceived in an atmosphere of fasting, praying, and communing attests to the attractiveness of marriage. Until then a married couple was permitted to share a dwelling and some intimacy short of sexual intercourse. Since that time sexual intercourse has been permitted in order to increase the population from within, and a number of children have been born since then. The economic situation of the community is now so healthy that an increase in children does not impede economic expansion.

Couples need Mel's permission, however, in order to marry. They must convince him that their love is spiritual and not based on physical attraction. He has refused permission in several cases. In 1975 he drew up a list with names of members who should marry each other. I am not sure to what extent the list consisted of same-sign couples. It does suggest, though, that in addition to peer pressure and spontaneous enthusiasm for the sign-endogamy rule, there were other factors at work which prevented the marriage or engagement of couples from different signs until November 1974. Indications that at least some members felt frustrated in their attractions to persons from different signs come from the recollections of several ex-members, who had been told, "If you were only from the same sign as I am." Instead of challenging the rule and displeasing Mel, members kept their nonconforming relationships hidden or inconspicuous. It sometimes surprised me to learn that a special relationship existed between a male and a female when I had never observed them together.

Conclusion

The willingness of members to subject themselves to the constraints and rules imposed by the belief system, even if their compliance brought more frustration than commitment, argues for a desire and a need for more structure in their lives. Most members had spent some time in countercultural environments where old conventions were jettisoned. It was often a time fraught with indecision and insecurity. On joining the Brotherhood they were ready to trade the relative freedom from rules and constraints for new rules and obligations in order to gain security and the certainty of being a part in a very important task. Daner (1976:104) came to a similar conclusion in her study of the Hare Krsna movement. Moore (1975:222) has recently commented that sometimes

> a whole community consciously organizes itself according to a set of explicit principles and rules. Such a community may enthusiastically turn to rule-making processes and orderly symbols as if thereby girding itself against the amorphous uncertainty of indeterminancy, trying to prescribe against it as against contagion.

In the Brotherhood such enthusiasm is visible in the adoption of sign endogamy. Charismatic authority fans the enthusiasm. For those who accept Mel's words as "the Truth," the concepts and rules are internalized and act as motivations for behavior. For others compliance with the rule is achieved by peer pressure or motivated by what Garfinkel (1967:70) has called "anticipatory anxiety." Colson (1974) has also pointed out that fear is often the motivation for traditional or compliant behavior.

The ideal of male dominance and female submission also corresponds closely with behavioral reality. Female members who might have had hopes for equal participation with the brothers acquiesce after initial attempts to introduce change, rather than challenge Mel's charismatic authority. Sanctions are used to keep the ideal of chastity plausible; known transgressors are punished, and intimidations create guilt and fear in others.

What is a loss of freedom for the individual member is a gain for the community. As Kanter (1972) pointed out, successful communities in the past (as defined in terms of longevity) have regulated intimacy among their members through either free love or celibacy. Free love was not equated with complete sexual freedom, but was often controlled by requiring members to forego exclusiveness in their relationships as, for example, in Oneida. Kanter suggested that the practice of either free love or celibacy has the consequence of freeing the individual from the commitments to a family or a mate and thus of increasing the individual's availability to the whole community. In the Brotherhood the chastity rule functions also to discourage strong dyadic bonds and thereby increases social cohesion. It seems, however, that Mel was concerned foremost with the increase in work output when he imposed the chastity rule. His apparent belief that sex "dissipates strength" and his call for hard work argue for such an interpretation. The remark by a brother that the energy freed by conserving the "life force" can be used instead to serve God lends further support. This belief is similar to Slater's argument (1970), and Freud's before him, that restrictions on sexual gratification increase the amount of energy that can be expended for the creation of material wealth. Insofar as sexual attraction directs a person's attention toward the object of his attraction, there probably is a distraction from work. Bion (in Veysey 1973:332) expressed a similar view, for he identified pairing as one of three patterns that interfere with the productivity of work groups. By minimizing pairing, the chastity rule and sign endogamy may have functioned in achieving a greater work output. Furthermore, a number of pregnancies, which might have imposed financial and other burdens, were prevented. Beyond these functions the chastity rule is a means for manipulating and controlling members, as can be seen in Mel's use of illness to promote guilt among the members.

Wagner (1976) suggested that the male-supremacist ideology in the "Haran" commune functions to discourage strong dyadic love bonds and to create male solidarity. Although the idea of male supremacy is much less pronounced in the Brotherhood than it is in Haran, it seems that strong bonds among some leading males do exist. The brothers' meetings, which excluded sisters, are reminiscent of Tiger's "aggressive organizations" (1970:171); they provided a forum for the discussion of aggressive behavior. It may very well be that this male solidarity contributes to stability, as Wagner (1976) suggested in the case of Haran. But from the point of view of the community's charismatic leader, the conceptual system of inequality is an attempt to reestablish a balance of masculine and feminine forces in the universe.

ACKNOWLEDGMENTS

I am grateful to Fadwa El Guindi, Jacques Maquet, and Michael Moerman for reading and commenting on an earlier version of this paper. To Jacques Maquet I owe special gratitude for introducing me to the study of intentional communities and for encouragement throughout my research. Finally, thanks are due to Jon Wagner, Fredrica Bernstein, and Roger Martin for suggestions to improve my English prose and to clarify some arguments. Responsibility for the shortcomings is mine alone.

REFERENCES CITED

Allegro, J. M.
  1956   The Dead Sea Scrolls. Harmondsworth, Middlesex (Eng.): Penguin.
Colson, Elizabeth
  1974   Tradition and Contract: The Problem of Order. Chicago: Aldine.
Daner, Francine Jeanne
  1976   The American Children of Krsna. New York: Holt.
Garfinkel, Harold
  1967   Studies in Ethnomethodology. Englewood Cliffs, NJ: Prentice-Hall.
Ginsberg, Christian D.
  1955   The Essenes—The Kaballah. London: Routledge and Kegan Paul.
Hayden, Dolores
  1976   Seven American Utopias: The Architecture of Communitarian Socialism, 1790–1975. Cambridge, MA: The M.I.T. Pr.
Kanter, Rosabeth Moss
  1972   Commitment and Community: Communes and Utopias in Sociological Perspective. Cambridge, MA: Harvard Univ. Pr.
Moore, Sally Falk
  1975   Epilogue: Uncertainties in Situations, Indeterminacies in Culture. *In* Symbol and Politics in Communal Ideology, ed. Sally Falk Moore and Barbara G. Myerhoff. Ithaca, NY: Cornell Univ. Pr.

Murdock, G. P.
  1949   Social Structure. New York: Macmillan.
Slater, Philip
  1970   The Pursuit of Loneliness. Boston: Beacon.
Talmon, Yonina
  1972   Family and Community in the Kibbutz. Cambridge, MA: Harvard
         Univ. Pr.
Tiger, L.
  1970   Men in Groups. New York: Vintage.
Veysey, Laurence
  1973   The Communal Experience: Anarchist and Mystical Counter-Cul-
         tures in America. New York: Harper and Row.
Wagner, Jon
  1976   Male Supremacy: Its Role in a Contemporary Commune and Its
         Structural Alternatives. International Review of Modern Sociology
         6:173–80.
Yalman, Nur
  1963   On the Purity of Women in the Castes of Ceylon and Malabar.
         Journal of the Royal Anthropological Institute of Great Britain
         and Ireland 93 (pt. 1):25–58.
Yogananda, Paramahansa
  1946   Autobiography of a Yogi. Reprint 1973. Los Angeles: Self-Realiza-
         tion Fellowship.

-4- HANS A. BAER

Sex Roles in a Mormon Schismatic Group

The Levites of Utah

AMONG THE NOVEL SOCIAL EXPERIMENTS WHICH emerged during the nineteenth century in American society, one of the most successful was the Mormon Church. The Mormons developed a unique social system—one which combined communalism, plural marriage, and theocratic leadership. One of the many ironies of Mormonism has been its shift from a radical and innovative movement to a conservative bastion of American values and middle-class respectability. Although the Mormon Church has never advocated sexual egalitarianism, it is interesting to note that Utah was the second territory or state (following the earlier example of Wyoming) to grant suffrage to women. Conversely, today the Mormon Church has in large part been responsible for the failure of the Utah state legislature to ratify the Equal Rights Amendment. Like other well-established religious organizations, the Mormon Church has spawned a number of splinter groups. The purpose of this essay is to describe and analyze sex roles in one of these groups, known as the Levites of Utah. Like other Mormon sects, such as those which continue to practice polygyny, the Levites believe that they are revitalizing Mormon principles which were emphasized during the nineteenth century but which have become dormant in Mormonism during the present century.

The Levite sect, officially known as the Aaronic Order, is a small communal group which was founded by Maurice L. Glendenning during the 1930s. Many of the members of the Aaronic Order believe that they are patrilineal descendants of Aaron or Levi, or of both, of Old Testament times and that they are to perform special religious functions prior to the Second Coming of Christ, which, it is claimed, will occur before A.D. 2000. The Aaronic Order consists of the following branches: (1) a congregation in a suburb of Salt Lake City and serving the Salt Lake Valley; (2) a congregation in Springville (about fifty miles south of Salt Lake City) serving the Utah Valley area; (3) the Eskdale commune in western Millard County, a few miles from the Utah-Nevada border; and (4) a cooperative community called Partoun in western Juab County, also a few miles from the Utah-Nevada border.

The Levites, like the Mormons, subscribe to an extremely patriarchal ideology. Among the topics to be discussed in this essay will be the historical background and the symbolic and organizational manifestations of this ideology. The former includes the Mormon heritage of most of the early Levites and the conservative Protestant background of the founder-prophet of the sect. The latter includes the politico-religious hierarchy, the dress uniform, affiliative ties, the sexual division of labor, and education. Despite the male-supremacist perspectives of the Order, there are situations and times when women in the group have played a more prominent role in the economic, political, and religious spheres of the community than might be expected. I shall argue that this tends to be the case during situations of economic necessity (that is, a temporary absence of personnel who are expected to carry out "men's" jobs), within the context of informal religious rituals and meetings, and during periods of religious change (that is, changes in the ideology or rituals of the sect). On the other hand, periods of relative structural and ideological normalcy or routinization tend to be characterized by a return to traditional sex roles as defined in Western society. Parallels of these patterns are found in other communal groups such as, for example, the Israeli *kibbutzim* (Spiro 1970; Talmon 1972) and, as will be shown, also occurred in Mormon culture.

The data presented in this essay are part of a larger study on the Levites which was conducted primarily between October 1973 and December 1975 (Baer 1976a). Between January and June 1975, while I was involved in full-time fieldwork among the Levites, I frequently visited the desert communities of Eskdale and Partoun, attended worship and study classes at the Salt Lake and Springville branches, and interviewed various members in all the branches. Some follow-up work was done between January and July 1976. Unless otherwise stated, the ethnographic present for purposes of this essay will be 1975. Most of the data presented here were obtained through participant-observation.

In addition to undertaking participant-observation, I conducted formal interviews with the leaders and with many middle-aged and elderly members—many of whom have been affiliated with the Aaronic Order since the 1940s and some of whom were followers of Glendenning in the 1930s. A fair amount of the information presented in this paper was obtained from Aaronic Order in-house booklets, letters, newsletters, and scriptures which were given or lent to me by various Levites or which were available in the Church Historian's Office of the Church of Jesus Christ of Latter-Day Saints in Salt Lake City. Data were collected also in both formal interviews and casual conversations with over thirty-five individuals who converted to the Aaronic Order.[1]

The Levite Community: A Historical Overview

The historical roots of the Aaronic Order lie largely in Mormonism. The majority of the early followers of Maurice Glendenning were members of the Church of Jesus Christ of Latter-Day Saints (more commonly called the Mormon Church). Glendenning and his wife, Helen, joined the Mormon Church in 1929; prior to this time, they had been members of various Protestant groups. Before his arrival in Utah in 1928, Glendenning had worked at a variety of occupations, including farming and chiropractic. Shortly after Glendenning joined the Mormon Church, he began to inform various individuals that he was receiving revelations from a supernatural source. These were not regarded favorably by various members of the Mormon hierarchy and resulted in Glendenning's being excommunicated from the church. Glendenning claimed that he was a literal descendant of Aaron and that he had received revelations from the Angel Elias. The revelations given to Glendenning directed the Levites to restore the House of Israel and to prepare the Tribes of Israel for the Second Coming of Christ. Despite the opposition of the Mormon Church, some people continued to follow Glendenning, and eventually in 1943 the Aaronic Order was legally incorporated in the State of Utah.

[1]For an in-depth analysis of the Levite conversion experience, see Baer (1978).

In the spring of 1949 the Levites began the establishment of Partoun, their first community in the desert of the Great Basin. Thirty-seven homesteads (each 160 acres) were filed for, some by non-Levites, and of these, thirty were actually settled for some time. Most homesteaders were required to install a deep well, which would provide water for farming, and have 40 acres under production within five years of their settlement before they could receive title to the land. Ex-servicemen could receive title to their homesteads by establishing and residing on them for one year. Eventually, fourteen families or individuals obtained title to their homesteads, six of the titles being obtained through the provision for ex-servicemen. Five "families" who were unable to improve their land according to the government regulations took advantage of an option to purchase five acres of their original homestead claim for a nominal fee; one family purchased an additional 35 acres. One of these "families" consisted of two unmarried sisters who had converted to the Mormon Church in Sweden and who later immigrated to Utah.

Partoun was established as a cooperative rather than a communal venture, although participants theoretically were to consecrate their property and possessions to the Aaronic Order. According to one elderly man who has resided at Partoun since 1949, it was to become eventually a United Order, or communal venture.[2] Small groups of men worked cooperatively in the establishment of various homesteads. Partoun also had a female carpenter who constructed her own house and did carpentry work on some of the other homesteads. One man sank five wells about one hundred feet deep to provide water for irrigation purposes for the community. Because of financial pressures many of the male residents would work for wages during the week in the Wasatch Front area and improve their homesteads on the weekends. Some men were able to find work, often temporary, on nearby ranches or at Fish Springs National Wildlife Refuge. Occasionally young Levite men from the Wasatch Front area would visit Partoun and work on its development. This employment situation for Partoun men meant that their wives now found themselves performing most of the work maintaining the homesteads, some wives even becoming involved in the heavy work of road construction.

[2]United Order refers to the various cooperative and communal experiments that the Mormons established in both the Midwest and the Intermountain West during the nineteenth century.

Because of inadequate funds to sink deep wells and to develop the land, the alkalinity of the soil, and the lack of agricultural expertise on the part of many of its residents, Partoun had many economic problems. Only a few homesteads were able to become somewhat productive. Some of the older residents were, and still are, able to subsist from social security payments, pensions, or various types of public welfare. In 1955, when Partoun had a population of about sixty individuals, Eskdale commune was established. Some Levites moved from Partoun to Eskdale, taking equipment and some small wooden buildings with them. In addition to some of the problems that have been mentioned, there was a certain amount of conflict among the early residents of Partoun. The current Chief High Priest claimed that one problem Partoun had was that too many people wanted to be leaders. According to one longtime female resident of Partoun, it had barely reached "first base" before Glendenning decided to establish Eskdale. Several individuals and families, most of them elderly, still live at Partoun, certain that some day this portion of the Snake Valley will be populated by thousands of refugees from the cities.

In December 1954 Glendenning and some other Levites investigated the central portion of the Snake Valley in western Utah to determine the feasibility of establishing a commune there. Two cabins from Partoun and a house trailer acquired elsewhere were moved to the new community, Eskdale, in mid-June 1955 to house its first settlers. One cabin served as a cook house and dining hall, and the other as a bunk house; the trailer was used for sleeping accommodations (Beeston 1969: 219). Eskdale was established under the guidelines of the Desert Entry Act, which enabled the community, as was not the case at Partoun, to concentrate the residences in one area rather than to establish a homestead on each of the ten entries, each of which was 320 acres. Eskdale gradually gained population, developed its land for agriculture, and added new buildings.

By 1975 Eskdale had grown from a community with a handful of residents to one with a population close to one hundred. Eskdale consists of thirteen houses arranged in two semicircular rows on the eastern portion of the community grounds, two small trailers housing two widows, and several public facilities. Except for the grade school, all the public buildings are located on the western portion of the community grounds. These include the dining hall-kitchen-laundry complex, a small high school building, the auditorium-school-music facilities complex, the Montessori school, and the school dormitory. The dairy is located southeast of the community center and the shop buildings are directly north of it. In contrast to the Salt Lake and Springville branches, which are located in the heavily populated Wasatch Front area, Eskdale and Partoun are located in the Great Basin, one of the most remote sections of the western United States.

Although a minority of the Order members are residents of the Eskdale commune, it is the center of Levite activity. The Eskdale commune is the principal Levite economic endeavor and the place where social and religious ideals are actualized. It is at the site of the Aaronic Order's educational and musical facilities and of the annual June convocation. The commune serves as a model for the other desert communities which the Levites plan to establish eventually. Eskdale and the other desert communes which will be established are the places where the Levites will be "purified as gold and silver" and will prepare for the Second Coming of Jesus Christ. Just as the Salt Lake Valley was viewed as Zion by the early Mormon pioneers, the Levites view the Snake Valley, referred to as Shiloah, as a refuge from the "wickedness" of Babylon.

The Aaronic Order as a Modern Revitalization Movement

Utilizing Anthony F. C. Wallace's concept of "revitalization movement" (1972), I have argued that the Levite sect emerged as an attempt on the part of its initial members to resurrect the *Gemeinschaft* ethos, which they perceived to have been characteristic of nineteenth-century Mormonism (Baer 1977). The Aaronic Order initially appealed to a certain alienated segment within the Mormon Church because, through its accommodation to the larger society, the latter no longer effectively met the needs of many of its members among the lower and working classes.

One of the major characteristics of nineteenth-century Mormonism was its emphasis on cooperation, egalitarianism, and provisions for the needy. Despite their failure to live communally in United Order, both during their early settlements in Kirtland, Ohio, and in Independence, Missouri, and later in the Intermountain West, the Mormons developed a number of cooperative institutions in the West, including irrigation cooperatives, stores, industries, cattle and sheep companies, and the Women's Relief Society. After the proclamation of the Manifesto in 1890, there was an appreciable decline of Mormon cooperative efforts. Individualism, laissez-faire capitalism, and social inequality were accepted by members of the Mormon hierarchy. Whereas nineteenth-century Mormonism had drawn many of its converts from the "disinherited," and often had substituted religious for social status, twentieth-century Mormonism achieved middle-class respectability and made religious and social status congruent (Davies 1963). Positions of leadership in the church hierarchy became progressively more difficult for the "common man" to acquire, particularly in the urban areas, and tended to be granted to the successful businessman or professional. In response to this accommodation, various attempts to revitalize Mormonism, including the Aaronic Order, emerged.

Most early members of the Order were individuals of relatively low socioeconomic status. According to several longtime members, many who showed an interest in the revelations received by Glendenning had been particularly adversely affected by the Great Depression. Some features of the Levite politico-religious organization suggest that it has served as a compensation for low social status. Whereas the Mormon Church may offer the "comman man" only a minor position within its hierarchy, the Aaronic Order may make him a high-ranking member in the priesthood and in the councils of the House of Israel. The emphasis of the early Levites on cooperation and egalitarianism, and their belief in the imminence of the millennium and in modern-day revelation (all Mormon beliefs which have been held "in abeyance")[3] is indicative of their strong desire to revitalize Mormonism.

Once a religious organization comes into existence and becomes somewhat stabilized in terms of its social structure and ideology, its development may become dependent on forces very much different from those responsible for its origin. In the case of the Aaronic Order, two factors that were especially significant in its development

[3]Early Mormons were certain that they were living in the "latter days," would live to establish Zion, and would see Jesus Christ return and take charge of his millennial kingdom on earth (Whalen 1964:104). Although a sense of millenarianism still exists among the Mormons, it has been relaxed considerably since the nineteenth century. Furthermore, while Mormons generally still claim that their prophet-president receives revelations, it appears that the mechanism for divine communication has changed since the nineteenth century. According to O'Dea (1957:160), "organizational procedures under the direction of a strong authoritarian leader largely replaced visions and revelations, a process that had already started in the last days of Joseph's rule in Nauvoo."

were the dynamic and charismatic leadership of Maurice Glendenning and the group's contact with various fundamentalist Protestant groups and individuals. Consequently, the Order has undergone
an appreciable shift from Mormonism and even from its own early
religious system to fundamentalist Protestantism. Unification of beliefs among members of the Aaronic Order tends to occur on a gener-
ational level rather than on a groupwide level. The differences
between the first-generation level and that of the third generation
are considerable, the first generation being a product of Mormon
culture and the third having very little exposure to formal Mormonism. The second generation stands with a foot in two camps,
many of its members having been raised in Mormonism but also
exposed to fundamentalist Protestantism in late adolescence or
early adulthood.

As a result of contact with a Pentecostalist group from California,
beginning in the fall of 1973, the young Levites were drawn into the
Jesus People movement. Although at first the older Levites were
concerned about the emotionalism and glossolalia exhibited by the
younger Levites, gradually they began to accept the "revitalization
within a revitalization movement" (which began to blossom during
the summer of 1974) and often participated in it. By the fall of 1975,
however, the ideological differences between fundamentalist Protestantism and the Aaronic Order became apparent to many young
members and even to some middle-aged members. These differences
resulted, beginning in December 1975, in a major schism, in which
over twenty-five of Eskdale's residents and a number of young Levites residing on the outside left the Aaronic Order.

Composition of the Aaronic Order

The Levites maintain that they are not to count the members of
their group. In order to determine the size of the Levite community,
however, I attempted to count them. Members of the Levite community were divided into two main categories—active and inactive. For
purposes of this census, "active" members included (1) individuals
who attend Levite activities at least once every two months and (2)
individuals who did not attend Levite activities at least once every
two months because they reside outside the state of Utah or because
of old age and poor health but still express a relatively strong commitment to the Aaronic Order. Individuals (except for young chil-

dren) who did not meet one of these qualifications were classified as inactive members. Table 1 presents census figures for mid-1975.

Because I was unable to make contact with most inactive adult members, their children were usually not included in the census. When adults are inactive members, in nearly all cases, their children under eighteen years of age are not active members of the Levite community. Since I usually had to rely on information given by active members in identifying inactive members, the census figure for the latter is probably somewhat conservative. Inactive members can be divided into two subcategories—those who maintain some contact with the Levite community, often because they are related to active members, and those who apparently have broken most or all ties with it.

Table 2 presents selected demographic characteristics of the Eskdale commune in early May 1975. In the case of the nuclear families, the man is a metallurgist who works in Idaho and plans to move to Eskdale in the near future. Because Eskdale has an appreciable number of school children whose parents are not residents of the community, its population is appreciably lower during the summer months. A few of the school children are not members of the Aaronic Order. Although most Levites reside in Utah, the Order also has members who reside in Idaho, Wyoming, Oregon, Colorado, Arizona, and Nevada on a permanent basis.

Whereas the older Levites were, or are, primarily members of the working class, younger Levites have considerably more education and have in many cases gravitated to professional occupations. During the summer of 1975, I compiled data on the occupational and educational status of the active members of the Aaronic Order between twenty-five and fifty years of age. Out of twenty-one males, ten were laborers (generally skilled), six were teachers, one was a medical doctor, one was an engineer, and one was a graduate student

Table 1
A Census of the Levite Community

Sex	Active Members		Inactive Members
	Over 18 Years	Under 18 Years	Over 18 Years
Male	56	50	51
Female	71	52	57
Total	127	102	108

Table 2

Selected Demographic Characteristics of
the Eskdale Commune

Number of nuclear families with children	9
Number of couples without children	3
Number of widows	4
Number of bachelors	6
Number of school children whose parents are not Eskdale residents	17
Total Population	94

in animal science. Five of the males had advanced graduate degrees. Except for one individual who held a high school degree, all the males in the sample had some formal education beyond high school. Another male, who was under age twenty-five during the summer of 1975, now is a veterinarian. Out of twenty-four females, four were professional teachers and one was a law student (now a graduated lawyer). Five women had undergraduate degrees, one had a master's degree, and one had not graduated from high school. During the 1950s Glendenning encouraged many young Levites to attend a Bible college in Colorado as well as state and private colleges and universities. He was an important influence in determining the philosophy of the Aaronic Order, whose motto is "education unlimited."

Historical Roots of the Levite View of Sex Roles

An analysis of the Levite view of sex roles would be incomplete without a discussion of its roots in Mormonism. Despite denial by the Levites that their organization is a Mormon "offshoot" or schism, there are strong similarities between Levite and Mormon beliefs, values, and behavioral patterns. Many of these s5similarities are apparent in areas such as sex roles, familial relationships, norms regulating sexual behavior, and the role of men and women in religious activities. According to Anderson (1942:426), except for the unique Mormon doctrine of celestial marriage (which encompassed both marriage for eternity and polygyny), the nineteenth-century Mormon family was little different from the family of New England. Whereas the traditional concepts of sex roles in Western society have been supported by the teachings of Saint Paul, the Mormons have buttressed and expanded upon these. To the Mormon people, patriarchal authority has been divinely ordained and is explicitly set forth in church doctrine. Joseph F. Smith, a former president of the Mormon Church, is quoted by Widtsoe (1939) as follows:

> There must be a presiding authority in the family. The father is the head or president, or spokesman of the family. . . . A home, as viewed by the Church, is composed of family groups, so organized to be presided over by the father, under the authority and in the spirit of the priesthood conferred upon him. . . . The position which men occupy in the family is one of the first importance and should be clearly recognized and maintained in order and with the authority which God conferred upon man in placing him at the head of his household.

Sociologist Kimball Young, one of Brigham Young's grandchildren, gives the following description of the Mormon conception of familial relations:

> In family life, the Mormons accepted and extended the patriarchal system. On the religious side, the males were accorded the rights and duties of the divinely established priesthood—the lower, or Aaronic, and the higher, or Melchizedek, and women could attain salvation by becoming members of the church—through repentance, baptism, and the "laying on of hands for the gift of the Holy Ghost." For them, however, the full glory in this life and in the hereafter could be obtained only through certain sacred rituals perfomed "by those in authority" involving marriage for "time and eternity." These marriages linked the wife to the husband forever and made it possible for her to share in his status during this life and in the next. But such status was not complete or satisfactory to God unless the women bore many children not only "to people and replenish the earth" but also to afford the waiting souls in heaven an opportunity to take on the flesh and go through "probation" of living on earth. [1947:375][4]

[4]It must be noted that many beliefs and rituals which are found in Mormonism and the Aaronic Order differ radically from those of traditional Judaism and Christianity. While this has become progressively less the case for the Aaronic Order, it is particularly true of Mormonism with its belief in polytheism and its emphasis on temple work or rituals for the dead. Both Mormons and some Levites adhere to the doctrine of the progression of gods as is expressed in the maxim, "As man is, God once was; as God is, man may become." In other words, both god and man are subject to the laws of progression; gods may become greater gods, and men may become gods. In Mormonism a god is married to one or more female deities; the greater the number of wives a god has, the greater will be his "exultation" (Whalen 1964:92). This was the ideological rationale for the Mormon practice of polygyny in the nineteenth century and also the reason that occasionally a man is "spiritually" married to other women in the temple.

Mormon males are expected to become husbands, fathers, economic providers, and agents of God in the larger society. Whereas the young Mormon male is incorporated into the priesthood at the age of twelve and prepared for position of ultimate authority within the nuclear family, the female is socialized into a role of dependency and submission. She is expected to value marriage, bearing and rearing children, homemaking, and giving support to her husbands. Church leaders have long stressed that women should not work outside the home, especially when there are young children to care for. In a study of the role of the Mormon woman, Wise and Carter (1965) found that, although nearly forty percent of the women in their sample were working outside the home, nearly one-fourth of them wished they were not employed. Mormons regard the enactment of prescribed sex roles to be necessary for harmony in society and for the attainment of perfection both in this life and in the next.

The Levites, like the Mormons, subscribe to the view that the man is the head of the family; and the mother, the head of the children. The husband-father is regarded by both groups as the patriarch of his family. According to Bushman (1971:6), the standard model for Mormon womanhood is "the supportive wife, the loving mother of many, the excellent cook, the imaginative homemaker and the diligent Church worker, a woman whose life is circumscribed by these roles." In many ways this model also applies to the women of the Aaronic Order.

Although Glendenning attempted to draw the Levites away from certain Mormon beliefs and behavioral patterns, he did not encourage a drastic redefinition of either traditional Judaic-Christian or Mormon concepts of sex roles. For the most part, the revelations which he received did not explicitly comment upon this matter. On the other hand, Glendenning attempted to extinguish the strong interest of some early Levites in polygyny, or plural marriage. Section 206 (undated) of the Book of Elias, which was published in 1944, states that "a Levite shall be the husband of one wife in the flesh." Later, in 1947, Glendenning received a revelation which declared that " . . . those of the House of Aaron shall have but one wife in the flesh and so long as she liveth in the flesh, there shall be no other" (Book of New Revelations 1948 ch. 4: 18–19). Glendenning sent a letter, dated November 6, 1953, to his cousins condemning polygyny and referring to the Mormon Church as the "reformed Brighamite Mormon Church" and as an "abominable church with such abominable teachings." Still later, on April 28, 1960, Glendenning issued another letter entitled "To Whom It May Concern," which also condemned polygyny.

As will become apparent later in this essay, many of Glendenning's policies were intended to reinforce traditional views of sex roles. It is likely that Glendenning's fundamentalist Protestant background as much as anything conditioned his patriarchal views. Also, it appears that his model of communal living was based on that of another patriarchal group, the Hutterites. Years before Glendenning moved to Utah, he had a chiropractic office in Yankton, South Dakota. Among his patients were Hutterites from the nearby Bon Homme Colony, the first Hutterite community in North America. In 1948, just prior to the establishment of Partoun and several years before that of the Eskdale commune, Glendenning initiated contacts (which have lasted for many years) with various Hutterite colonies in Montana. The Levites feel a close relationship with the Hutterites and, based on a revelation received by Glendenning, believe that the Hutterites are "Northern Levites" (Disciple Book 1955:15).

Symbols of Male Dominance and Female Subordination

Geertz (1973:89) has defined culture as "an historically transmitted pattern of meanings embodied in symbols, a system of inherited conceptions expressed in symbolic forms by means of which men communicate, perpetuate, and develop their knowledge about and attitudes toward life." If for the moment we can regard "culture as a symbol system," perhaps we may arrive at some deeper insights into the Levite world view, particularly as it relates to sex roles. I shall consider two cultural complexes, namely, the Levite politico-religious hierarchy and the Levite dress uniform. The first will be viewed as a "symbol of male dominance," and the second as a "symbol of female subordination." Because these designations are obviously complementary and somewhat arbitrary, I have chosen them strictly for heuristic purposes. It is very likely that many Levites would not regard these two complexes as being symbolic of their view of sex roles. Symbols, however, often have meanings in addition to ordinary ones which do not appear at the level of consciousness but are expressed through certain rituals, proscribed forms of behavior, and institutions.

Although the Levites claim that their politico-religious organization is identical to that of the ancient Israelites, it bears some striking similarities to that of the Mormon Church. Divine authority is believed by the Mormons to be delegated to the prophet-president of the church and by the Levites to the Chief High Priest of the Aaronic Order. The Mormon Church has a hereditary position for a male of the Smith family whose function is to dispense special "blessings" to church members and to determine their lineage. In the 1940s the Order also had a Patriarch who had a similar task, but now this responsibility is carried out by the Chief High Priest. Advancements in the religious hierarchy of the Aaronic Order are made by "calls" in a manner similar to that of the Mormon Church.

Both the Mormon Church and the Aaronic Order claim the Aaronic and Melchizedek priesthoods just as did the ancient Israelites. Mormons believe that the Aaronic, or "lesser," priesthood was conferred on Joseph Smith and Oliver Cowdery by John the Baptist. In the Mormon Church the Aaronic priesthood is ranked into three grades in order of importance—deacon, teacher, and priest—which are generally assigned to males between the ages of twelve and eighteen years. When a Mormon male reaches eighteen years of age, he can enter the Melchizedek priesthood, which is ranked in order of importance into the grades of elder, seventy, and high priest.

Unlike the Mormon Church, the Aaronic Order presently places strong emphasis upon the Aaronic priesthood, but gives minimal attention to the Melchizedek priesthood. The Levites believe that the Melchizedek priesthood became corrupted after the time of Malachi and, according to one male informant, has not been yet "set to order." Unlike the males of the same age-group in the Mormon Church, young males designated to be "of Aaron" are not permitted to officiate as priests until they reach their early twenties.

It is believed that God gave the Levitical priesthood to Levi and his male descendants. Later God gave the Aaronic priesthood to Aaron, the great-grandson of Levi and the elder brother of Moses, and his male descendants. Consequently, all Aaronites are Levites, but not all Levites are Aaronites; the Aaronic priesthood "comprehends the Levitical priesthood" (Beeston 1957:207). Levites not of Aaron are to assist the Aaronites in their priestly duties. Also, others referred to as the "sons of Aaron by adoption" were given the right to assist in the lesser offices of the Aaronic priesthood after the coming of Christ (Beeston 1957: 207–8; Book of New Revelations, ch. 7:24–25).

In addition, it is believed that only one lineage of the descendants of Aaron did not "pollute their inheritance"—the sons of Zadok. Consequently, according to Levite belief, only males who are lineal descendants of Aaron and Zadok can hold the Aaronic priesthood today. Furthermore, all Aaronites are born with the priesthood which is hereditary and which was "ordained" to them in the "preexistence," but can only officiate in it if authorized, or "given the keys," as one generally is after one has reached twenty years of age.[5]

Table 3 indicates the priesthood hierarchy and its relationship to other members of the Aaronic Order. The Levites believe that Jesus Christ is the Great High Priest of the Aaronic Order and the True Church of God. It is through him that the authority of the priest and of the councils of the Aaronic Order is delegated. The Chief High Priest is in charge of the "spiritual affairs" of the Aaronic Order, and the First High Priest is in charge of "temporal affairs." The authority of these two offices is "almost equal" (Beeston 1966:64). Both these two offices have been held by Robert Conrad since the death of Glendenning in 1969. The Office of the Second High Priest consists of a principal Second High Priest and his assistants, also technically referred to as Second High Priests. The Second High Priest and his assistants are responsible for the performance of certain ordinances. At the present time, the Aaronic Order has four Second High Priests, three of whom, including the principal Second High Priest, are brothers. The former principal Second High Priest, now deceased, was the father of these three men.

The Priest of the Branch is responsible for the "spiritual and temporal affairs" of a particular branch. The Salt Lake and Springville branches both have a permanent Priest of the Branch. The branch priest of the Eskdale commune is called the "acting priest," a position which is rotated every three months among the priests residing in Eskdale. The branch priest is assisted by other priests and disciples in the performance of ordinances and other branch functions. Although Partoun has had resident branch priests in the past, it presently does not have one. A male resident of Partoun,

[5]Both Levites and Mormons believe that before one is born and receives a body, he lives as a spirit in the "preexistence."

Table 3

Priesthood Hierarchy in Relation to Aaronic Order Membership

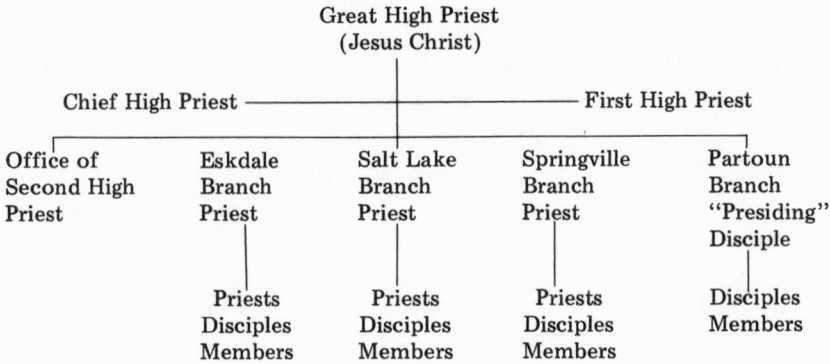

Great High Priest
(Jesus Christ)

Chief High Priest ————————————— First High Priest

Office of Second High Priest	Eskdale Branch Priest	Salt Lake Branch Priest	Springville Branch Priest	Partoun Branch "Presiding" Disciple
	Priests Disciples Members	Priests Disciples Members	Priests Disciples Members	Disciples Members

referred to as the "lead," or "acting," disciple, carries out many of the spiritual and temporal functions which a branch priest ordinarily conducts. An attempt is made to have priests from the Eskdale commune visit the Partoun branch at least twice a month so that certain rituals may be performed.

Fully consecrated males generally are disciples, and male disciples are organized into a "brotherhood" which regularly meets in the various branches. Female disciples are not presently organized into a "sisterhood," but, according to the Chief High Priest, they may be so in the future. All priests and male disciples in the Aaronic Order at the present time are married. Table 4 shows the distribution of priests and disciples and married men not holding these positions in the Aaronic Order.

The Aaronic Order has an elaborate system of councils which, it is believed, will some day administer to the religious needs of the Tribes of Israel. At present, because of the relatively small size of the Order, the Order is utilizing an abbreviated version of this system of councils. Table 5 indicates the council system and its relationship to other Levite offices and organizations. The Supreme Council is the legislative body which passes rules and regulations and which controls the funds of the Order. It consists of ten members, including a chairman, who must be Aaronite priests and fully consecrated. Either the Chief High Priest or the Supreme Council may appoint the chairman of the council, but both must concur on the appointment. The principal Second High Priest is always a member of the Su-

Table 4
Distribution of Politico-religious Positions
among Active Married Males in Aaronic Order

Branch	Priests	Disciples	Males neither Priests nor Disciples
Eskdale	9	5	3
Partoun	0	4	1
Salt Lake	5	1	2
Springville	2	1	1
At Large	4	0	0

preme Council. According to the Chief High Priest, the "real power" of the Aaronic Order lies in the Supreme Council. The Chief High Priest and First High Priest review and can approve or veto the decisions of the Supreme Council, which in turn can override a veto.

The Interceding Council coordinates the affairs of the four branches and "shall pass the desires and pleadings of the people to the Supreme Council" (Book of New Revelations, ch. 22:62). It consists of ten members and is chaired by the Second High Priest. According to the Chief High Priest, the Interceding Council is a "grass-roots" organization which must have representatives from all the branches. Both priests and disciples are members of the Interceding Council. The Chief High Priest noted that an attempt is made to avoid a situation where an individual is a member of both the Supreme and the Interceding councils. A relatively large proportion of the members of the Supreme and Interceding councils are

Table 5
The Councils of the Aaronic Order in Relation
to Other Offices and Organizations

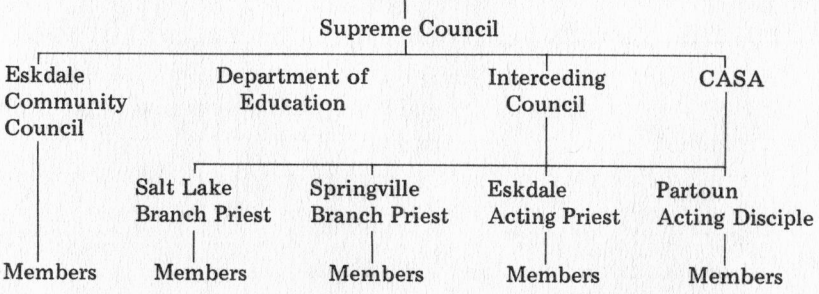

Eskdale residents—forty percent in both cases. It is interesting to note that three Eskdale residents hold membership on all three councils of the Order, namely, the Supreme Council, the Interceding Council, and the Eskdale Community Council. Council meetings are closed to nonmembers except secretaries, who are obligated not to discuss proceedings with others.

Each branch and council has a secretary who is generally a female; the secretary of the Supreme Council, however, is a young male. The work of the various secretaries is supervised and coordinated by the National Secretary, who has been a female Partoun resident for many years. She is assisted in her office by a member of the Salt Lake branch and reports directly to the Chief High Priest. The appointment of the various branch and council secretaries is made by the National Secretary and the respective branch priests and councils.

Although it officially is a lower-level council, the Eskdale Community Council is an extremely important formal decision-making agency. In the spring of 1975 the Community Council consisted of eight of the eleven married men who were permanent residents of the Eskdale commune. Two of the three married men not on the council were recently married and are in their early twenties. Individuals are "called" to the Community Council by its members.

The Community Council generally meets every other Sunday evening (comparable to Monday evening in the larger society), and the Chief High Priest is usually present at these meetings.[6] The Community Council exercises much latitude in making formal decisions for Eskdale and is seldom overruled by the Interceding Council or by the Supreme Council. According to the Chief High Priest, the Community Council is "very autonomous" as long as its decisions and policies are compatible with those of the Aaronic Order. An Eskdale priest noted that council decisions act as precedents for future decisions.

The Community Council receives input from the residents of Eskdale at the community meetings, which are conducted once a month. During these meetings the council may announce new policies or recent decisions and present community financial reports. The residents of Eskdale may discuss community needs and take a vote on proposed recommendations to the council. All fully consecrated members of the community over twenty-one years of age may vote.

[6]The Levites observe Saturday as their Sabbath.

The two major "official departments" of the Order are the Christian Aid Service of America (CASA) and the Department of Education. At the present time the CASA is somewhat comparable to the Relief Society (a female organization) of the Mormon Church. The CASA sponsors sewing and quilting sessions for women in the various branches and is also responsible for the storage of used clothing at Partoun. The Department of Education is responsible for the religious and musical education of the Order and the operation of the Eskdale school system.

The complex system of offices and councils found in the Aaronic Order acts to legitimate the dominance of males. Although the Levites subscribe to basically the same bilateral-descent system as the larger society, their claim of being Levites and Aaronites is based on a patrilineal principle. In a sense, patrilineal ideologies view women as being unnecessary or superfluous. Among the Levites, the genealogical status of women is seldom a matter of serious concern. Women are either Levites because their fathers are or because it is presumed they are "Levites by adoption." When the Chief High Priest determines whether an individual is of Levi or Aaron, that individual is always male. All major statuses and most minor statuses in the Levite politico-religious hierarchy are monopolized by males. The few women who are permitted to attend council meetings are required to remain silent about the proceedings both during and after the meetings. Although women may become disciples, their being such does not permit them to qualify for certain councils which are open to male disciples. In addition, while male priests and disciples in the Order receive a certificate acknowledging their status, female disciples do not receive such a document. Women who do hold an office have to be "called" or approved by the men.

It is likely that many Levite males consciously recognize the politico-religious hierarchy as a symbol of their dominance, but it is probably less likely that many males view the Levite dress uniform (and associated grooming practices) in the same light or as a symbol of female subordination. Nevertheless, various regulations associated with the wearing of the uniform reveal some of the more subtle nuances of Levite attitudes concerning sex roles.

For the active Mormon, the observance of the Word of Wisdom—a proscription forbidding the consumption of alcoholic beverages, coffee, tea, and tobacco—and certain styles of underclothes or temple garments provide powerful symbols indicating membership in a particular group. Many Levites, but not all, demonstrate their membership in the Order of Aaron with a distinct style of uniform, which females, particularly, are encouraged to wear. Rationales given for wearing a uniform are that it is a method of "witnessing for Christ" and that it unifies the Levites. An additional rationale which is given for women is that the uniform is more "modest" than secular dress styles.

The uniform for males, quite ordinary and not especially distinct, consists of a blue or white shirt with the word "Aaron" or "Levi" embroidered on the pocket. Only a male who has been designated as a lineal descendant of Aaron can have the word "Aaron" inscribed on his shirt; all other males can use the word "Levi." A fair number of males, particularly those who do not demonstrate a strong commitment to the Order, do not follow this practice. Males are free to wear whatever style of pants and suits they choose. According to an elderly female informant, at one time it was proposed that the males wear white overalls and white shirts, but the proposal met with general opposition on the part of the men. This informant maintained that Glendenning was willing to wear the proposed uniform at Eskdale, but not in non-Levite settings. The Levites assert that in the future their priests will wear white robes while performing various rituals.

A uniform for female members was formally proposed in late 1948 when Helen Glendenning announced to a group of women that the Chief High Priest had said that it was time for the women of the Order to wear one. The Aaronic Order has three basic uniform styles for females. One, which is regarded by some as the "official" Aaronic Order uniform, consists of a light blue dress with buttons in the front and a ribbon with fringe above the breast. The fringe serves as a reminder to keep the "commandments." According to many Levites, this uniform is the only style which a woman should wear when she is involved in the performance of certain "ordinances," or rituals. A uniform consisting of a blue jumper and a white blouse serves as a "work uniform" or "school uniform," although this is the only uniform many females generally wear. The most recent uniform to be designed—one with many practical advantages and which is probably the most stylish by secular standards—consists of blue slacks, a blue tunic, and a white blouse. Most widows wear a white uniform similar to the Order dress, but, to do so, they must make a pledge that they will never marry again. All uniforms are required to cover the knees; girls attending Eskdale grade and high schools are required to wear uniforms, even if they are not members of the Aaronic Order.

Part of the complete uniform is the "cap of honor," which is modeled after the Mennonite cap but has a visor with the word "Levi" embroidered in gold thread. Once a female decides to wear the cap of honor, she makes a pledge that she will never take it off (except in certain situations such as washing one's hair or bathing) and will never again cut her hair. The act of removing the cap after one has made a pledge is considered to be a fairly serious offense, but it appears that the only forms of social control to deal with it are disapproval and gossip.

Females under the age of thirty seldom wear the Order uniform. Some women in the Aaronic Order, all nonresidents of Eskdale, seldom wear the uniform, and others wear it primarily to Levite meetings but not elsewhere. Some of the younger and middle-aged women feel self-conscious about wearing the cap in non-Levite settings. When a young Levite, who attended the University of Utah and worked in its library where she had much contact with non-Levites, decided to wear the cap, members of the Aaronic Order expressed enthusiastic approval. Some women modify the uniform to make it more stylish by secular standards. Some women have made "uniforms" that resemble the long dresses currently fashionable among Mormon women in Utah.

The pressure to wear the uniform and particularly the cap has been relaxed in recent years. Some young women ceased wearing the uniform after they left Eskdale to attend college or to work on the outside. The uniform has been the source of a certain amount of controversy. Some women have argued that the expectation that they wear a uniform is a denial of their "free agency," the Mormon term for "free will." Several years ago one male refused his sister-in-law permission to attend his wedding because she did not wear a cap. Glendenning apparently exerted considerable pressure on women to wear the uniform as in the case when he photographed the women, placing those wearing the cap on one side, and those not on the other side. An interesting exchange took place when a man suggested at a study meeting that some women allow their hair to hang to their shoulders rather than rolling it under their cap. A woman with this latter style protested by noting that, when a Levite woman in her eighties wore her hair to her shoulders, she was asked by someone whether she was attempting to "catch a husband." Several years ago a woman wrote the following in the Aaronic Order newsletter: "Husbands in the Order should teach their wives to wear the uniform. Some say it is not written. It has come from the Office of the Chief High Priest and we say that we believe he is the servant of God. . . ." On the other hand, another Levite female more recently found it ironic that the men generally expect the women to wear a uniform but are not willing to do the same.

The dual standards applied to the wearing of a uniform clearly reveals an attempt by the males to reinforce their dominance and to subordinate the females of the Order. The decision that the females wear a distinctive garb came from the founder-prophet of the group and has been accepted almost unanimously by Levite males. On the other hand, despite the fact that some Levite females unequivocally accept this system of dual standards, many others directly or indirectly resist it. One ingenious adaptation has been the modification of the uniform so that it conforms more closely to current dress styles. Despite these mild forms of protest, it appears that for the most part women who wear one or more of the various types of uniforms presently used in the Order have internalized their subordinate status.

Structural Expressions of the Levite View of Sex Roles

It was pointed out earlier in this essay that, although a minority of Levites reside at the Eskdale commune, it is the center of Levite activity. Many members of the Aaronic Order who live in towns and cities plan to move to Eskdale or to the other Levite desert communities which are planned. The Levites maintain that a large number of communities, similar to Eskdale, will be established in the Snake Valley before the Second Coming of Christ. In the meantime, urban Levites are expected to give support—financial, physical, and moral —to the Levites who are already living in the desert. Unlike most communal ventures, Eskdale is part of a larger group with three noncommunal branches. Although Eskdale is striving to become economically self-supporting, it has not been so since its establishment over twenty years ago. The Eskdale commune is to a large extent maintained by the financial tithes and contributions of the noncommunal Levites. A mass exodus of these members to the Snake Valley at the present time would be a maladaptive phenomenon. Eskdale also has a relatively high turnover rate in that some families will reside there for several years and then will return to an urban area. Fortunately, however, the Aaronic Order has a pool of noncommunal members who are committed to a communal ideology and who fill vacancies as they arise at Eskdale. This practice does not completely eliminate the problems that are associated with high turnover rates, but it does ease them.

The scope of this paper does not permit further discussion of the various reasons for the failure of the Levites to create a relatively self-sufficient community at Eskdale. Nevertheless, the Eskdale commune is regarded as an expression of Levite ideals and goals. In this section I shall focus on three structural expressions of the Levite view of sex roles, namely, those in the areas of affiliative ties, economic organization, and education, particularly as they are exhibited at the Eskdale commune.

Affiliative Ties: Family and Marriage

Most of the Levites belong to a small number of interrelated families. Many offspring of the pioneers intermarried, and their offspring have in turn started to intermarry. Endogamy is preferred, but it is not uncommon for young Levites to marry non-Levites, particularly Mormons. In many cases marriage with outsiders results from a lack of commitment to the Aaronic Order. Another factor, of course, is a limited number of potential mates to choose from within the Order. It is not uncommon for Levites who marry outsiders to drift away from the mainstream of the Order. In some cases Levite-Mormon marriages result in a variety of tensions which may endure for many years. In some other cases a young Levite with little initial commitment to the Order marries an outsider but later decides that he or she should return to the fold; such a situation also may cause certain marital tensions. Since there are relatively few young converts to the Order, most committed young Levites attempt to find their partners within the group.

The Aaronic Order attempts to instill a sense of familism among all its members. Several informants stated that they feel that the Order is their "family." Like Mormons and many other small Christian groups, Levites address each other as "Brother" or "Sister." Unlike the Mormons, the Levites do not use forms of address which distinguish members on the basis of their status in the politico-religious hierarchy. The exception to this rule was Maurice Glendenning, who was addressed as "Bishop." Even the Chief High Priest is addressed as "Brother Bob" by both young and old. Although there is an attempt to create a sense of familism, some Levites admitted to me that they feel somewhat marginal because they have no or few relatives in the Order.

Each nuclear family at Eskdale has its own separate dwelling unit, although some of the children of these families live in the school dormitory. Most social interaction among adult residents of Eskdale occurs in work settings or at religious meetings. Although children visit each other in their homes rather frequently, such visiting does not occur often among adults. It appears that the residents of Partoun are more receptive to visiting than those of Eskdale. That they are may be related to the distance between homesteads at Partoun, the greater amount of leisure time that many of its residents have because they are retired, and the fewer opportunities for social contact. According to an Eskdale widow, after the chores and community activities are over, there is little time for visiting. Some Eskdale residents expressed a desire for more visiting in homes among the adults. Also some Partoun residents stated that they sometimes feel like intruders at Eskdale or that the residents of the commune are indifferent to their visits. A male resident of Partoun told me that he feels that there is more "fellowship" in his community than at Eskdale and that some Eskdale residents give him the impression that they prefer not to be visited at home. I personally found much more visiting in homes among adults when I did fieldwork in a Hutterite colony in South Dakota (Baer 1976b).

Just as is the case among the Mormons, the Levites place a great emphasis on large families and greatly value children. Rapport with the Levites, particularly with the women, was greatly enhanced as my wife evidenced pregnancy and our son was born. Although the Order implicitly encourages the procreation of many offspring, it permits each married couple to decide on the size of family they wish to have. This policy tends to follow the one which has been followed by the Mormon Church in recent decades. Although the church theoretically forbids birth control, it avoids open campaigns on the issue and appears generally to ignore the matter (O'Dea 1957:141).

The socialization of the young has been a source of major controversy in the Aaronic Order. Both Glendenning and the current Chief High Priest repeatedly encouraged Eskdale residents to allow their children to be raised communally by a small number of responsible adults. At the present time preschool children between ages two and six spend a large portion of the work day in the Montessori school. For mothers who wish to use it, a small nursery for infants is also available in the Montessori school. Eskdale couples rotate as "dean" and "matron" of the school dormitory about once a month. While some grade school and high school children live in the dormitory, others continue to live with their parents. The children whose parents do not reside at Eskdale have no other options, but those whose parents do often continue to live with them. At one time the community adopted a policy which permitted each adult to correct any child's behavior. This policy, however, also has failed because of the strong objection on the part of some Levites. Young Levites who were raised in the dormitory often note that discipline is not nearly so strict today as it was at certain periods in the past. A number of young people complained, for example, that one dormitory dean required transgressors of certain rules and regulations to wear red rings in their noses. Another dormitory dean made concerted efforts to separate boys and girls and forbade teenagers of the opposite sex to hold hands. The current Chief High Priest and his wife, however, felt that these practices were too extreme and brought an end to them.

Social relations at Eskdale indicate that there is a continuation of strong familial bonds among its members which in a number of respects interferes with the communal ideals of the Order. Kanter (1973) cites a number of studies of communal ventures, such as the Israeli *kibbutzim,* the Moravian intentional communities of the eighteenth century, and the Oneidans of the past century, which "support the proposition that communalism and familialism are antagonistic principles; that there is an inverse relationship between strength of community and strength of family" (282). However, it should be pointed out that most Levites have been living communally less than ten years and that concepts which they previously held about privacy are probably deeply ingrained. Eskdale's high school principal noted that it is relatively easy to construct some buildings, but it takes more time to develop a sense of "brotherhood and community," a quality which he feels has been strengthened gradually at Eskdale. Even though tensions may exist between individuals or families, a resolution to overcome or resolve these is not infrequently expressed in religious meetings, particularly during testimony meetings or at times when people spontaneously decide to give testimonies. Since the beginning of the religious revival, there has been more public expression of love and concern for one another and a desire to work in harmony.

Sexual Division of Labor

Eskdale's primary economic activities are crop and dairy agriculture. The commune had about 750 acres under cultivation and 21 wells, which vary in depth from about 40 to 200 feet. Eskdale's principal crop is alfalfa, most of which is used to feed the community's cattle, but some of which is sold commercially; generally there are three or four alfalfa crops a year. Other crops grown at Eskdale include corn, wheat, and barley. Eskdale also has two vegetable gardens which provide potatoes, corn, onions, carrots, beans, peas, pumpkin, squash, beets, and parsnips for the community and other members of the Order. Eskdale owns about 70 milk cows and about 100 calves, springers, and dry cows. Several years ago the commune owned about 30 head of beef cattle, but this number has decreased to a handful.

For the most part, Eskdale's sexual division of labor follows the one which has been traditionally defined in Western Society. Table 6 lists Eskdale's full-time work force. The composition of the work force shifts from year to year, primarily because bachelors may move in and out of Eskdale at any time of the year. The work manager is voted into office for a period of one year and makes the work assignments for the men. Bachelors are generally members of the work pool, which means they may be assigned to agricultural work, construction, repair work, dairy work, and so forth, for temporary assignments depending on the need. Male high school students are part-time members of the work pool and may be assigned specific tasks such as milking and cleaning the dairy. Although married males are assigned specific tasks, they are also part of the general work pool and may be given temporary assignments. The males conduct a meeting each work day after breakfast to discuss work assignments and problems for the day. All Eskdale teachers function under the Department of Education of the Aaronic Order.

Eskdale females, except those who are full-time school teachers, are members of the "center" work pool. The term "center" refers to a small group of buildings which include the communal kitchen and dining hall, the communal laundry, and the storage area. The kitchen supervisor prepares the center work schedule, meal menus,

Table 6
Eskdale's Full-time Work Force

Males	Positions	Females	Positions
A	Music teacher, beekeeper	A	Grade school teacher
B	High school principal	B	Grade school teacher
	and teacher	C	Kitchen supervisor, home
C	Work and shop manager		economics teacher
D	Gardener	D	Montessori school
E	Agriculturist		directress
F	Agriculturist	E	Community secretary,
G	Work pool member		center pool member
H	Work pool member	F	Community accountant,
I	Maintenance work		center pool member
J	Work pool member	G	Student music teacher
K	Work pool member	H	Montessori school teacher
L*	Dairy manager	I	High school teacher
M*	High school teacher, work	J	Center pool member
	pool member	K	Center pool member
N*	Asst. shop manager, work	L	Center pool member
	pool member	M	Center pool member
O*	Work pool member	N	Center pool member
P*	Work pool member	O	Center pool member
Q*	Work pool member		

*Indicates that an individual is a bachelor. All other individuals in the full-time work force are married.

and the grocery shopping list, shops once a month in the Salt Lake Valley, and coordinates the state-funded school-lunch program. Previously, the kitchen supervisory position was rotated every three months, but recently this assignment was extended for an indefinite term in order to eliminate the confusion which resulted from a frequent turnover of kitchen supervisors. The community council selects the kitchen supervisor.

Most center pool tasks are performed on a rotating basis. Two different women are scheduled to prepare meals each day. Women wash their family's laundry at assigned times, but the dormitory laundry is washed several days a week on a rotating basis, two women assigned to each day. During the 1974–75 academic year, there were three dormitory wash days, but during the previous academic year, there were five wash days because of the greater enrollment in the grade and high schools. Bread making and butter making are also rotated assignments, the former being done daily by a different woman every day and the latter being done perhaps three days a week by a different woman each day. Two women are assigned to community secretarial and bookkeeping tasks two days a week and are consequently assigned to the center work pool schedule only three days a week. Because the dormitory matron is expected to be in the dormitory most of the time, she usually does not participate in the center schedule.

Both grade and high school girls work in the communal kitchen and dining hall, usually starting to wash dishes in the first grade and graduating to more complicated tasks as they mature. The girls generally prepare breakfast and supper, but the women prepare the main meal of the day, eaten about noon. Generally on Fridays the girls prepare dinner so that they gain the experience of preparing the main meal of the day. Every Wednesday evening the women and the high school girls clean the community center. Some elderly women at Eskdale have no specified work assignments but can work when they choose to. Sometimes women are assigned to work in the community nursery when it is in operation. Preschool children spend much of the day in the Montessori school. During the summer months women and high school girls can vegetables which are raised at Eskdale and fruits which have been picked and purchased elsewhere, perhaps the Salt Lake and Utah valleys. According to the kitchen supervisor, Eskdale budgets about $1,000 per month for groceries, which provides for about half of the community's food consumption. The Eskdale commune produces its own meat, milk, butter, eggs, and vegetable produce, but must purchase some canned vegetable products because it does not have facilities for pressure-cooking vegetables.

Although Eskdale is characterized by a traditional sexual division of labor, there are incidents and situations in which it is not adhered to. One woman operated a tractor at Eskdale for a while, and one of the men noted that women are more careful with the farm machinery than are the men. Another woman worked in the irrigation ditches with her husband for part of a summer. Some female high school students work in the dairy with the males, and it is not uncommon to see girls riding horses for pleasure. Although males rarely work in the communal kitchen, the Chief High Priest and another priest from the Salt Lake branch occasionally clean dishes. While one woman supervised Eskdale's school-lunch program, her husband was assigned to work in the kitchen. Apparently some of Eskdale's males have defined working with the commune's small flock of chickens as "woman's work." This task was assigned first to a young man who later was "promoted" to a more prestigious occupation, and later to a young bachelor who was expected to assist an elderly woman with it. It is interesting to note that both males exhibited a great disdain for this assignment.

The Levite Educational System

A central focus of the Eskdale commune has been its school system, which presently consists of a Montessori school for children between the ages of two and six years, a grade school, and a high school. The Montessori school is directed by a woman who was trained at a Netherlands-based Montessori institution in Phoenix; she is the first person in the state of Utah to have been certified as a Montessori teacher. She is assisted by a young woman who graduated from Utah State University with a bachelor's degree in education with an emphasis on child development.

In February 1975 the Eskdale grade school had twenty-two students, about half of whom were children of people not residing at Eskdale. The grade school enrollment fluctuates appreciably from year to year, as is made apparent by the fact that it had thirty students during the 1973–74 academic year. In February 1975 two students were children of non-Levites, and in the past there have been as many as six to eight non-Levite students in the grade school. Apparently some non-Levites in the Snake Valley have preferred from time to time to send their children to either the Eskdale grade school or high school. The grade school has two college-graduated and certificated female teachers; one covers grades one to four, and the other covers grades five to eight.

The Eskdale high school is the only high school between Delta, Utah, and Ely, Nevada—a distance of 147 miles. The size of the student body and faculty of the high school also fluctuates from year to year. During the 1974–75 academic year there were approximately twenty-five students in the high school with two graduating in May, whereas during the 1973–74 academic year there were thirty-two students with seven graduating. The high school enrollment has approached forty students in previous years. During the 1972–73 academic year the high school had eight full-time and part-time teachers, six of whom had college degrees, but not necessarily in education. Table 7 summarizes the composition of the high school faculty and its qualifications during the 1974–75 academic year.

Although the grade and high schools lack many of the facilities of outside schools, the low student-faculty ratio apparently helps to compensate. Eskdale graduates generally have been readily accepted by colleges and universities, despite the fact that the high school lacks accreditation. A proportionally high number of Eskdale graduates received college scholarships, and many students pass tests granting them the equivalent of one year's college course work. Levite college students, particularly those whose families live at Eskdale, must support their own education with scholarships and part-time work.

One of the chief sources of pride for the people of Eskdale and the Order is the music program and community orchestra. The Levites believe that, because the Levites of Old Testament times were musicians, they must continue this tradition. Piano instruction is the basis of the music education program and begins for many students in the third grade. Students may be involved in one to four hours of musical instruction and practice daily. In 1973 the school orchestra became the community orchestra after some adults expressed a desire to learn how to play a musical instrument. Consequently, the community orchestra consists of grade and high school students, young people who recently graduated from high school, and adults —most of whom are females. The forty-five–piece orchestra plays primarily religious and classical music and has performed at numerous locations in Utah and eastern Nevada, including the University of Utah and Brigham Young University.

Table 7
The Eskdale High School Faculty, 1974–75

Teacher	Sex	Degree of Teaching Activity	College Degree	Teaching Certificate
A	male	full time*	yes	yes
B**	female	full time*	no	no
C	male	full time	yes	yes
D	female	full time	yes	yes
E	female	part time	no	no
F	male	part time	no	no

*music teacher who also teaches grade school children
**music education major who is student teaching

Of the various formal organizations in the Aaronic Order, it is in the educational system that the females begin to approach an equal status with the males. It must be noted, however, that the ultimate control of the educational system lies with the Supreme Council— an all-male organization. In addition, the various principals of the Eskdale high school, who also have been supervisors over the other schools in the system, have been invariably men. Nevertheless, a large proportion of teachers are, or have been, women. It appears that in recent years it is the females who have been more likely to go on to college or university. This trend is indicated partly by the fact that in the spring of 1975 there were six bachelors (all adolescents or young adults) and no unattached females of the same age range residing at Eskdale. Although it was not uncommon for young unmarried women to visit Eskdale on the weekends or during vacations, many of them were attending college. While it is true that Levite women tend to be attracted to disciplines which traditionally have been associated with females, one woman was a law student (now a lawyer) and another was an engineering student. There appeared to be little or no objection to these women's entering professions which have been traditionally associated with males in American society. Furthermore, the status of teacher and the possession of musical skills, unlike the larger society, are considered to be highly desirable attributes among the Levites. Consequently, the relatively high representation of females in these two areas is a marked improvement over their subordinate status in other areas of Levite life.

The Role of Women in Fluid Situations

Sex roles in the Levite community tend to follow closely the traditional model prescribed in Western society. As I have pointed out, however, there are situations in which adherence to this model is relaxed. I shall argue that this departure from the traditional model tends to be true in four situations or contexts: (1) times of economic need or necessity; (2) religious rituals and discussions; (3) recruitment of new members; and (4) periods of ideological change. It is my proposition that, although Levite women do not necessarily become the social equals of Levite men in these settings, they do make significant gains over the status level they hold in more structured settings.

Periods or Situations Involving Economic Need

Incidences in which women worked at traditionally defined male jobs have been cited already in this paper. These include the two female immigrants from Sweden who established a homestead and the woman who worked as a carpenter at Partoun. When many of the males were away from Partoun because they had to earn income from other jobs, women maintained the homesteads and did road work for the new community. Although this pattern has not been so pronounced at Eskdale, there have been cases in which females have driven tractors and worked in the irrigation canals and the dairy. Both Partoun and Eskdale have been pioneer communities which often experienced a shortage of personnel in certain critical economic areas. While there has been an abundance of teachers in the Order, there has existed a serious shortage of qualified agriculturalists, construction workers, and mechanics in both communities. Many of the young men who periodically visit Eskdale are primarily urban dwellers who are unfamiliar with the skills that are necessary to establish a desert community. In some cases female Levites have possessed these skills or exhibited an ability to acquire them quickly. At times the leaders of the Eskdale commune have recognized the women's abilities and have been willing to relax the traditional definitions associated with sex roles.

Religious Rituals and Study Meetings

Formal religious rituals of the Aaronic Order—many of which are modifications of those of the Mormon Church—tend to be highly structured and definitively prescribed. Priests, sometimes with the assistance of male deacons, are the only individuals who are permitted to perform these "ordinances." The Levites also observe a number of rituals which are much more informal and loosely structured. Females generally play a more active and expressive role in this second category of rituals than do the men. The one exception is the sermon, which is a standard part of the Levite worship service and in almost all cases is delivered by a male. Although the sermon may be delivered by the branch priest, it is often given by another male member of the local branch or of another branch. Most sermons tend to drift from one topic to another without any apparent organization or continuity. It is not unusual for individuals to state that they attempted during the past several days to organize a sermon but decided to resort to an impromptu address and place the matter in "the hands of the Lord." The exception to this general pattern occurs at the Springville branch, which has fewer male adults than particularly the Eskdale and Salt Lake branches. Consequently, a woman will be asked occasionally to deliver the sermon.

Women play a particularly expressive role in the testimony sessions and in the prayer circles. The former, which occur on the first Saturday of the month and spontaneously from time to time, is a carry-over from Mormonism. The prayer circles, which often occur after regular services or in people's homes, appear to have been borrowed from fundamentalist Protestant groups. Although these are occasions when members of the Order express their dependence on the Order, perhaps even more pronounced is their use as cathartic mechanisms which permit particularly women to release feelings of frustration and anxiety. Testimonies often take the form of a confession of one's transgressions against others and of one's failures to conform to the group's norms. Some women await the testimony session with great anticipation; one woman, for example, was almost always the first person to testify when the worship service at the Salt Lake branch moved into this phase. Many of her testimonies revolved around the frustrations of being the mother of ten children. It is not unusual for women to cry during or after their testimonies. Although males also deliver testimonies, they generally do not express strong emotional feelings and often give brief, impromptu sermons. One middle-aged man, who often cried when he gave a testimony, told me that he felt embarrassed about his behavior and was sometimes reluctant to testify because he was afraid that he would cry. During testimony and prayer sessions, individuals experiencing marital or economic problems, doubts, temptations, and so forth, are prayed for or given some kind of moral support. The love one feels for the individual with a problem is often stated at these times.

Women also play a very active role in the study classes, which are conducted on Saturday mornings and on various evenings of the week, depending on the branch. Women not only participate actively, but often are also responsible for leading the classes. It is also not uncommon for women to be better prepared to discuss some of the intricate doctrines of the Levite religion. It appears that women spend on the whole more time than the men studying the Mormon scriptures, the sacred books of the Aaronic Order, and the Bible.

Recruitment of New Members

A study which I conducted of the Levite conversion experience included twenty-three females and twelve males who joined the Aaronic Order (Baer 1978). Partly because my sample was not entirely random, it is likely in reality the male-to-female ratio of converts is more balanced than the numbers indicate. Three of the females in the sample are widows whose husbands were also converts to the Order. The Levite husbands of two other elderly converts were unable to be interviewed. Nevertheless, there appears to be a somewhat greater tendency for females to join the Order (and also to attend religious meetings) than for males. Some females joined the Aaronic Order after they were divorced or widowed. In most cases these women did not remarry a member of the Aaronic Order. The Order provides widows with opportunities for social interaction which are not often provided in larger society.

Levite females have had a strong influence in attracting their husbands, parents, children, relatives, and friends or acquaintances to the Aaronic Order. Whether their influence in this regard has been proportionately greater than that of males is difficult to determine. Nevertheless, it appears that their proselytizing efforts have equaled those of males. The current Chief High Priest, for example, joined the Aaronic Order about ten years after his wife had done so. Although couples in marriages consisting of a Levite and a non-Levite (usually a Mormon) seldom live at Eskdale, the current Chief High Priest resided there for about a year before he decided to join the Order. Women in particular request that group prayers be said for the conversion of their husbands to the Aaronic Order. It should be noted that not all of these attempts to induce one's spouse to join the group are successful. For example, two women have been praying for the conversion of their husbands for about twenty-five years.

Periods of Religious Change

Earlier in this essay I pointed out that there has been a considerable amount of ideological shift in the Aaronic Order from Mormonism to fundamentalist Protestantism. Although Glendenning and some other Levite males, particularly one who was not reared a Mormon, played an important role in bringing about this shift, a large number of Levite females, especially younger ones, have also contributed to ideological change in the Order. For example, in 1963 a Levite woman attended a revival meeting in the Phoenix area at which Jerry Owens, a Protestant evangelist, was preaching. Shortly afterward this woman took Owens to meet Glendenning, who often spent winters in Arizona for health reasons. Glendenning and Owens immediately took a liking to each other, and arrangements were made to have Owens speak to the Levites in Utah. Over the years Owens himself and the groups to which he introduced the Levites were influential in bringing about religious changes in the Order. Although the woman mentioned was only indirectly involved in these changes, her receptivity to Gentile non-Mormon beliefs and rituals was one among a number of events in which Levite women have acted as agents of religious change.

Some of the Protestant groups with which the Order has had contact have been of a Pentecostal orientation. Although the Levites have had contact with these groups as far back as the mid-1950s, only a small number of Levites had "spoken in tongues" prior to the summer of 1974. Speaking in tongues was usually done privately or in very small groups who were sympathetic to the practice. Glossolalia in large group settings was disapproved of and ridiculed, even though a fair number of Levites had witnessed the phenomenon in various fundamentalist Protestant congregations.

During the summer of 1974, a Pentecostal, or "charismatic," revival occurred among the Levites at Eskdale and spread to the other branches of the Order. The emergence of the charismatic movement within the Aaronic Order was largely stimulated by contacts with a Jesus People group from California known as the Order of the Lamb. A young man, who had joined the Aaronic Order several years earlier but who was of a Protestant rather than a Mormon background, emerged as the informal leader of the charismatic movement. In his efforts to win other Levites over to the revival, he was supported by his wife, the daughter of a high-ranking priest. Because she had been an excellent student, was amiable and cooperative, and had scrupulously abided by community norms, she was regarded by many to be the paragon of young Levite womanhood. While an appreciable number of males were involved in the revival, many young and middle-aged females were particularly receptive to the informal and expressive rituals of the Pentecostalists such as impromptu prayer meetings, glossolalia, prophesying, and healing. It appears that in these rituals, in contrast with the formal religious services of the Order, the females approached equal status with the males.

Despite the initial reservations of many Levites, it seemed for a while that in the long run the charismatic movement would serve a cohesive function. It integrated into the Order many of the young Levites who had not experienced the pioneering efforts of the older Levites. It transcended the cleavages which existed among the generations of the group. Especially noteworthy, considering our focus on sex roles in communes, the movement provided a new opportunity for Levite females to participate actively rather than passively in religious activities.

These points of unification, however, proved to be temporary and were negated by the schism of many young Levites and some middle-aged Levites from the Order. Although many factors contributed to the schism, the precipitating one appears to have been the research activities of two women, namely, the wife of the informal leader of the charismatic movement and one of her younger sisters. These two women compared the Bible and the Levite scriptures, concluded that serious contradictions existed between them, and maintained that the latter were largely in error. During the fall of 1975, the heated debates which followed these discoveries culminated in the expulsion of the informal leader of the revivalists and his chief disciple from the Eskdale commune. The wife of the informal leader followed him, as eventually did many others, including the other woman who engaged in the controversial research. Although he was extremely reluctant to do so, the woman's husband—the supervisor of the Levite educational system and a high-ranking member of the Order—also left the Eskdale commune at the end of the 1975–76 academic year, largely because he did not desire to be permanently separated from his wife. The role of these two women in the schism again illustrates the prominent role which Levite women have played during times of religious change.

Shifting Definitions of Sex Roles among the Mormons

A parallel of the relaxation of sex-role definition that occurs in certain situations among the Levites occurred among the Mormons during the nineteenth century. Although the Mormon definition of sex roles has always been patriarchal, their pioneering efforts and their practice of polygyny, or "plural marriage," at that time contributed to this relaxation.

> Mormon women were probably more independent than most Western women. For one thing, the men were often away on missions of one kind or another so that the women had to provide a livelihood for themselves and their children, as well as send occasional expense money to their husbands. For another thing, the practice of plural marriage insured that, in the case of many families, the husband could not manage his farms and other enterprises on a day-to-day basis; this had to be done by its various wives and their children. The women often had cooperative "bees" to build houses, canals, and fences and to make quilts. Finally, the inhospitable nature of the Great Basin and the isolated character of most of the settlements must have required women to be more self-reliant and self-sustaining than settlers in less harsh areas. [Arrington 1971:23]

During the nineteenth century, sex roles often merged as Mormon women confronted situations in which they had to assume as much responsibility for agricultural tasks such as plowing, planting, digging irrigation ditches, and harvesting as they did for domestic chores. In many ways the frontier life of Utah women resembled that of other women on the expanding American frontier. In addition, women were encouraged by one no less than Brigham Young himself to enter male-dominated occupations. "We have sisters here who, if they had the privilege of studying, would make just as good mathematicians or accountants as any man," he affirmed.

> We believe that women are useful, not only to sweep houses, wash dishes, make beds, and raise babies, but that they should stand behind the counter, study law or physic [medicine], or become good book-keepers and be able to do the business in any counting house, and all this to enlarge their sphere of usefulness for the benefit of society at large. In following these things they but answer the design of their creation. [Quoted in Arrington and Bitton 1979:227–28]

Some Mormon women became independent entrepreneurs, operating small businesses such as millinery shops, bakeries, and private schools. The Relief Societies established in 1869 under the auspices of the church hierarchy not only convened to produce clothing, quilts, and carpets, but also operated cooperative stores for the sale of various home manufactures and were engaged in silk-producing and grain-storage programs. During the first two decades of Utah's settlement, a number of self-trained women acted as midwives and physicians, relying particularly upon botanic medicine for their cures (Lobb and Derr 1978:344). Young encouraged both men and women to obtain medical degrees from eastern medical schools. Deseret Hospital, which was operated from 1882 to 1890 and which was the first Mormon hospital in Utah, was managed by a female board of directors and was staffed by four female Mormon doctors. Mormon women were also admitted to administrative and teaching positions in elementary and secondary schools. When the University of Deseret (the forerunner of the University of Utah) opened its doors in 1869, it registered eighty-eight women along with ninety-nine men (ibid.:341).

Although some Mormon women were able to enter occupations traditionally occupied by men, it is important to note that Brigham Young was concerned that the coming of the railroad to Utah would lead to Mormon dependence on Utah's growing Gentile population as well as on eastern commerce. For example, in 1869 the Relief Societies were directed to organize Retrenchment Associations in order to produce garments so as to avoid reliance on imported clothing (Arrington and Bitton 1979:228). The expansion of occupations and economic endeavors for Mormon women was not so much a matter of shifting attitudes toward sex roles per se as it was a response by the church hierarchy to the encroachment of the larger society upon the refuge that the Mormons had created in order to escape the larger society.

As mentioned earlier, Utah has the distinction of having been the first state or territory in the United States in which women exercised suffrage. What on the surface may appear to have been a progressive move on the part of the Mormon Church must be viewed within the context of the federal government's unrelenting campaign against plural marriage. According to Warenski (1978:144), "... if polygamy and women's suffrage seem unlikely partners, an unraveling of the tale reveals that suffrage came to Utah more because of polygamy than in spite of it." While their eastern sisters struggled for voting rights largely on their own, the vote was simply given to Mormon women by the male priesthood leaders who viewed it as an important strategy in countering the efforts of the larger society to stamp out polygyny in the Intermountain West. Warenski (ibid.:164) goes on to say that "it is unlikely that the women of Utah would have promoted suffrage for themselves at that time, nor is there any evidence that they took any significant part in its passage." Unlike the eastern feminists, the Mormon women did not generally question the male-controlled priesthood authority. Although Utah Mormon women sent delegates to the National Suffrage Association meetings beginning in 1879, they did so only under the approval of the church hierarchy.

Once the necessity of utilizing women in various spheres of the Mormon economy and the crisis surrounding the practice of plural marriage passed, the Mormon Church reverted to more traditional definitions of sex roles. This shift is summarized in the following remarks by Jeffrey (1979:178):

> And with the church's accommodation to the Gentile world, the leadership no longer had the same requests to make of Mormon women and no longer furnished the same support for expanded female roles. In fact, during the twentieth century, Mormon women lost respect and power, rather than acquired them. Even their organizations ceased to play the independent role they once had. By the mid-twentieth century, indeed, Mormon women had become the bulwarks of social and sexual conservatism.

Perhaps this transition is best exemplified by recent efforts by the Mormon Church to thwart the efforts of the women's liberation movement. When the Utah state conference of the International Women's Year met in Salt Lake City in June 1977, church leaders encouraged Mormon women to attend (Beecher and MacKay 1978:583). Under the influence of ultraconservative political activists, most of whom were Mormons, women were warned against the alleged conspiratorial tactics of the organizers of the conference. As a result of these efforts, voting on the Equal Rights Amendment at the conference was about 6,000 to 400 against ratification. A similar voting pattern occurred against elective abortions, public funding of birth-control centers, sex education in schools, daycare centers, and other related issues.

Summary and Conclusions

In one of the few overviews of sex roles in American communal groups, Kanter (1973) suggests that there exists an association be-

tween communalism and sexual egalitarianism. An examination of
Levite sex roles adds to the growing amount of evidence which indicates that communalism and a male-supremacist perspective are
often combined (Wagner 1976). Maurice Glendenning, the founder-
prophet of the Levite sect, did not envision overall a drastic redefinition of traditional sex roles. The only significant innovation which
he proposed in this regard was communal childrearing—a pattern
which has been only partially implemented at the Eskdale commune. In fact, if anything, Glendenning reinforced traditional concepts of sex roles which have been associated with both Mormonism
and Protestant fundamentalism. That he did so is particularly evident in the case of the politico-religious hierarchy which he borrowed and modified and in the great emphasis that he placed on a
distinctive dress uniform for Levite females. Glendenning's major
innovation involved an attempt to revitalize Mormon cooperative
and communal endeavors rather than to redefine existing concepts
in sex roles.

Although Levite women appear to be relatively satisfied with traditional Western sex roles, there appears to be some diversity of
opinion on issues such as the feminist movement. An elderly Levite
woman, one of the first members of the Aaronic Order, favors passage of the Equal Rights Amendment and complained about the job
discrimination she experienced on the outside because of her sex.
Although stating that career-minded females have "gotten off base
somewhere along the line," a middle-aged woman admitted that the
women's liberation movement is "good" for some women who make
better business people than they do mothers. The decision of a few
young Levite women to enter occupations which have been traditionally assigned to males has not encountered great opposition in recent years. Although the Levites attempt to shun the larger society
in a variety of ways, they are not immune from its changing definitions of sex roles. In addition, it must be noted that some of the
childcare facilities of the Eskdale commune such as the Montessori
school and the exchange of child tending responsibilities among
families frees many Eskdale women for various other endeavors
such as teaching, religious study, and participation in the community orchestra.

An examination of Levite sex roles indicates that females play a
greater role in informal settings and during periods of sociocultural
change than in formal settings and during periods of social stability.

Furthermore, an examination of Mormon sex roles reveals that sex-role definitions for females expanded during periods of political and economic expediency, whereas they contracted after Mormon culture had gone through a process of accommodation to the larger American society. This finding supports a model developed by Moore (1975: 210–40) which attempts to explain the baffling incongruence between ideology and social relations often found in utopian societies. Based on the "dialectical exercise" proposed by Murphy (1971), the basic postulate of her model is that the underlying quality of social life is one of "theoretically absolute indeterminacy." In addition to the factor of indeterminacy, Moore's model postulates an ongoing tension between "processes of regularization" and "processes of situational adjustment." Processes of regularization refer to those which attempt to fix social life, including the construction of rituals, regular formalities, laws, normative practices, customs, symbols, ideological models, and so forth. Conversely, Moore (1975:220) notes that "the cultural, contractual, and technical imperatives always leave gaps, requires adjustments and interpretations to be applicable to particular situations, and are themselves full of amibiguities, inconsistencies, and often contradictions." Processes of situational adjustment permit a certain degree of interpretation of the group's conception of an ideal social system. The Levite social system and ideology are often characterized by inconsistencies and tension. While the Levite perspective is basically patriarchal, there are certain situations in which it is economically expedient to allow women a greater participation in spheres usually relegated to males. In addition, it is in loosely defined settings such as certain rituals or study sessions and during periods of ideological flux that women play a more predominant role than would be indicated by Levite cosmology. Apparently these tendencies also have been present in at least some other communal or cooperative ventures, including nineteenth-century Mormonism and the Israeli *kibbutzim* (Arrington 1971; Spiro 1970). Whether this pattern holds true for most utopian or communal movements remains to be determined.

Friedl (1975:4) maintains that male ethnographers gather incomplete data as to the relative power of men and women, particularly since they talk to mostly men. In the case of my own fieldwork among the Levites, although I spoke with many females as well as with males, it would be foolish to argue that my own sexual status did not affect the data which I was able to obtain or which I chose to gather. A more complete view of sex roles among the Levites would require the work of a female ethnographer to complement my own research. She might discover spheres in which women exert a greater influence than I was able to detect.

ACKNOWLEDGMENTS

I extend special thanks to Robert Conrad, Chief High Priest of the Aaronic Order, and the many members of the Aaronic Order, whose assistance made my research possible. Although undoubtedly many Levites will disagree with much of my analysis of their group, I should like to add that their ideals of egalitarianism and communalism are ones toward which I am deeply sympathetic. I am also grateful to Seymour Parker for first telling me about the Aaronic Order and for giving me support in my study of the group.

REFERENCES CITED

Anderson, Nels
  1942 Desert Saints: The Mormon Frontier in Utah. Chicago: Univ. of Chicago Pr.
Arrington, Leonard J.
  1971 Blessed Damozels: Women in Mormon History. Dialogue: A Journal of Mormon Thought 6:22–31.
Arrington, Leonard J., and Davis Bitton
  1979 The Mormon Experience: A History of the Latter-Day Saints. New York: Knopf.
Baer, Hans A.
  1976a The Levites of Utah: The Development of and Recruitment to a Small Millenarian Sect. Ph.D. diss., Univ. of Utah.
  1976b The Effect of Technological Innovation on Hutterite Culture. Plains Anthropologist 21:187–97.
  1977 The Levites of Utah: A Twentieth Century Attempt to Revitalize Mormonism. Proceedings of the Central States Anthropological Society, Selected Papers 3:9–16.
  1978 A Field Perspective of Religious Conversion: The Levites of Utah. Review of Religious Research 19:279–94.
Beecher, Maureen Ursenbach, and Kathryn L. MacKay
  1978 Women in Twentieth-Century Utah. In Utah's History, ed. Richard D. Poll, Thomas G. Alexander, Eugene E. Campbell, and David E. Miller. Provo, UT: Brigham Young Univ. Pr.

Beeston, Blanche W.
  1957 Now My Servant. Caldwell, ID: Caxton.
  1966 Purified as Gold and Silver. Caldwell, ID: Caxton.
Book of New Revelations
  1948 Salt Lake City: Corporation of the President of the Aaronic
        Order.
Bushman, Claudia Lauper
  1971 Women in Dialogue: An Introduction. Dialogue: A Journal of Mor-
        mon Thought 6:5–9.
Davies, J. Kenneth
  1963 The Mormon Church: Its Middle-Class Propensities. Review of Reli-
        gious Research 4:84–95.
Disciple Book
  1955 Salt Lake City: Corporation of the President of the Aaronic
        Order.
Friedl, Ernestine
  1975 Women and Men: An Anthropologist's View. New York: Holt.
Geertz, Clifford
  1973 The Interpretation of Cultures: Selected Essays. New York: Basic
        Books.
Jeffrey, Julie Roy
  1979 Frontier Women: The Trans-Mississippi West, 1840–1880. New
        York: Hill and Wang.
Kanter, Rosabeth Moss, ed.
  1973 Communes: Creating and Managing the Collective Life. New York:
        Harper and Row.
Lobb, Ann Vest, and Jill Mulvay Derr
  1978 Women in Early Utah. In Utah's History, ed. Richard D. Poll,
        Thomas G. Alexander, Eugene E. Campbell, and David E. Miller.
        Provo, UT: Brigham Young Univ. Pr.
Moore, Sally Falk
  1975 Epilogue: Uncertainties in Situations, Indeterminacies in Culture.
        In Symbol and Politics in Communal Ideology, ed. Sally Falk
        Moore and Barbara G. Meyerhoff. Ithaca, NY: Cornell Univ. Pr.
Murphy, Robert F.
  1971 The Dialectics of Social Life. New York: Basic Books.
O'Dea, Thomas F.
  1957 The Mormons. Chicago: Univ. of Chicago Pr.
Spiro, Melford E.
  1970 Kibbutz: Venture in Utopia. New York: Schocken.
Talmon, Yonina
  1972 Family and Community in the Kibbutz. Cambridge, MA: Harvard
        Univ. Pr.
Wagner, Jon
  1976 Male Supremacy: Its Role in a Contemporary Commune and Its
        Structural Alternatives. International Review of Modern Sociology
        6:173–80.
Wallace, Anthony F. C.
  1972 Revitalization Movements. In Reader in Comparative Religion, ed.
        William A. Lessa and Evon Z. Vogt. 3d ed. New York: Harper and
        Row.

Warenski, Marilyn
    1979   Patriarchs and Politics: The Plight of the Mormon Woman. New
           York: McGraw-Hill.
Whalen, William J.
    1964   The Latter-Day Saints in the Modern Day World. Reprint 1967.
           South Bend, IN: Univ. of Notre Dame Pr.
Widtsoe, Leah D.
    1939   Priesthood and Womanhood. Salt Lake City: Deseret.
Wise, Genevieve M., and Don C. Carter
    1965   A Definition of the Role and Homemaker by Two Generations of
           Women. Journal of Marriage and the Family 27:531–32.
Young, Kimball
    1947   Sex Roles in Polygynous Mormon Families. *In* Readings in Social
           Psychology, ed. Theodore M. Newcomb and Eugene L. Hartley.
           New York: Holt.

-5- BARBARA MATHIEU

The Shiloh Farms Community

A Case of Complementarity in Sex-Role Dualism

THE FOUNDING OF THE SHILOH Farms community coincided with the United States' entry into World War II. E. C. Monroe, a successful ship designer and businessman forced to retire at age sixty because of poor health, established the community of Shiloh in Chautauqua County, New York, in 1941. It was his stated intent to provide a "refuge for the rehabilitation of man." Among those who were first attracted to Monroe and his "perfectionist" theology (influenced by the writings of J. H. Noyes), prophetic teachings, and concept of a self-supporting, residential religious community were a number of newly uniformed servicemen. For the young serviceman the benevolent but moralistic Monroe symbolized strength, security, and stability. His fatherly counsel gave assurance and courage to those who were facing uncertain times.

The Shiloh "family," though then small in number, sustained an active correspondence with all its members as well as with prospective members who were serving in the armed forces. Active communication by mail and phone with absent members and friends is still a top priority at Shiloh. Several long-term members told of traveling from California to New York to spend their leave time with Monroe and the Shiloh family. These same members planned, while still in uniform, to become permanent residents of Shiloh once their tour of duty was complete. The current leader, Father James, was first introduced to Monroe and the Shiloh family while serving in the U.S. Navy.

Another class of persons attracted to the charismatic Monroe was the socially labeled "derelict"—individuals who saw their lives made up of successive personal failures. Monroe offered these persons the hope of fulfillment of their goals along with the assurance of his support, spiritual and material, so long as they proved themselves worthy and demonstrated a desire for reform.

Monroe incorporated into his community's charter traditional American ideals and values: patriotism, free enterprise, the work ethic, monogamous marriage, technological progress—values which were undergoing revitalization at that time in response to the war. Though an exemplar of American secular ideology, Monroe found himself in opposition to the major denominational churches, which he accused of being rigidly doctrinaire, thereby not allowing for "new revelations of the holy spirit."

Opposition to the established churches was also based on what he declared as a dangerous emphasis on the "social gospel," in which church members were encouraged to be involved in social issues and concerns. Monroe insisted that the proper focus of religious practitioners should be on individual spiritual development, not on social ills.

As the United States entered the war, threats to the traditional social order loomed. The establishment of the Shiloh community at that time could be interpreted as an attempt by a small number of persons to stem the tide of social change by reaffirming their conventional values and by offering an environment for individual spiritual enlightenment and development.

Information on the early history of the community, recorded in newspaper clippings kept in Shiloh scrapbooks, reveals a skeptical climate in the society that surrounded the newly established Shiloh community. As is common to most historical and contemporary communities in which there are identifiable boundaries separating members from outsiders, the impingement of external prejudices and disdain served to strengthen the internal bonds of solidarity and reinforce the original motivation for community. Several articles seemingly were written as apologetics attempting to justify and explain Shiloh's origins and philosophy and to repudiate rumors that Shiloh was a community "solely for derelicts and misfits." To counter the rumors, the articles projected an image of Americanism and good will.

In 1968 the well-established Shiloh Farms community moved from the state of New York to northwest Arkansas. The decision to move was prompted, according to charter members, by prophetic revelations interpreted by the community leadership. The change of location promised to be advantageous to the then expanding health-foods distribution enterprise, which continues to be the successful support of the community. Despite prophetic decree and the recognized potential for increased self-sufficiency in a region with a longer growing season, nearly half of the New York membership left the community rather than resettle in Arkansas.

The community is now situated on a grassy knoll overlooking a small Ozark town. The physical center of the community is an imposing stone structure which houses the bakery, administrative and business offices, kitchen, dining hall, and several single residential rooms. The original structures at Shiloh, built from locally quarried stone prior to Shiloh's occupancy, lend an aura of protection and strength. This site originally had been an elegant health spa at the turn of the century and later was used by the John Brown Military Academy.

Parents and children have their own quarters within residences which house from 12 to 25 persons. Each building except for the nearly completed sanctuary-education building bears a biblical name. Frequent moves among residences is not uncommon for some members, as changing spatial requirements of nuclear family units have priority.

In 1977 the Shiloh community had 102 members ranging in age from 6 months to 84 years. There were 21 married couples, 21 single adults, including widowed and divorced persons, and 39 children. Of the single adults, 8, including the spiritual leader, were men. Father James, the third successive leader in the 34 years of Shiloh history, has remained celibate since 1963 when his wife was killed in an auto collision four months after their marriage. One member speculated that Father James might consider remarrying as the founder, Father Joshua, had done, should the "right person come along."[1] In a private conversation Father James admitted that he had given remarriage some thought, but recognized that his time commitment to his role as leader would be a hardship on a prospective family.

Shiloh has maintained a sizable and stable membership despite major changes including (1) a major shift in its economic base (from

[1]In 1979 I received a long-distance telephone call from a Shiloh member telling of Father James' betrothal to a woman who had been a missionary in Tanzania and who had had some previous contact with the Shiloh family over the past eight years. When I registered my surprise, my informant said he believed that Father James' intended had initiated the marriage proposal.

a retail bakery business to nationwide wholesale distribution of health foods), (2) relocation from New York to Arkansas (the nearly halved membership at the time of relocation has doubled in nine years), and (3) rapid and widespread social changes in the society at large.

The membership is homogeneous in its white middle- and lower-middle-class origins, but in specific social background and life experiences there are large differences. For example, one longtime member was active in Washington, D.C., society before joining Shiloh, whereas another person stated he had "been to the pits" as a former heroin addict, ex-convict, and mental patient. Another person had been labeled mentally retarded by mainstream society; at Shiloh she was fully integrated into all aspects of community life and was competent in fulfilling her role in daily maintenance activities and in the community's business office.

Factors identified by members as contributing to Shiloh's success as a community include the quality and dedication of its former and present leadership, the business acumen demonstrated by those few who have held continuous responsibility in this area, the flexibility of social organization (visible social interaction) within a rigid social structure (implicit and underlying principles of social interaction), and the total collective participation in the continuing, daily building and maintenance of the community.

In the summer of 1977, I entered Shiloh Farms as a participant-observer, having made previous contact with a member family through mutual friends. I was unaccompanied by my own family during the summer I was in residence. All members were informed of my role as an anthropologist. Communitywide knowledge of my intent as a researcher most likely influenced my reception in the community, which was congenial. The degree of disclosure and the kind of information offered undoubtedly was aimed at presenting a positive view to an outsider. The literature on the presentation of self (see Goffman 1971, 1973; Lofland 1972; Karp 1973) has treated the individual's desire to project an acceptable image even to strangers, and the importance of a favorable "presentation of self" can be assumed for the collective identity of a community as well as for individual identity of self.

When I was formally welcomed by the community, the leader encouraged all members to extend themselves in any way required to make the time profitable for the research effort. Although it was suggested that I introduce myself to Shiloh history via scrapbooks and conversations with charter members, there were no restrictions as to with whom I was permitted to speak, what subjects could be discussed, nor what could be observed. Nevertheless, no matter how "open" and self-aware a community deems itself to be, it is often the case that the participant-observer learns more than the host community anticipates or desires. This obviously was so in my case, as I was asked by the leader how I had learned certain facts which he read in my thesis presented to him a year following my summer's research. At that time he offered to "correct" some of the "surprising" information.

Observation through participation in daily life at Shiloh occurred in the context of both formal and informal activities (work in the bakery, office, primary school, and kitchen; attendance at daily meetings, communal meals, out-of-town shopping, delivery trips, recreation and leisure activities), which led to some degree of interaction with each of the 102 members.

The advantage of gathering multiple perspectives through participant-observation is illustrated by the following example: one couple had stated that their primary reason for joining Shiloh had been to alter their orientation away from positions of leadership and management, roles which they had always held in mainstream society. They desired to be in more subordinate roles and relationships so that they might learn the humility and submission they believed necessary to attain their spiritual goals. Furthermore, they stated that they wanted to resocialize themselves and their children to less materialistic values. Ironically, both husband and wife were in key leadership positions in the community and as a family enjoyed the most attractive residential quarters at Shiloh. Conversations with other members revealed that, during the year prior to their joining Shiloh, this family had experienced occupational difficulties and had incurred large debts. The stated reasons given by the couple may have accounted for only part of their motivation to join Shiloh, which, it was rumored, had provided them with a way out of their financial dilemma.

In addition to carrying out informal observation, I held structured interviews with thirty Shiloh residents, a sample constituted of different age groups, sexes, levels of education, marital status, backgrounds, and life experiences. This sample, though not chosen according to random statistical procedures, was selected with a concern for representativeness.

Social Relationships at Shiloh

The Shiloh community traces its origins to the charismatic leadership of E. C. Monroe. Those who entered Shiloh in the early years made a commitment which placed them in a relationship of dependence to Monroe. Monroe assumed responsibility for the spiritual, psychological, and physical well-being of his followers in return for their submission to his authority (not unlike the "covenant of the Old Testament God with the Israelites," I was told) and their cooperative participation within the framework of communal life. Many persons told of having "felt compelled by the power, insights, and spirit of love which emanated from Monroe" and of being "unable to make any choice but to live in Shiloh."

As noted earlier, Monroe himself was in a transitional period in his life, having been forced to retire for health reasons in the midst of a successful career. The formation of the community gave a focus to the last part of his life. The establishment of a refuge for those "in need" provided Monroe with an avenue of expression for his Christian philanthropic principles and allowed him to exercise his talents for designing environments, physical and social, and for executing his visions and plans. Finally, the acclaim and respect he gained from his role as prophet-leader (he assumed the name Father Joshua, symbolic of a new role as a "warrior for God") added to his fulfillment during the remainder of his life.

As judged from the "life histories" of thirty Shiloh residents, reasons for joining Shiloh could be placed in two categories: (1) some members had perceived themselves to be inadequate for successful adjustment to mainstream society; and (2) some perceived defects in American society as a whole which prevented them from achieving successful self-integration. A number of the sample referred to themselves as former derelicts or n'er-do-wells who had been unable to make it on their own. Others had joined Shiloh because they had found a group of people who "lived what they believed." There were a number of individuals who reported that they had always lacked close, enduring primary relationships within their own families, with spouses, or with friends. Some of the men told of having been reared without male role models. The present leader had been raised by his grandmother and maiden aunts after the death of his father and mother before his ninth year.

Many of the older members reported having been drawn to Shiloh in its formative years by the charisma and personal ministry of Father Joshua, just as more recent members spoke of the personal interest and support Father James has given them in times of crisis and need. One man, for example, said he had been a "flounderer" all his life, "unable to ever get a grip on my life." He came under Father Joshua's influence at a time when he was close to alcoholism. His family, he said, had not been able to help him. When he made the decision to become a member of the Shiloh family, he was told that he must follow the ways established for the community, that the path would require much of him, but Father Joshua assured him that, if he were sincere in his desire to rehabilitate his life, he would "walk into hell with me if need be." And there were times, he confided, "when Father Joshua was called upon to do nearly that, but he *never* let me down."

One woman, who lives at Shiloh with her three daughters, first heard of the commune when she was in a financial and emotional crisis. Her husband was an alcoholic and a gambler, and had sexually molested their two eldest daughters. She had been in poor health at the time and was unable to provide for her family independently. She said she had always had a very low self-esteem and that her situation had seemed hopeless to her. When first introduced to Shiloh, and even during her "probationary visit," she was skeptical about the community's religious and social practices. She had come from a Roman Catholic background and was unaccustomed to the neopentecostal orientation of Shiloh. But, she stated, she found herself among people who cared about her well-being and whom she could trust. She was pleased with the positive response of her daughters to the new environment and felt that she had experienced a "rebirth." After three years of living at Shiloh, she claimed enough self-confidence "to make it on my own on the outside if I wanted to." She had learned valuable skills working in the Shiloh business office and meeting the public (she served as tour guide for clients and visitors to the community) as well as proper personal nutrition and health measures. She boasted a thirty-pound weight loss as a result of learning to eat properly.

By the time a person is "rehabilitated" at Shiloh, he or she is well integrated into the social and psychic life of the community so that there has been a very low attrition rate, according to the leader and other members. As in the case of the woman just described, many persons experience a sense of meaning and purpose at Shiloh Farms, often for the first time in their lives.

Sex-Role Relationships

According to Turner and Shosid (1976:995), "one of the features of effective organization is that roles are clearly and stably identified so that the ambiguity and interchangeability principles cannot operate." At Shiloh sex roles are well defined, and there is a high level of consciousness and consensus concerning the basis and behavioral concomitants of sex roles.

Shiloh's sex-role prescriptions are based on a literal interpretation of the New Testament Epistle to the Corinthians, in which Paul declares that the "anointed one," Jesus Christ, is the "head" of the man and that the man is the "head" of the woman. The leadership role for the community is legitimized on the same basis; it is seen as a "fatherhood" office and carries with it ultimate responsibility for decision making and implementation at every level of community life. Sex roles in Shiloh follow the traditional American prescription of male dominance–female submissiveness. Cognizant of the issue of sexual equality in contemporary society, Shiloh members, male and female, defended their institutionalized relationship of female dependency. It is not, they repeatedly stated, grounded in a concept of fundamental inequality between the sexes. They explained the ideal thus: wholeness in a complementary relationship is achieved when both male and female aspects harmoniously fulfill their respective roles; both are viewed as worthy and important, whereas, in a superior-inferior relationship, recognition is only of the worth of one and denigration of the other.

Monroe, greatly influenced by the writings of Noyes, found Noyes' philosophy of sexual equality in matters of spiritual and social fulfillment compatible with his own life experience. Both of Monroe's wives had been educated, professional women. Monroe did establish male dominance in spiritual and corporate leadership, but because there is a greater number of single women (divorced and widowed) presently at Shiloh, it is specifically in the marriage relationship that women are expected to subordinate themselves to their husbands in temporal matters.

It was my observation that several of the married women often struggled to suppress their own better judgment in matters so as not to be in disagreement with a husband who may have had nothing more to weight his position than that he was the male "head of household." One woman confided to me that she was certain that it was her own strong will which impeded her husband in making a full commitment to the Shiloh community and to a more spiritual life.

Sex differences in role prescriptions and role behaviors, according to a Shiloh precept, have only to do with God-ordained functions for males and females. Father James has called this precept "opposite equality." Bennett (1967:114), in his study of the Hutterian Brethren, describes the "role components of the sexes" as follows:

> Hutterian men are colony citizens first, executives and managers second, and laborers third; Hutterian women are housewives and mothers first, light laborers second, and citizens third.

In Shiloh, by contrast, both men and women are community citizens first. Each, ideally, enjoys the same rights and responsibilities as the other in the general life of the community. The only role not open to any woman is that of spiritual leader, and this restriction is based on the literal translation of Scripture cited above. The current leader, Father James, has reported that though there are no women presently holding any of the symbolic offices known as the "hand of God," there is nothing which would prevent a woman from being selected by him to fill such an office.

The male-female dualism at Shiloh is not unlike the dualism expressed in the yin-yang symbol. The division between the two aspects is clearly distinguishable, yet together they form a stable whole depicted visually by a perfect circle. The achievement of wholeness, unity, and harmony in family life is through the complementary interaction between the husband's responsible exercise of authority and the wife's trusting submission and obedience. This same model, according to Father James, is the one to be applied to the larger Shiloh Family.

Although women are expected to take subordinate roles at the institutionalized levels of marriage and religious office, some Shiloh wives are more disposed to leadership and management roles than are their husbands. One woman told me that she had to work daily on her "addiction" to taking over as the family manager ("addiction" is a euphemistic term used by Shiloh members meaning "problem"). This woman, along with others who had skills and personal characteristics appropriate to leadership and administration, was given community tasks in which her qualities and abilities were channeled into productive benefits for the entire community.

During the period of research, there were more women than men serving on the council, the decision-making body of the community, and the person who appeared to me to have the greatest influence on Father James concerning general matters was a woman. There was not a male member whom I would have expected to challenge her wisdom, counsel, and authority.

There is continual socialization at Shiloh for interdependence and submissiveness. The primary task "on the pathway to Christ consciousness is submission of the egoistic will to the divine will" present in each person. The submission of one's willful nature to a higher order is not an abstract concept at Shiloh; it is part of the daily interaction between leader and member, and between member and member. Shiloh members find they must subordinate their own wills to those of others on a daily basis. For example, one woman told of her request for a washing machine after the birth of her fourth child. Her family was the only family which lived over a mile away from the community proper in a single family house at the edge of a small farm which Shiloh had recently purchased. In discussion with another Shiloh woman, the new mother was told that the persons who worked in the central laundry facility might not have any other way of contributing directly to her family except in doing her family's laundry. Though transporting her heavy load of soiled laundry may have been a hardship, she recalled this incident to me as an illustration of the importance placed on the interdependence and exchange among Shiloh members.

In the daily meetings Father James repeatedly stressed that submission of one's egoistic will was, for both men and women, the most important step leading to "Christ consciousness," or spiritual perfection. Submission and subordination, it was stated, did not imply an inferior or negative condition, nor did it refer to one's station in life, but was essential for spiritual development.

The socialization of females and males, particularly of the more recent members, promoted assertiveness for males and submissiveness for females at the level of interpersonal interaction. A young, unhappy married woman threatened to leave Shiloh and take her three children with her if her husband would not consent to their leaving as a family. She said she believed that, if she actually packed her things, her husband would realize the depth of her despair and determination to leave and would then join her. To her dismay she found him willing to let her go, but without him or their three children. Faced with that choice she capitulated.

Father James was then called in, and this woman reported that it was his sensitive counsel and supportiveness which helped her to realize that the root of her troubles was in her own "willful nature." It was her intention then to look more to the community for the emotional support she found lacking in her marriage and to become more actively integrated into community life. The forming of the new primary school provided her with an appropriate vehicle for involvement. She volunteered to me that her marriage had improved since she had learned more "self control and submission," yet remarks to other members revealed continuing difficulties in the relationship.

A young, single male member reported that he had been counseled by Father James to be more assertive in circumstances in which, he complained, he felt excluded from the activities or conversations of married couples. He had been told that if he felt "left out" he was the one responsible for both the feelings and the corrective measure of actively engaging himself in social interactions of which he wanted to be a part.

In both the cases described above, the individuals were held responsible for their own dissatisfaction, but, whereas the young woman had been admonished to become more submissive, the young man had been instructed to be more assertive.

Men and women at Shiloh are assigned jobs more or less according to conventional norms. Women are the primary caretakers of small children, and men do the heavy work. But all males, with the exception of Father James, who contributes voluntarily as his schedule allows, participate on an assigned rotation basis in some aspect of food preparation, serving, or cleanup. Proportionately, women at Shiloh spend time in more nondomestic tasks than do their counterparts in mainstream society. During the work day childcare is available so that mothers and fathers are free to pursue community tasks. During the daily morning meeting, children over the age of three do not sit with their parents or siblings. Expected to be present in the morning meetings, teenaged girls are each assigned to sit with one or two children and to be responsible for their comportment.

Women sit on the left side of the sanctuary with the children, and men sit on the right. At the Sunday morning worship service, families can choose to sit together. When a member was asked about the spatial division of men and women at the daily morning meetings, she replied that this custom made it easier to focus on the proceedings of the meeting. If one were seated next to one's spouse or children, one would be tempted to think about domestic matters at a time that should be reserved only for community concerns.

Nuclear family identity is strong at Shiloh and is given legitimate recognition in the overall community organization, but there are times when family concerns are expected to be subordinated to that of the community. There is a high degree of interaction among family members during the workday and in other contexts, probably more so than for the average American family. Father and son or daughter may be assigned to dishwashing schedules together, just as mother and daughter or son may both work in the warehouse filling customer orders.

During the time of research there were those who were trying to solicit support to vote for more leisure time for one's family. They wanted two fewer communal meals on the weekend and one morning per week in which attendance at the six o'clock meeting would not be compulsory. It was recognized by everyone that more individual time could be granted only at the expense of community time. This became a hotly debated issue following the researcher's departure.

Marriage as an Ideal

During the period of observation, Father James spent considerable time in biblical exegesis and discussion on the subject of male-female relationships. This topic was of timely interest because of the planned marriage of two Shiloh members. According to Father James' interpretation, mankind's "original sin" was not related to sexuality (that is, the pollution of male by female), but to an acquired knowledge of, and belief in, evil. Prior to the "original sin," there was only knowledge of good. Humankind introduced the concept of dualism into the world, thereby negating the principle of the divine and complete unity of "Yahweh." "Christ consciousness," the stated spiritual goal for all Shiloh members, is a condition in which all dualities are resolved into unity. Marriage, accordingly, is a tangible manifestation of creating unity from duality. Though marriage is a social ideal and is symbolic of a higher spiritual unity, it is not a prerequisite for the attainment of spiritual goals.

While there is no expressed value favoring married persons, in practice those in the community holding the most responsible positions are either presently married or widowed. Divorced persons, as well as unmarried persons, are invariably found in the less important administrative or work roles.

Despite the positive value placed on marriage, dyadic relationships are not expected to prevail over community consciousness. For example, betrothal of a couple can be made only after public prophecies by several community members give sanction to it. When couples or families travel away from Shiloh on business, a third person nearly always travels with them. Couples and families never dine without inclusion at their table of other Shiloh members. In fact, during the first year of residence at Shiloh, a new family will be seated along one side of the head table, as will be all visitors, facing not one another, but facing Father James or other charter members.

Unlike conventional American marriages, wherein women and children have been economically dependent on the husband-father, the family organization at Shiloh has no such dependence built into it. Instead, economic dependence is on the community. All members, adults and children, receive allowances directly from the community. The allowance is of equal value for male and female adults. Families can, of course, set up their own financial-management strategy, but an equally apportioned allowance is a tangible symbol of the community's view on the equal contribution made by males and females. This method of monetary allocation emphasizes the interdependence between an individual member and the community, a mechanism which fosters group cohesion rather than dyadic or familial dependency.

Shiloh Dialectics

At Shiloh one is impressed with the ongoing dialectics between (1) machine and nature, (2) reason and intuition, and (3) spiritual progress and material resource. In these dialectical relationships there is no overt attempt to suppress either element, but a seemingly

conscious awareness of both. The expressed primary goal for Shiloh
members is spiritual development and perfection, but this can only
be realized if the community sustains itself by fulfilling mundane
requirements. Zablocki (1971:169) states that "in any strongly value-
oriented collectivity, it is important to ensure that adherence to the
values does not conflict too much with the actions necessary to survival."

At Shiloh the dialectical oppositions are readily apparent in the
daily life of the community. There is an expressed preference for
that which is "natural" and "organic," and all foods bearing the
Shiloh label or consumed by the community are regarded by them
as such. Yet the sophisticated level of electronic technology (numerous microphones, an elaborate amplification system, and a complete
recording studio) employed at Shiloh for communicating and recording their world view and collective proceedings is at once impressive
and overwhelming to the outsider and appears incongruous with the
advocacy of a natural, organic way of life.

The daily morning meetings are devoted primarily to instruction
by Father James in the proper steps to be followed on the pathway
to "Christ consciousness." He stated repeatedly that spiritual development was not to be attained through any power associated with
reason or the intellect, but would be achieved through the intuitive
grasp of life experiences. Yet a contradiction appeared between the
medium and the message. His message that spiritual perfection
could be achieved following the subordination of that which is
analytical and rational was delivered in a painstakingly methodical
and discursive mode. In fact, there was little, if anything, in the
collective meetings which could be described as spontaneous, not
even the regularized ritual of "speaking in tongues."

Rather than renounce material assets and comforts (member-
recruits are not required to give up their personal property as a
condition for membership), Shiloh members pride themselves on
their very high standard of living. One member declared that he
would have to earn a minimum of $20,000 a year on the outside to
provide his family with the same material standard of living they
enjoyed at Shiloh. Counterpoint to the value of acquiring material
goods (which, it is rationalized, allows the community to aspire more
successfully to spiritual goals) is the recognition of the price paid for
material security. A rhetorical question frequently posed by Father

James to the assembled community was "Are we running the business, or is the business running us?" This revealed his continuous consternation over the extended absences of some community members for business purposes.

The nominal identification of fully committed Shiloh adult men and women is symbolic of hierarchical and functional differentiation. Once designated by Father James, men are addressed as "Elder ———[first name]," and women as "Mother ———[first name]." The title "Elder" denotes seniority, rank, experience, and wisdom. The title "Mother" denotes nurturance, intuitive insight, and sensitivity. Shiloh ideology would ascribe characteristics of gentleness, compassion, and intuitive sensitivity to femaleness, and rationality, leadership, and physical strength to maleness. Father James stressed on several occasions that the above-mentioned feminine and masculine qualities can and do exist in both males and females, and ideally the development of *both* gender qualities in men and in women is encouraged as part of the process of becoming whole, complete persons. Men should not be uncomfortable expressing compassion or being nurturant, according to Father James, nor should women be afraid of showing their physical strength. But, he warned, men and women should be cautioned against assuming the "God-given" functions of the other.

Conclusion

In this descriptive analysis of a successful community, we have traced some of the antecedent variables present at the time of founding, specifically, the social milieu and the individual characteristics and motivation of both the founder and member-recruits, to see how they pertain to role relationships in the present-day Shiloh Farms community. We ought to note also that, just as there are traceable patterns, change is an inevitable factor resulting from the ongoing dialectic present in any human organization, both at the micro-level of interpersonal interaction and at the macro-level of such processes as commerce with an external market, accommodation to a neighboring body politic, and so on.

Monroe's personal philosophy was not in opposition to such conventional American values as free enterprise, the Judeo-Christian work ethic, and male dominance. Instead, he conceptualized his task in founding Shiloh as that of reestablishing American ideals in a spiritual context. Like J. H. Noyes, Monroe did not consider women less worthy or capable of achieving spiritual perfection than men. Certainly the independent success achieved by both of Monroe's wives had contributed measurably to his respect for women. Sexual equality is reflected in some aspects of the socialization process which aims at investing all persons with a sense of worth by providing ways in which individuals can make tangible contributions to the whole community.

Role relationships are conceptualized as containing both complementary and symmetrical elements which contribute to equilibrium in the social system. It is taught that one subordinates oneself to another, not for the purpose of elevating another's ego, but because subordination and submission enables one to shape one's own ego in preparation for greater spiritual development. It is believed that the more submissive one becomes, the more detached one can become from personal whims, desires, and material possessions. Father James is acclaimed by members as the prime exemplar of this philosophy. It was reported by several that he had foregone a number of personal pursuits such as a once-active study of music; he fasts one day a week, takes almost no time off for himself, and sleeps less than five hours, rising in the predawn hours to prepare for his community responsibilities. Clearly, then, submission and subordination of the self does not, for Father James, entail inferiority. Similarly, the subordination of women to men does not, in the world view of Shiloh, imply that women are spiritually inferior to men.

Conceptualization and enactment of sex roles in the Shiloh Farms community occurs within a framework of sexual dualism based on complementarity rather than on conflict. The complementary sex-role model at Shiloh promotes a relationship of dependence between the sexes. While institutionalized roles of male superordination and female subordination exist, these role prescriptions do not have their bases in a premise of generalized male superiority–female inferiority. Furthermore, a number of symmetrical elements in sex relationships tend to stabilize the social system existing at Shiloh Farms.

It is difficult to apply an external sexual-equality standard which ignores the internal logical coherence of a closed social system such as that of Shiloh. The women interviewed, both married and single, spoke of opportunities for fulfillment of self since becoming Shiloh community members, in contrast to their earlier life situations. Of the six college-age persons at Shiloh in 1977, the one female was the only one who was away at college, fully supported by the Shiloh corporation. During the year's time in which I had the most continuous contact with the Shiloh community, I knew of three persons who had left—two males and one female. None of the three was self-defined or defined by others as earnestly committed.

According to my own evaluation, the one person whom I perceived as having the most autonomy, personal freedom, and influence was the senior woman mentioned earlier. Her status, I believe, was directly related to her substantive endowment to the community at the time of her joining during the formative years of Shiloh. Her former home in College Park, Maryland, had served as a retreat for Monroe when he was in the area on business or vacation. Today, when visitors comment on the lovely furnishings, fine china, and silver visible in the "big house," which houses the leader and twenty-one others, including this woman, they are proudly told that those things had come from Mother Lois' home.

It could be concluded that the salient cleavage between persons at Shiloh is not gender-specific, but appears to be based on a fact of economic and material benevolence to the community. Therefore, in their capacity for spiritual development, as in their economic functions, women of Shiloh enjoy more equality than the community's patriarchal philosophy would at first suggest.

REFERENCES CITED

Bennett, John W.
  1967 Hutterian Brethren. Stanford: Stanford Univ. Pr.
Goffman, Erving
  1972 Relations in Public. New York: Harper and Row.
Karp, David A.
  1973 Hiding in Pornographic Bookstores. Urban Life and Culture 1 (4): 427–51.
Lofland, Lyn
  1972 Self-Management in Public Settings. Urban Life and Culture 1 (1):93–108.
Turner, Ralph H., and Norma Shosid
  1976 Ambiguity and Interchangeability in Role Attribution: The Effect of Alter's Response. American Sociological Review 41:993–1006.
Zablocki, Benjamin
  1971 The Joyful Community. Baltimore: Penguin.

-6- *BRYAN PFAFFENBERGER*

A World of Husbands and Mothers

Sex Roles and Their Ideological Context in the Formation of the Farm

> I ask if men ever baby-sit. "Sure,
> they help out when they can. Our
> men are good to us." When I press,
> "Yes, but do they have assigned turns
> like you do?" they look at me
> perplexed, as if I were a misplaced
> androgynous creature in this world of
> husbands and mothers.
>
> KATE WENNER, "How They Keep
> Them Down on the Farm"

THE FARM, A COMMUNAL UTOPIA LOCATED IN rural Tennessee, is probably the largest and most successful commune to emerge from the Haight-Ashbury movement during the late Sixties. Twelve hundred people now dwell on the commune's 1,750 acres, and ten branch Farms account for another 1,400 followers of the Farm's teachings (Wenner 1977:74). Farm members acknowledge Stephen Gaskin as their spiritual teacher and try to put into practice his highly systematic procedures for obtaining religious salvation, or as they term it, "enlightenment." The ideology is a remarkable syncretism of several religious and philosophical traditions, including Tantric Hinduism, Mahayana Buddhism, Zen, Christianity, and humanistic psychology. These traditions are woven together into a single faith that, in Stephen's view, expresses the essence of all religions. The Farm's success and its fascinating ideology deserve scholarly attention, for it is clear that the commune represents one of the most successful, and enigmatic, utopian movements of the twentieth-century American communitarian renaissance.

Few observers of the Farm have failed to note its paradoxical quality. Emerging from the sexually open and freewheeling atmosphere of the Haight-Ashbury, the Farm has nevertheless reinstituted precisely those sexual restrictions from which people were turning away during the Sixties. Marriage, held in low esteem by the advocates of the "hippie" movement, or counterculture, is at the heart of the Farm's prescription for a happy and fulfilling life. Whereas the hippies of the Haight-Ashbury encouraged sexual freedom and "nonattachment" to a particular sexual partner, promiscuity of any kind—including premarital sex and adultery—is forbidden at the Tennessee commune and its several branches. Artificial techniques of birth control are also forbidden. Another apparently traditional theme of Farm life is a rigorous sexual division of labor, buttressed by beliefs about sex-ascribed attributes and potentialities. Wenner has summarized the Farm's paradoxical transformation by noting that its members "seem to have fulfilled their ideals of the Sixties by turning dramatically away from the very freedoms that gave birth to these ideals" (1977:74). Robison, echoing Wenner, notes that at the Farm "the onetime 'hippies' now adhere to old-fashioned values and strait-laced strictness" (1977:46). Just how is it that the Farm developed such a rigidly restricted system of sexual relationships?

It is tempting to argue that, faced with the turmoil and antinomian fervor of the Sixties, Stephen and his followers sought security and stability by instituting traditional modes of social relationships. But there is evidence that this view, although it seems to account for monogamy and sex-role differentiation at the Farm, is fundamentally mistaken. The Farm's models for sex roles are, to be sure, at least partly rooted in the traditional American family, but in other respects the commune is innovative and departs significantly from the traditional mold. The commune expects, for example, that women will cook and clean, but the "macho" pattern of male aggressiveness, promiscuity, and dominance is actively discouraged through the use of formal sanctions. Furthermore, the commune has experimented with group marriage. It appears quite clear that the Farm has not sought security and viability by merely asserting traditional modes of sex roles and sex relationships.

The literature on communal utopias suggests that, far from embracing traditional sex roles and relations, a commune seeking permanence and viability would avoid both monogamy and sex-role differentiation. Kanter, for instance, has argued that few successful communes encourage monogamy because it interferes with an individual's commitment to the group as a whole. A successful commune tries to cut off alternative objects of a person's commitment, so that "person and group are inextricably linked" (Kanter 1972:66). The formation of strong couple bonds, Kanter has stressed, poses a threat to the community, should one member of a couple feel more allegiance to the other member than either of them do to the community as a whole. Should these two commitments come into conflict, the couple may withdraw from the community. Free love as well as celibacy were common institutions in the successful nineteenth-century communes because both prevented couple formation and thereby helped ensure commitment. Kanter argues that communes permitting couple formation are not likely to persist for twenty-five years, which for her is the criterion of commune success.

From the standpoint of the literature, the Farm, in asserting a rigid sexual division of labor, has insisted on a social institution that ought to consign it to dissolution. Conover (1975), for example, argues that "dedifferentiation" of sex roles must be emphasized by any commune hoping to legitimate its stress on sharing and equality. Ramey (1972) has argued that sex-role differentiation will, inevitably, generate tensions contributing to a commune's downfall. Kanter (1972) suggests that, by emphasizing differentiation in family and sex-role relationships, a commune throws away the opportunity to involve family members in a wider sphere of social relationships, and therefore invites couple withdrawal. Yet the Farm places central emphasis on male-female differences and on the family roles of husband and mother. The Tennessee commune appears to have instituted precisely the modes of social relations identified by scholars of the communal movement as antithetical to commune success.

The Farm, then, is truly enigmatic. The commune has not only moved sharply away from the open sexuality of the Haight-Ashbury; it has also veered away from the traditional models of American sex-role relationships. Furthermore, it has adopted models for its social order that, according to the major theoreticians of communal movements, should doom the commune to an early demise. How can we account for this enigmatic community, its curious blend of traditional and innovative social relationships, and its apparent success?

If we are to understand the Farm, we must begin, as have Wenner and Robison, by acknowledging its paradoxical transformation from the open sexuality of the Haight-Ashbury to the closed, exclusive monogamy of the Tennessee commune. But we must not make the mistake of thinking that Stephen and his followers simply have returned to traditional modes of family relationship. While the commune accepts monogamy and sex-role differentiation, other aspects of the traditional family, such as male dominance and "macho" aggressiveness, are explicitly identified as barriers to spiritual progress.

The Farm asserts a rigid social order, but its *raison d'être* is religious, and, I shall argue, its social relationships cannot be understood apart from their ideological context. The Farm, I wish to show, represents an attempt to conserve, within the bounds of its sharply circumscribed role relationships, an ideology that attaches a religious value to human fellowship. This ideology arose in the commune's structural antithesis: the Haight-Ashbury, where thousands of people, temporarily stripped of their traditional roles, celebrated for a few brief months the idea that all kinds of people were beautiful and deserved love. Stephen's teachings outline a rigid social system that attempts to preserve the Haight-Ashbury's values. By carrying out their social relationships according to Stephen's teachings, commune members believe that they have been able to retain the *spirit* of the Haight-Ashbury, *sans* its unfortunate tendency to wind down into disillusionment and violence. What appears to outside observers as nothing more mysterious than traditional sex roles is, in the view of Farm members, a design for social relations that helps to preserve and to radiate a holy, transcendent power—one that, if tapped, could save our society from doom. To understand this remarkable group, we must try sincerely to understand not only its social relations, with their apparently traditional form, but also the ideology in which these relations are situated. We must begin, therefore, by examining Stephen's ministry in its historical context, and I shall trace its origins and evolution prior to discussing sex-role institutions at the Farm today.

Stephen's Life Prior to the Revelations

Like many other charismatic leaders, Stephen does not seem to regard his biography as being particularly significant in itself, save for what it might demonstrate in support of his teachings. One interviewer asked him, "You were a teaching aide to Hayakawa at San Francisco State, a semanticist . . . ," to which Stephen replied, interrupting the interviewer rather brusquely, "Well, I'm trans-semantic now. That means on the other side of. Semantics is an effort to try to figure out where it's at if you don't know where it's at" (Cantwell and Gross 1971:146). The past, in Stephen's view, is not important, and excessive attention to the past "makes you paranoid" (Gaskin 1976:30). Yet Stephen, in his lectures, has stressed the themes of his past that appear to him to be important as illustrations of the wrong ways to live. He identifies the strategies that he once used for coping with life—secularism, materialism, individualism, irresponsibility, and pleasure-seeking—and argues that they ensure unhappiness. He reminds his followers that he has already tried all of these strategies, and stresses that, because of his long experience of imperfection and unhappiness, he is uniquely suited to be a spiritual teacher for our times: "The universe is [not now] necessarily in need of someone [peaceful and naive] who stepped out of a lotus blossom and said, 'From this place get cool' " (Cantwell and Gross 1971:209).

Stephen, born in 1935, emphasizes that persons truly spiritual were missing from his childhood, and his followers echo this belief. In their view, a truly spiritual person would manifest the beauty and, what is more, the *power* of divinity. Stephen was told as a child that Christ was only a very good man who lived a long time ago; no mention was made to him of what Stephen now believes were Christ's considerable powers (Link 1970:21). In school Stephen was taught the materialist doctrine that there is no spiritual plane of existence and that spiritual powers such as telepathy do not exist:

> When I was in high school, the universe was wrapped up. They knew how many elements there were, and they said it was all a material plane trip, and there was nobody coming around being telepathic and really heavy and really stoned. [Gaskin 1984a:n.p.][1]

Among Stephen's followers who went to church, the feeling is strong that established religions are insincere and lack true spirituality. One informant told me:

[1]Most of Stephen's publications are not paginated. They are transcriptions of his lectures, which, to be properly appreciated, should be read in their entirety. Most are available by mail from the commune's Book Publishing Company, in Summertown, Tennessee. Grammatical errors in the original are reproduced as they were printed; they are, in fact, one aspect of Farm language (for example, the resolute usage of "to be" in the singular regardless of number disagreement).

> You get this brief pelting of the Bible and the spirit and all this
> kind of brotherly love, you know, oneness ... you get all these
> fantasies and then when you grow older you find out that God is
> just kind of a Santa Claus figure, just, you know, who *is* he, I don't
> know where these people *got* this.... You can read the Bible, but
> you've got to practice what you preach.... I always thought people
> didn't do that, like preachers and stuff. I always thought they
> spouted all this stuff, but you know, what the hell. After the
> church, they could do whatever they wanted. Cheat on their in-
> come tax, or whatever.

A person who seeks true spirituality learns very quickly that the
quest should be kept secret, because people would not understand
them or would think their behavior odd. One of Stephen's followers
told me, "I think I had some mystical experiences when I was very
young, like in connection with the Catholic trip. But they closed up
inside of me, there's no one who would understand. I used to write
them down in little notebooks. Another informant, who says he first
learned about the universe's divinity and beauty by observing the
Sierra forest of California, said he did not tell anyone that "what I
really wanted to do was to go up into the woods and watch the forest
do its thing. They'd think I was some sort of homosexual or something—here's this creepy, creepy cat, you know. I had to kind of like
vibe along with everybody else and kind of like, steal away, by
myself...."

Stephen and his followers say that American culture, since it is
based on the premise that there is no spiritual plane and that material reality is the only valid one, values only material goods and
encourages an unhealthy competition among persons in pursuit of
material rewards. Stephen's Haight-Ashbury followers identified
the competitive theme of American culture as particularly dangerous:

> I hated sports. I like swimming and stuff, but competition (whew)
> really devastated me. It wasn't losing, but this constant, get in
> there and win it, you know, from the coaches and everybody else.
> All of this expectation from everybody. I hadda get out. Luckily I
> did that, I would've gone crazy if I'd stayed in.

A common complaint among informants was that the competitiveness and individualism encouraged by American culture interfered
with solidarity in the family as well as at school. One informant told

me that, in his family, "they kind of talk about each other like, 'he's a good guy but you wouldn't want to enter into a business agreement with him.' "

The competitive and individualistic atmosphere of American social life encourages, according to Stephen's followers, a persistent avoidance of real communication among people. One informant said that, in high school,

> I . . . was very conservative with how I let things out. I would find out what the situation was. Every once in a while, I'd fool 'em, I'd trick 'em, and let something else out, you know. But it was all gamey, you know, gamey. I could see their game and I thought, "I'm going to play a more complex game." So it was just all these games happening. So my early friends, there was not any, there wasn't *any* spiritual contact.

Stephen constantly emphasizes that, without real communication, responsible relationships are impossible. A responsible relationship is one that is characterized by commitment, but a person who is not willing to communicate honestly and openly is not likely to commit himself or herself deeply and honestly to a relationship. The life of such a person is littered with broken ties. Stephen, for example, left his home in 1952 at the age of seventeen because, he says, "I couldn't get along with my mother and father" (Gaskin 1970:n.p.). Yet, he says, he was incapable of taking care of himself because of his irresponsibility. "I threw myself on the mercy of the Marine Corps to support me" (ibid.). After his discharge from the Marines, Stephen married, but the marriage failed, he says, because he and his wife were unable to communicate sufficiently well to reach an agreement about their commitment to one another (ibid.).

Since a person who cannot keep commitments is not, according to Stephen and his followers, likely to find fulfillment in his or her social relationships, "kicks"—pleasure and amusement—are sought in drinking, in sex, in material goods, and in sadism or masochism. In Stephen's view these avenues of pleasure seeking are unfulfilling and dangerous, because it is always necessary to increase the effect or to seek novelty: a person seeking pleasure will say, " 'Something new, this will get me off, something new, this will get me off, something new, this will get me off. . . .' But that something new will get you off once or twice and you'll have to go off to the next thing" (Gaskin 1974a:n.p.). In pursuit of kicks, Stephen bought sports cars and motorcycles; he tried alcohol, fencing, archery, and deer hunting; finally, just before the Haight-Ashbury era, he sought "kicks" by working as a bartender in a Hell's Angels' bar and as a private detective specializing in divorce surveillance. He says he savored, rather sadistically, the misfortunes he witnessed (Cantwell and Gross 1971:209).

The themes of Stephen's youth—secularism, materialism, individualism, irresponsibility, and pleasure-seeking—epitomize for him the problems imposed on us by the socialization, or "programming," characteristic of modern American culture. This programming produces individuals who are unable to see the beauty of the universe around them, to speak truthfully, to honor their commitments to others, to forge fulfilling relationships, or to find fulfillment. It was precisely this kind of sentiment about American culture that motivated people to join the Haight-Ashbury movement, and Stephen, who had tried every avenue for fulfillment available in mainstream, or "straight," society, was to become one of the movement's leading spokesmen. He was to argue eloquently that people should repudiate the pleasure strategies of American culture and try to build a new kind of social system that destroys, instead of encourages, the walls separating people from one another.

The Haight-Ashbury

San Francisco's Haight-Ashbury movement, which reached its pinnacle during the 1967 "Summer of Love," found adherents among people who, like Stephen and his followers, felt that the traditional American blueprints for living accomplished little more than to alienate people from one another. Among the thousands of persons who flocked to "the Haight" in 1966 and 1967 were many who were prepared to abandon completely the traditional American roles, statuses, and values, and it was among such persons that there occurred some very remarkable explosions of what Turner calls "spontaneous *communitas.*" *Communitas,* in Turner's view, is a stirring experience of "mankind as a homogenous, unstructured, and free community," and it is very likely to occur where people confront one another stripped of their mundane identities (1974:169). Such confrontations may occur during pilgrimages, during the liminal phase of *rites de passage,* and during times of social change.

Departure from American society's system of roles, statuses, and values was indeed a central preoccupation for the "hippies" of the Haight-Ashbury who "dropped out" of the anomie-producing mainstream society. Instead of materialism, "planning for the future," and individualistic aggrandizement, they stressed spontaneity, immediacy, and the quality of personal relationships (Turner 1969:112–17). The rituals of the Haight were, unmistakably, manifestations of *communitas.* The "Be-ins," for example, were celebrations of the essential beauty and dignity of all people. The ritual of sharing drugs, especially passing around a marijuana cigarette, was important to the setting in which *communitas* emerged. An informant recalls:

> The couple of friends I had, a few of them I dragged along on the trip. I said, "Come on and do this, it's really great." The communion thing when we started taking drugs was just unbelievable, you know, just *unbelievable.* Instant friendship with people, you know, *people* you just didn't even know before. That was our whole family trip. It was the communion that happened between us. So strong, you know.

The Haight's hippies forthrightly rejected many of the mainstream society's models for social relationships as irrelevant to what they were trying to accomplish, preferring instead to bask in what they described as a "beautiful" feeling of community and openness that prevailed among their groups of drug-sharing friends. These groups came to be seen as more important and more fulfilling than their members' natal families; indeed, as stated by the informant quoted above, many of these friendship groups came to be called "families," though their members were not related by kinship.

Though there were said to be many beautiful moments of communion in these groups, participants felt strongly that they were exploring an unknown realm and that they did not know the rules. Mainstream society could not provide any guidelines. As one of Stephen's early followers told me, "There's no background for that kind of thing. Where do you look for models? In *their* world, where you look there's just weird stuff. There's nothing, yeah, nothing." Lacking guidelines, the small groups had their ups and their downs:

> The first few times you're experimenting with [these small "fami-
> lies"] like a lot of things come out. You're still working with your-
> self while you're working with other people. All these ego things
> come out. Once in a while, there were times like, just as together
> as I've ever seen. There were other times that weren't so pretty.

Despite the difficult moments, followers of the movement per-
sisted in the optimistic belief that it was possible to overcome all
human foibles through love. It was with this passionate conviction
that those who joined the Haight-Ashbury movement tried to overcome racism, war, and jealousy. Open sexuality, for example, was
practiced in the belief—regularly contravened by actual experience
—that jealousy could easily be defeated if the parties to a triangle
would only try to love one another. For a time, failure to overcome
such obstacles was interpreted not as a sign that the essential beliefs
of the Haight were wrong, but merely that people, in their early
childhoods, had not been given the kinds of values and behavioral
guidelines that they needed to build a successful community.

There thus arose a search for appropriate values and models in
other cultures, and there was an explosion of interest in Native
Americans, Zen, Yoga, Taoism, Cabalism, and mysticism. Texts from
these spiritual and mystical traditions were read avidly, but with
little comprehension; there was only an awareness that, somehow,
they were very important and that they held the key to gaining
control over the new and exciting, if dangerous and upsetting, world
that had been created in the Haight. It was in this exceptionally
experimental, sexually open, and rather confused setting that Stephen, by this time a graduate student at San Francisco State College,
was to begin his ministry. It met with striking success. By 1970
Stephen spoke before crowds of up to two thousand people.

The Revelations

Stephen was enrolled in a graduate program at San Francisco
State during the beginning of the Haight-Ashbury era (ca. 1966), and
he worked closely with the renowned semanticist S. I. Hayakawa,
who was later to become the president of the college and a U.S.
senator. Hayakawa recalls:

> Steve was that kind of brilliant student that whatever subject he
> studies, he puts his own interpretation on. I never knew for sure
> whether he understood semantics, but I had to give him an A. He
> talked more than his share, but he was always witty and enter-
> taining. . . . Every once in a while, Steve'd put his arm around me,
> as if he were a tall son. . . . [Quoted in Link 1970:21]

Stephen distinguished himself in his studies by his exceptional creativity. Hayakawa was so strongly impressed by Stephen's creativity
that he thought his student would become a successful writer: "His
stuff was so good that I felt within a year he would be writing *New
Yorker* quality fiction. He had the promise of becoming one hell of
a writer" (ibid.:22). Stephen's creativity has very much to do with the
success of his ministry. His creative synthesis of Oriental mysticism
and other religious traditions provided the drug-sharing "families"
with a plausible interpretation of the confusing texts and with the
behavioral guidelines they sought.

Another factor in the success of Stephen's ministry was his teaching experience. Having received his master's degree from San Francisco State, he continued with his studies and served for two years
as a teaching assistant there, and it was during this time that he
developed the main elements of his leadership style. It is important
to stress here that, although Stephen now conceives of himself as an
inspired spiritual teacher, he does not use the culturally provided
model of the ecstatic, haranguing storefront minister. On the contrary, Stephen's style is much more reminiscent of everyone's favorite professor: the affable, witty, sloppily dressed, and charmingly
eccentric teacher who lectures with spontaneity, conviction, and
insight. As a teaching assistant, he was friendly with his students,
became involved with them socially, and started smoking marijuana
with them. He found that some of them were leaving school without
the slightest ambivalence, and wondered what it was that they had
found more rewarding than academia.

Stephen's first experience with psychedelic drugs, especially LSD,
caused him some confusion. Taking LSD "blew a bunch of minds—
including mine. I was really nutty for a while," he states. "I'd go
around, I'd try to put people on to what I was seeing, and they'd say,
'you're crazy, man,' and I'd say, 'All right.' But the next time, I'd look
and there it would be again" (Gaskin 1972:n.p.). What astonished
Stephen on his LSD trips was the phenomenon of telepathy, which,
he states, is very vividly revealed to persons under the influence of

psychedelic drugs. A person who is high on LSD can, he maintains, communicate a state of euphoria (a "contact high") to another person who had not taken any drug. Furthermore, just as one person can get another person high through a telepathically communicated contact high, it is also possible for a person to "bring someone down," or destroy others' euphoria (and one's own, as well). Stephen found that

> if you said something that was a downer [while high on LSD] it ran the juice [that is, euphoria] out . . . if you were mean to someone you'd drop your energy, if you went on an ego trip you'd drop your energy . . . it would get weird. If someone who was on the trip with you wasn't being straight with you it would get the trip weird for everybody. [Gaskin 1972:n.p.]

Between LSD trips, Stephen eventually discovered that telepathic relations existed among people who were not "high," even though they typically refused to admit it.

Stephen's revelations were, initially, a source of confusion and discomfort to him. Like many of his students, he dropped out of San Francisco State. He traveled to British Honduras, where he stayed for seven or eight months, he has stated, to regain his sanity (ibid.). Yet on his return to San Francisco he continued his experiments with LSD, and these experiences brought about a renewal of the revelations. Like many of his future followers, Stephen found that drug experiences could break down the walls separating people and bring them together in a beautiful, heartfelt communion underscored by telepathic understanding. One informant, for example, said of her early drug experiences: "There were times when we took acid (LSD) when we were really hooked in, zap, telephone lines between our heads. If one of us said a word or anything, we would all know just what they were talking about."

Stephen, who at this time was also developing a "family" of drug-sharing friends, had a very similar experience:

> None of us were planning it . . . we just got stoned together. We were so high we got telepathic and inside each other's heads. A cut glass platter that Maggie [Stephen's wife] had used to bring refreshments caught the light, splintering it into four directions, a beam piercing each heart. We started glowing. Michael and Maggie turned white and me and Ina May did some psychedelic change things and we looked at each other with looks like, "Wha-a-at?" We didn't say anything, but we all thought this thing and were

afraid to say it! Shortly after, they decided to call it a night. 'Soon
as we went to bed, I asked Maggie what happened 'cause I didn't
want to prejudice her mind. So she told me what happened and it
was the same thing, you know; it was what I knew happened too.
Then we knew together that if we both knew that, we'd better go
talk to them. So we went to talk to them and they knew that. And
then we agreed to it. But it fell on us . . . bang! . . . just chonk! . . .
and what we agreed to was that it was such a heavy thing that
we'd keep straight with it. It was such a beautiful, perfect, clean
telepathic thing, that, among other things, we're like a living
monument to that communication—that that communication
took place and we will swear to it to this degree. [Quoted in Link
1970:24]

The four friends may have been reluctant to concede the existence
of telepathy the moment it occurred, but they vowed never to let
such an oversight occur again. They decided to form a group marriage (a "four-marriage," in Stephen's terminology), and they agreed
to stay together for the rest of their lives in commemoration of that
beautiful evening.

Stephen's revelations about telepathy challenged the materialistic, secular themes of his socialization. He came to believe that an
unseen, telepathic field of communication really existed, and he
believed his thoughts really did have an impact on other peoples'
happiness and well-being. He concluded that what people thought
and felt about one another mattered very much indeed. For Stephen
the romantic ideals of the Haight-Ashbury were transformed into
absolute imperatives: people *must* love one another deeply, because
if they do not they cause material and physical harm to themselves
and others around them by telepathic means. It occurred to him that
the cause of human suffering is that people did not send out loving,
healing vibrations to one another through telepathy. If a group of
people who conceded the existence of telepathy and its effect on
other people got together, it seemed to him possible to create a
community that would give energy and health to one another in a
beautiful communion. To test this idea Stephen decided to set up an
experimental college class at San Francisco State. He called the
class "Group Experiments in Unified Field Theory," indicating his
interest in testing his ideas about vibrational fields among people.
There was a slot open on Monday nights, and during February 1967
Stephen began the Monday Night Classes that were to continue for
nearly four years.

The Monday Night Class

The intention of the Monday Night Class was, as Stephen recalls, to find out the "ground rules" of a new territory—a world in which what people feel and think about each other has a definite impact on them:

> We started thinking. . . . *What is the etiquette of a telepathic society?* How does one order one's mind when you live in a universe where there is not a wall around your head, where your skull is not the limit of your consciousness, but that you actually share space with other people—that you *interpenetrate.* . . . What is the political science when we can all be in the same place at the same time? [Gaskin 1976:22; my emphasis]

A search for such a "political science" was carried on by reading mystical and spiritual texts: "We read all the books we could on the Tarot and the I Ching and yoga and Zen and fairy tales and science fiction and extrasensory perception, and a whole area of stuff that suddenly looked like it had juice in it that didn't look that way before" (Gaskin 1974a:n.p.). At that time, as Stephen recalls, the class "knew little more than there was something other than the material part of existence." But gradually a pattern emerged: "We realized that all the best minds in history had been devoted to religion and all of the records that had been preserved the longest had been devoted to religion and everything that seemed to be central to all cultures was religious" (Gaskin 1974b:8).

The importance of religion is that, in Stephen's view, it contains models and guidelines for dealing with the fact of human telepathy, and every religious tradition contains within it exactly the same procedures for bringing about, and maintaining, a state of beautiful ecstasy—a "high," or a state of "stonedness"—in which a person sends out loving and beautiful vibrations. Much of Stephen's lecture on a typical night would be taken up with an explication of some tradition in terms of this assumption.

The Monday Night Class meetings opened with a religious theme. The entire group chanted a Hindu sacred syllable (a *mantra, om*) for several minutes. Stephen then requested questions from the audience. Aside from the taunts of hecklers, most of the questions dealt with perplexing aspects of the mystical and religious texts that Class members were reading with great interest and, evidently, little comprehension. No matter what he was asked, Stephen would instantly supply an answer that, in the view of Class members, added additional credibility to his basic premises about telepathy. During the next two years he was to draw upon several religious traditions to synthesize an ideology that, in his view, expressed the essence of all religion.

Stephen, in putting together his architectonic ideology, utilized the potent talents of creativity that Hayakawa had already noticed in him. He states that he understood each religion in a sequence of "intuitive flashes":

> It's like when you learn one foreign language it helps you learn the next one. I first understood the nature of what was going on in an intuitive flash. And that was my first way of understanding —an intuitive flash in which I saw the way the thing works. Then I worked my way, as it were, through a yoga model, since the first person I found who talked that language was my yoga teacher. And I ran through that model until I could see my way through it in yoga terms. Then I could do it in Buddhism and Christianity. When I did it in Buddhism I found out about Zen, and I did fall in love with Zen somewhat, because Zen is so clean. It's a very clean and simple thing. [Gaskin 1972:n.p.]

Yet, just as he had done previously in studying semantics, Stephen always put his own interpretation on the religious traditions that he studied. He drew from them the concepts that supported his basic premises about telepathy, but set aside the aspects of the religions that, in his view, departed from what he saw as a universal religion: "The thing about all those religions is that you can stack them all up together like IBM cards, and you can look at them and see which holes go all the way through. And that's the trip we're trying to do, the one with all the holes that go all the way through" (ibid.).

The success of Stephen's charisma—his personal magic and power as a religious teacher—should be understood as an interaction of three factors. The first is that his audience was composed mainly of college students and dropouts who were trying to understand the confusing texts and who found his lucid, professorial manner familiar and convincing. A second factor in his charisma is the creative genius he possesses. Stephen's rhetorical style combines lucidity with a rough-and-ready confidence and, moreover, an ability to transform any exigency or counterargument to his advantage. Finally, his teachings, while ranging throughout all the complexities of the texts being read, really boiled down to a very simple, straight-forward proposition: "If you really want to change the world, you have to change your soul—you have to change things on a spiritual level" (Gaskin 1974:11).

The Revolution

The *communitas* ideals of the Haight-Ashbury readily translated into opposition to the American political and military systems and the Vietnam War. From the Haight, the war appeared to be nothing more than a manifestation of ethnocentrism—the blind destruction of a foreign culture and economic system simply because American society could not understand or tolerate it. The Haight's ideals of tolerance and communion led to a consensus that the Vietnam War must be stopped. But just how should the campaign to end it be organized?

There were two schools of thought on this issue. The first advocated terrorism and violent struggle against the capitalist order. The second position, of which Stephen was the most articulate spokesman, held that, simply by becoming peaceful and nonviolent themselves, the people of the Haight could change the whole world. From Stephen's view, no revolution could succeed if its advocates had violence or hate on their minds. A person thinking about violence or hate sends out violent or hateful vibrations, thus injuring other people and creating in them the same thoughts and feelings. Violent revolutions are always unsuccessful, in Stephen's view, and he cited in his talks the examples of Russia, Mexico, China, and other countries which had experienced revolutions but which were still not free. A nonviolent revolution was the only alternative, and Stephen saw himself as the "strongest, clearest beatnik voice for peace that's happening in this country right now" (quoted in Cantwell and Gross 1971:142). In Stephen's view "the over-all consciousness of mankind is at fault for the evils of any given age" (Gaskin 1972:n.p.), and the Vietnam War was nothing more than a manifestation of our own hatefulness and inability to love. If we want the war to end, Stephen argued, we would have to learn how to love each other more deeply.

Student revolutionaries countered this position with the argument that suffering is caused by the military and by the capitalists who control the decision-making process. There can be no peace until such people are killed, they said. Stephen, in replying to this argument, denied that anyone is in control of American society: "What I'm trying to tell you is this country's out of control, it's up for grabs. Nobody's in control" (quoted in Cantwell and Gross 1971:208). He agreed that American society is characterized by suffering, but he maintained that the suffering was caused not by intention but by ignorance. Ignorant people do not realize that their consciousness is responsible for the evils they experience, and therefore they should be regarded not with hate but with compassion. Regarding someone with compassion, argued Stephen, is the same as loving them, and ultimately this strategy will end the war. "It feels to me that if we're going to do it, we're going to have to have all hands aboard. You can't say the boat will float better if you throw somebody over the side" (Gaskin 1974a:n.p.). If we are to have a peaceful and beautiful society, we *must*, admonished Stephen, try to love even those who appear to be responsible for war and ugliness.

The early period of Stephen's ministry culminated in the massive Monday Night Class meetings at the Family Dog Ballroom near the beach in San Francisco (May 1969–October 1970). Crowds of up to two thousand persons gathered to hear Stephen's charismatic, articulate, and entertaining talks. By this time Stephen had synthesized into a systematic whole the various ideological and religious traditions he had studied, producing an architechtonic world view that not only explained the source of suffering but also offered a very clear guideline for transcending it. Stephen demanded of people that they change themselves immediately or accept that they will continue to harm themselves and the rest of the universe, and hundreds of people found his exhortation sufficiently convincing to change their lives.

Enlightenment: Here and Now

By 1969 Stephen had identified what he saw as the common themes in all religions and had taken the further step of charting for his followers a path for salvation. He announced to the Monday Night Class that he had become a spiritual teacher and that, if his followers were willing to do what he told them to do, they could stay "high" permanently. This announcement was not greeted enthusiastically by all listeners; indeed, many Monday Night Class regulars stopped attending. One informant told me that, in her view, Stephen had "gone off the deep end" and had become a "megalomaniac." But there were many who believed that Stephen had discovered the secrets of the universe, and they were prepared to put his teachings into practice.

Stephen's formula for salvation puts great emphasis on change right here and right now, and in this sense it departs fundamentally from many of the religious traditions from which he had drawn. While these traditions are concerned in large measure with the fate of the soul in the afterlife, Stephen virtually ignores the question of what happens after death. He has stated, in response to a question during the Monday Night Class, that the soul has an existence after death, but that what happens to it is of little concern to us because we cannot hope to understand it. What matters is our salvation right here and right now. If we are to experience heaven, it must be on this earth. Furthermore, heaven—a world of peace and communion—is available to us right now, he argues, if we will only take the responsibility to create it by sending out beautiful vibrations.

To send out beautiful vibrations a person should get "high," but being "high" involves much more than a drug-induced euphoria. A "high" person, as Stephen defines the state, is merry, honest, straightforward, disciplined, and sensitive to the beauty of the universe. But, most importantly, such a person can function happily and successfully: "You can tell who they are, because they look together and they're friendly and they're sane, and they're functional, and they're actually able to do things" (Gaskin 1972:n.p.). High people are also very handsome and healthy in appearance and radiate winning, appealing smiles. They are winsome and convert others' opposition to support merely by their attractive presence.

Most of us, as Stephen points out, do not think of ourselves as being so attractive and so appealing. Yet the power of his message inheres in his proposition that we *choose* to be the way we are. We can choose to be "high," and we can contribute toward the creation on earth of a heaven of peace and communion. Alternatively, we can choose to be paranoid, hateful, and unloving, in which case we create an ugly world and suffer in it. It is only in this choice, Stephen argues, that our free will resides.

Free Will and the Creation

We shall, according to Stephen, experience the reality we have ourselves created: "If you don't respect the Creation, you get a funky Creation" (quoted in Cantwell and Gross 1971:209). "You straighten up the universe," he says, "by straightening up yourself" (quoted in Anonymous 1970:48). People who do not realize this quality of the universe are ignorant. An ignorant person, though he or she might have failed to receive moral instruction, is nevertheless held responsible for their emitted vibrations. That to which a person chooses to pay attention will "get heavy"—that is, become imbued with energy: "That's what your attention is like—what you put it on will get heavy. What do you want to get heavy? Do you want streetlights and the signs on Market Street to get heavy? If you spend your time on Market Street, that's what will get heavy" (Gaskin 1970:n.p.).

Human attention, according to Stephen, *is* energy; it is the fundamental energy of the universe, manifested as a fertile, creative life force. By directing this attention people bring about the reality that they experience. Most people, of course, do not realize this and think that their attention has no effect on the universe around them. A person therefore has a choice: he or she can add to or subtract from the level of peace and communion in the universe by directing attention. The choice is a free one. No one will force a person to radiate beautiful vibrations or to put attention and energy into being peaceful and beautiful. But if we fail to do so we shall suffer.

Our act of directing our attention produces, according to Stephen, an immediate retribution that he calls "karma." Such acts include thought and feeling as well as overt, observable action. If a person thinks a hateful thought, he or she will experience hatred from others. A state of ignorance, in which a person denies or ignores the way the universe works, acts in a circular way, because the person experiencing bad karma does not take responsibility for it; therefore, he or she goes on to complain about how unfair the world is—thus producing more bad karma. One of Stephen's Haight-Ashbury followers told me:

> We thought stealing was OK, like, as long as it was from the big chain supermarket and all these little rationalizations. And then our karma was really crappy. We couldn't figure out why, we just didn't see the connection. We thought that was just the way life was. We were born into this *crummy* world.

By believing the world is "crummy," according to Stephen's ideology, we make it crummy.

Complaining about one's situation, no matter how bad it is, has a specific and regular effect on the quality of creation. As people complain about how miserable and unfortunate they are, they keep contributing to their own continued misery and misfortune. They create their own suffering. If they are to stop suffering, and if they want others around them to stop suffering, they must stop complaining and try to be beautiful. The creation of a beautiful and peaceful universe is our single greatest responsibility, Stephen argues; we must be beautiful and loving in our hearts and minds if we are to stop making ourselves and others suffer. As individuals, we can choose to change and to bring some joy and refreshing beauty to the world around us. But the effect multiplies when a community of people transcend ignorance and try to put Stephen's teachings into practice.

Community and Agreement

According to Stephen, when several people join together to form a community of beautiful vibrations, they can bring about a particularly refined, pure creation:

> If you've got a hundred people looking at an orange, and ninety-nine of them say it's an orange and one of them says it's a rutabaga, well, it's going to keep on being an orange, but it ain't going to be as perfect an orange as it would have been if all hundred folks said it was an orange. [Gaskin 1974a:n.p.]

A group of people who are in agreement about what they ought to put their attention into will experience communion. Yet this communion is fragile in the sense that if anyone joining in does not agree on its basic premises, the communion becomes less perfect.

People who do not know about the astral plane or about telepathy are likely to disrupt ("ripoff") communion and lower the quality of creation. Ripoffs arise most commonly from ignorance. But in Stephen's view it is very likely that, in every group to which he speaks, there will be a few persons who deliberately try to ripoff the communion. He terms such persons "juice freaks," because they are addicted to trying to get the "juice" (energy manifested as communion) directed toward themselves alone. This tendency to monopolize "juice" is, according to Stephen, natural, because human energy is very attractive and appealing when communion occurs. The appeal of this energy leads children, for instance, to try to focus it on themselves. The problem is that the disruption, whether intentional or not, destroys the attention responsible for communion. Ripoffs thus "fog the juice"; that is, they blur the purity of the created communion. Juice freaks, in particular, must be dealt with forthrightly and firmly.

In the Monday Night Class, Stephen learned to deal with the many hecklers—juice freaks—by using the authority model of the college classroom. He seldom stood, but there was little doubt that, like a lecturer, he was to be considered the focus of attention. Just as college teachers may try to persuade their students to pay attention while in class, Stephen argued that complete attention and cooperation were necessary if the group was to achieve its goals. But in this context the demand for full attention was more than a matter of convenience for instructor and students. On the contrary, it was a religious matter—a matter of maintaining the purity of the group's vibrations and communions.

One Monday night Stephen was explaining, in response to a question, that he had quit eating meat to get "high." From the periphery of the crowd, the usual source of juice freaks, a male voice called, "How high?" Stephen replied, "You can't measure that. What kind of ruler do you expect to measure something like that with?" "What kind do you have?" the heckler replied. Stephen admonished, "I was in the middle of saying something to her," referring to the woman who had asked the question, "and I felt that it was a ripoff for you to walk by and holler like that 'cause you popped a bubble that was happening at the time." "That's not what a ripoff is!" the man insisted. "That is what a ripoff is and the way that you do it is like walk around on the outside of the circle and just game along like that. You're on for energy games, you're not on for anything real" (quoted in Link 1970:20).

Another heckler, a self-styled revolutionary, insisted that good vibrations were impossible now because one had to prepare for violent, fascist repression. Stephen responded, "There's not enough communication in this exchange to support the amount of vibrations happening in it. You're putting out negative-uptight, negative-uptight, negative-uptight. What are you contributing to the system?" The revolutionary responded, "I'm putting out vibrations that are realistic." "Good vibrations are realistic too," Stephen replied.

"Now you say you want to help out. Here's a trick—how about a little mind ecology? This is an ecological system of mind that we are all sharing, and you're a smog producer" (quoted in Cantwell and Gross 1971:209).

People get to be "juice freaks" because they do not know how to ask for attention in an open and honest way. A visitor to the Farm, for example, tried to strike up small talk with a Farm member, who replied: "There's no need for this to be said, you're just trying to get attention, you're fogging the juice!" Yet if a visitor asks for attention directly and honestly, it will be given. "They'll come up to you and stroke you and hold you, and play music with you if you want."

A person can choose to become beautiful in the here and now, Stephen argues, and in so doing vibrations are produced that create a loving and peaceful life around one. He argues that our principal responsibility is to make this choice; indeed, he maintains, it is the only choice we can really make. It is difficult for us to believe, he says, that we can change right now. "Getting high" with drugs or with communion helps, in that we see that we are capable of the "high" state. But it is much more difficult to "stay high."

Staying High: Speaking the Truth

Stephen, by the closing phase of the Monday Night Class period, had foreseen the limitations of drugs as a way of "staying high." In the midst of the heaviest period of drug use, Stephen said:

> I find out that as I go along, the more I go along, that sometimes
> I can smoke some grass and not get high. And once in a real great
> while I can even take some acid and not get very high. But I find
> that if I tell the truth it gets me high ... every time. So if you find
> yourself going to a place where you think you're as high as you're
> going to get with the help of your chemical assistance, then back
> in behind a little truth, and start climbing the ladder by hand.
> Because you can get as high as you want on truth, just by telling
> it like it comes. It doesn't even have to be something heavy. Be-
> cause it's true it's heavy ... that's really right on. ... The Truth's
> gonna come out anyway, somebody's gonna speak it, you know.
> You might as well up and do it yourself—it gets you stoned to do
> it. [Gaskin 1970:n.p.]

Many of the people attending Monday Night Class did so with their "families," the small groups of drug-sharing friends bound together by their *communitas* experiences, but plagued and often decimated with jealousy, anger, and egotism. Stephen was to devote much of his lecture time during the last year of the Monday Night Class to the problem of these small groups, and his message to them was to try to work constantly within them to maintain a good feeling of trust, love, openness, and honesty. It is therefore necessary, he argued, for his followers to forget their cultural programming: "In most folk's ground rules it's impolite to notice that your conversational partner is neurotic" (ibid.). In "straight" society, people do not talk about their feelings and about how a situation feels, but in Stephen's view this lack of communication is deadly to maintaining a high.

If people refuse to talk about their often wounded and sometimes ugly feelings about one another, they will accumulate what Stephen calls "subconscious"—a store of resentment that sours and festers if it is not brought into the open right away. Such a store (or, in the drug-culture patois of the group, a "stash") translates into bad vibrations and therefore a poor creation. As one member of the commune put it, "something will come down [happen], and you won't cop to it [speak about it], and you'll find yourself not liking that person" (quoted in Kaplan 1978:384). Stephen cautions that "if you try to be polite and don't quite say what's in your head and you figure you'll work it out some other time, you're going to build up community subconscious until you explode" (Gaskin 1974a:n.p.).

People must therefore work closely together in their small "families" to try to speak the truth:

> I think what I spent the most time doing, of all the time I was high, other than the time that was spent grooving and digging it, was working in small groups of people trying to figure out, you know, how come you look that way? What's happening? Hey, what are the vibes like? Anybody else feel this way? What's going on? Working together in small groups of people like that, telling the truth, you can get high. [Gaskin 1970:n.p.]

His followers who had not yet formed such groups were advised to do so: "If you just go and do it right so you make friends—a circle of friends around you—you'll be all right" (quoted in Cantwell and Gross 1971:212).

Stephen insisted that such groups not be composed of only two persons. A couple, for example, would probably not be successful at keeping each other high:

> The thing about being married in two is that sometimes one part-
> ner will take an ego advantage on the other one and dominate.
> Once you lose your juice it's really hard to get it up. It's like one
> partner just ripped the other one off all his energy. Then they go
> along all through life like that, with one of 'em holding all the juice
> and the other not allowed any. And that can happen in a two very
> easily. That can't happen in a four very well because, like, if you
> get on a trip, there's a bunch of other folks who are going to say,
> "Hey, man, you're on a trip." You can't fool three people very well.
> It's hard to do. [Quoted in Cantwell and Gross 1971:208]

He pointed to his "four-marriage," with Maggie, Michael, and Ina
May, as the model for small groups:

> I got three other people who I'm married to, all of whom are
> interested in my being straight, and I'm interested in them being
> straight. And so we work at it all the time. We keep each other
> pretty well ripped off as far as attachments and stuff goes. Like if
> somebody gets out of line and starts getting on an attachment trip
> somebody says, Hey man, you're attached. We stay as high as we
> can all the time, and if we aren't high we're finding out why not.
> [Gaskin 1970:n.p.]

These groups, Stephen argued, should be permanent. It takes a lot
of work over a long period of time to achieve a permanent "high,"
and a long-term commitment is required. Furthermore, finding
someone who will tell you the truth should be seen as a great gift;
because "the best thing that you can depend on is somebody who will
tell you the truth. If you find somebody who'll tell you the truth
about where you're at, hang on to 'em don't let 'em get away" (ibid.).

Speaking the truth in small groups often manifests as criticism
of another's harbored resentment, and it is often the case that
the harbored ill feelings are replaced by newly wounded egos. A
wounded ego is just as dangerous as a "stash," since it results in bad
vibrations. In Stephen's view, a person would not feel wounded by
criticism if it were not for the fact that he or she nourished harbored
resentment; his followers, therefore, must welcome and accept the
criticism they are given. They are to transcend what Stephen calls
the "praise-blame trip," which is identified as a great barrier to
enlightenment.

Stephen teaches that one should not depend on others for approval
or seek to avoid blame and criticism, for in so doing one advertises
a willingness to be conditioned by rewards and punishments. Happi-

ness, in his view, can be obtained only by becoming independent of praise and blame, and his followers are admonished to refuse to bow down to either. If a person uses praise or blame in an attempt to condition one of Stephen's followers, Stephen tells the person to "state the implication of the remark as clearly as possible" (Gaskin 1974a:n.p.).

Much conditioning occurs when people speak to one another using double or veiled messages, and Stephen maintains that such messages, which contain some unspoken but nevertheless disturbing implications, are a central danger to the small group's communion. He advises his followers:

> One of my teachings is that when someone points a subtle implica-
> tion at you you're supposed to rip the top off it and say, "What's
> that?" I really think that's an important thing to do to keep your-
> self out of trouble. We don't let one speck of implications go by. As
> soon as somebody starts implying stuff, we'll try and state what
> the implication is as clear as we can. [Ibid.]

Some people try to protect their egos by arguing back when such prying occurs, but it is very important that they do not succeed at maintaining their "cover," or defenses:

> You've got to say what's true, you've got to tell the truth and fear
> no man. There's always folks that are going to want to shut you
> down [defeat you in argument] so you won't blow their cover [re-
> veal their stored resentment]. How we make it . . . is we don't let
> folks shut us down so you won't blow their cover. It works out that
> on the Farm everybody's uncovered . . . we're like a mental nudist
> colony . . . we don't believe in privacy, because we'd rather be sane
> than highly individualistic. [Ibid.]

This kind of criticism is disconcerting at first, "but in a little while you see that [criticism] go on commonly enough that you develop a sense of humor about it, and don't go into such severe praise-blame every time anybody says anything to you" (ibid.).

Yet criticism ought to be done with compassion. Stephen's follow-ers have to accept that, no matter how far out of line a person might seem, everyone is capable of "straightening up" and sending out beautiful vibrations. It is essential that the criticism be made not only with compassion but also without anger. An ex-Farm member recalls, "It's important that nobody fights . . . you have to keep the juice good. You can't keep juice good if someone fights." When a criticism is made, it must be done very evenhandedly with the attitude that the critic just wants to keep the juice pure. A critic should conceive of himself or herself as just "helping out," which is the maximum "extent of anyone's ego involvement in criticizing others" (quoted in Wenner 1977:83).

The purpose of telling the truth is to maintain the group's high, a sense of communion, and love for one another. If the bad situation and the bad vibrations can be cleared up by communication, then the group once again becomes a solitary unit. The restitution of communion is interpreted by Stephen's followers as a divine miracle and a direct result of following Stephen's teachings. They tell of remarkable transformations in the appearance of a scene in which truth has been spoken. Whereas previously the people interacting looked ugly and haggard, they subsequently became beautiful and rosy-cheeked. The healing vibrations produced in such an interaction are believed to affect the entire universe. Stephen maintains that the beautiful vibrations produced by his followers are enough to "integrate," or bring peace and beauty to, the entire country.

Stephen's recipe for salvation, with its strong emphasis on salvation here and now in small "families" of friends, offers a fulfillment of the Haight-Ashbury dream. His message about the necessity of realizing the Haight's ideals—*communitas* and peace—is buttressed by a highly systematic cosmology that explains suffering and that holds each and every individual accountable for the quality of the universe as a whole. He argues strongly that the only freedom that a person has is to embrace his teachings or to turn away from them, and the latter choice entails suffering for all other sentient beings. He demands an instantaneous conversion:

> If you don't feel that you're beautiful you may have trouble just changing your mind and deciding, I'm beautiful, right now. But you can change your mind and decide to tell the truth ... right now, anyone can. All you have to do is decide that you want to do it, and start working on it, and you'll get loving, and you will become just, and you will become beautiful, if you follow truth. It will take you to the same place. [Gaskin 1970:n.p.]

Salvation is available to everyone, no matter how horribly a person has suffered:

> None of the stuff that's happened to you has changed you or
> harmed you or hurt you in any permanent way whatsoever. Once
> you understand the unsulliable nature of the intellect, it's no
> longer necessary to seek absolutia for past sins. Dig that? That's
> a powerful spell. Anyone who understands that can be absolved in
> the here and now. [Gaskin 1974a:n.p.]

Stephen's religion, with its stress on *communitas,* change, and
commitment, lent itself readily to the creation of a confederation of
tightly knit, truth-telling "families" out of the anonymous sea of
individuals that attended the huge Monday Night Class during
1969–70. The practice of speaking the truth in permanent, solitary,
small groups, helping many overcome the disputes, jealousy, and
resentment they had experienced, led to strong sentiments of "family" fellowship and thus to the realization of the Haight's goals
(albeit on a small scale). His most enthusiastic followers formed
group marriages themselves and tried to emulate Stephen's "family." One informant told me, "I think he's just found out how to keep
himself and his family straight—and he works on that. . . . Just to
watch him do his thing, you're attracted by it. . . . We just had to do
it [too]. It's very simple." Many of the "families" emulated another
aspect of Stephen's lifestyle: living seminomadically in refurbished
schoolbuses. This pattern of emulation was to have considerable
significance for the formation of the Farm in Tennessee.

The Astral Continental Congress

When Stephen was invited in 1970 to speak at a number of
churches and colleges throughout the country, he suspended the
Monday Night Class meetings and prepared to embark on the tour.
Nearly two hundred people declared, unbidden, their intention to
follow him—a logical step since, in emulating Stephen's lifestyle,
most of these people had already moved into converted schoolbuses.
On October 12, 1970, a caravan of as many as sixty-three buses
(Fiske 1973:33) left San Francisco. Its departure was a significant
step forward in the formation of the Farm, since only the nucleus of
Stephen's most strongly committed followers followed him as "the
Caravan."

Prior to his departure, Stephen spoke of the trip as a test of his
divinity. He asserted that he was so high that he would receive good
treatment from the police wherever he went. He told a heckler

during one of his Caravan speeches that one should not be afraid of
the authorities:

> They treat me right everywhere and they'd treat you like that
> everywhere, if you did it the way I do. You know, I'll tell ya, three
> of our buses got busted for grass, and somebody remembered some
> cat gettin' ten years for a joint in New York not long ago. But two
> of the buses had to pay twenty-five dollar fines and the third just
> lost its grass. [Quoted in Cantwell and Gross 1971:208]

Despite these minor "hassles" the group did indeed return to San
Francisco without a serious "bust."

Stephen referred to the Caravan, during which he held over thirty
meetings, as the "Astral Continental Congress"—a national forum
for the creation of a new spiritual order. His lectures, conducted in
the usual question-and-answer format, were received with interest,
curiosity, and occasionally hostility. He was probably not successful
in getting his ideas across to most of the people who attended the
meetings, since the questions sometimes produced tangential re-
plies; but there is one function of the Caravan period (October 1970–
February 1971) that can be clearly identified: the experience forged
Stephen and his band of loyal, emulating followers into a solitary
group.

Upon their return to San Francisco, Stephen held one Monday
Night Class meeting, but it was not successful. Stephen, noting that
the Class meeting had failed to come to communion, remarked that
the spiritual impulse had left San Francisco and that San Francis-
cans had become "astral conservatives." Later the Caravan held a
meeting, and it was decided that they ought to stick together. They
had discussed previously the possibility of forming a commune, but
now the time appeared ripe. Stephen recalls:

> We'd become a community from working together, and we knew
> we could do heavy stuff from working together. The next Sunday
> we met and I said, "Man, we can't separate like this, because we've
> become a thing. We're something. We've shared so much karma
> and so much heavy stuff has gone down and we've done so much
> heavier stuff than we ever thought we could do. . . . Let's go to
> Tennessee and get a farm." [Gaskin 1974a:n.p.]

But why Tennessee? The group's publications state that they chose
Tennessee because they had previously been welcomed by the people

there. Certainly another factor was the low price of land. Yet at
Stephen's last San Francisco Sunday Service (February 10, 1971), he
reasserted that the group should test its divinity by going to the most
conservative part of the country and nevertheless merit a warm,
friendly reception from its residents.

In this test of its ability to make friends with the "hippies'"
nemeses—the "straights"—the group was partially successful. Not
long after arriving in Tennessee and purchasing a large parcel of
land, good relations were established with neighbors:

> Homer was going to run us out of the country the first time he saw
> us, because the last people he'd seen with long hair did stuff like
> peel out of the gas station without paying for the gas. But after he
> got to know us we were doing stuff like being partners with him
> in his sawmill and sending over a crew to help him maintain his
> farm. And a bunch of people who were shiftless, most of them
> being English majors and kilo dealers, and other worthless types
> that hadn't never worked, learned how to run tractors and saw-
> mills and learned how to farm. [Gaskin 1974a:n.p.]

Another neighbor noted that Farm residents are "honest to a fault"
(quoted in Fiske 1973:39). The sheriff of Lewis County, T. C. Carroll,
noted that "residents of the Farm stay to themselves and have a good
name" (ibid.). Carroll once told the crew at the gate, after asking
them whether there were any runaway girls at the Farm, "Sure is
good I could just come down here and ask you . . . rather than search
the Farm because you got a reputation for truth established. That's
a lot easier way to do it with you than to have to come inside and
look at everybody, and it feels good to do it like this" (quoted in
Gaskin 1974a:n.p.).

Yet Stephen was not totally truthful with his neighbors and with
the police: he did not tell them that the group was growing marijuana on the Farm. On August 31, 1971. Stephen and three of his
followers were arrested at the Farm when investigators found the
marijuana patch. They were convicted by a Lewis County court on
November 11, 1971. An appeal was attempted on the grounds of
religious freedom, since the marijuana was used in the group's communions. Stephen's appeal eventually came before the Supreme
Court of the United States, which refused to hear the case in October
1973. Later, a plea before a Tennessee court for suspension of sentence was also refused, and on February 22, 1974—three years after

his departure from San Francisco—Stephen, accompanied by three of his followers, was sent to a penitentiary in Tennessee (Gaskin 1974b), where he served a two-year sentence. Despite Stephen's arrest and conviction, the Farm remained stable during his jail term and, since his release, has grown considerably. Stephen promised Sheriff Carroll that no more marijuana would be grown on the Farm, and since that time the police have ignored the occasional use of the drug in the commune's churches (Fiske 1973:39). The Farm today is a thriving commune of twelve hundred persons, who conceive of themselves as living in a "family monastery." The group has tried to realize the *communitas* ideals of the Haight-Ashbury through the creation of a complex community of tightly knit households, or "families," of up to thirty individuals.

The Family Monastery

Stephen's religion establishes, as its ultimate concern, a "high" state of communion in small groups, the basic nucleus of which is a permanent marriage. During the latter phase of the Monday Night Class and during the period of the Caravan, many of these marriages were group marriages, but this experiment failed not long after the establishment of the commune. There was too much discord caused by jealousy. The *coup de grâce* to the four-marriage model was administered by Michael's departure from the Farm. The group returned to the two-marriage model. It should not, however, be thought that the group understands their current, two-person model of marriage as a replica of the institution in mainstream society. Though the Farm insists on sex-role differentiation, as does traditional American society, males and females are ascribed attributes that, in the view of commune members, differ considerably from mainstream society's conceptions. According to Stephen, male-female relationships in mainstream society are based on ignorant ideas that encourage suffering and irresponsibility. A two-person marriage can, he argues, become a vehicle for spiritual awakening, but *only* if the couple understand precisely the differing nature of male and female energies and submit to inclusion in a "family" of critical and compassionate sharers of their household.

In Stephen's view there are two features of sexual relationships in mainstream society that cause couples to suffer. The first is ignorance of the beautiful nature of female energy, an ignorance that is fostered by the "macho" ideology of male dominance and male aggressiveness. The second is that the pursuit of pleasure in sexual relations on a material level (that is, without attention being paid to the spiritual implications of sexual relations) leads invariably to sado-masochistic relationships and therefore to suffering.

American culture, according to Stephen, teaches a male to think that he alone has the "energy" in sexual relationships. A man likens his erection to a thunderbolt, believing—erroneously—that it is the result of his energy alone. With this idea in mind, he chases after women aggressively. Women, in turn, may—out of ignorance—encourage this aggressive, macho behavior because it flatters their ego. Stephen argues that it is really up to women to help men overcome their macho role tendencies:

> It's easier for the cats to take off their six-guns and quit being macho if their ladies don't polarize them into that and come on and expect them to be like that.... the male thinking that his erection is his lightening bolt ... makes him think that he's the cat with the juice. And that's what puts him on that trip, if the lady is on a corresponding trip when she says, "Oh, he's got that juice and he's chasing me, it's because I'm so neat," and she encourages him in that way. [Gaskin 1974a:n.p.]

Stephen maintains that a relationship predicated on this one-way flow of energy (that is, from male to female) will not satisfy either partner. In such a relationship the male expends his limited energy and the woman's is not even aroused; satisfaction lies beyond the reach of both. What couples fail to realize in traditional American sex relationships is that a woman's energy is like an electromagnet —it draws up the male's erection—and without it a man cannot hope to achieve an erection for a long time or to draw upon much energy.

In a low-energy state devoid of satisfaction, a couple may experiment with increasingly sado-masochistic techniques to try to achieve the fulfillment they want:

> If you keep striving after sexuality ... in a while the amount of sensation you require will become so great that the tissue starts breaking down and you'll be off into sadism and masochism and violence.... Extreme sexual perversions ... is just a heavier grade of sandpaper—just scratch yourself a little harder because you're jaded. That's how some folks get into weird stuff. [Ibid.]

A satisfying relationship must be predicated on the idea that a woman has a beautiful energy that a man can share. As long as this idea is kept in mind, there will be sufficient sexual energy to provide full satisfaction without getting involved in sado-masochism.

While explicitly denying that male energy is superior to female energy, Stephen nevertheless maintains that

> males and females have different signs on their electricity, like positive and negative. They both have energy, but the signs are different. The result of this is that you can take an uptight man and an uptight woman and let them both share the same energy and they can be made refreshed and relaxed—both of them, because the woman's minuses and the woman's pluses can cancel out just like an algebra equation cancels. [Ibid.]

But such an interaction can occur only if care is taken to make sure that the woman's energy is stimulated. Stephen instructs couples to "let the lady be a little bit aggressive in the beginning. This culture is so far overbalanced about the male being aggressive that the female needs to be kind of aggressive to get things happening" (ibid.). The male should see to it that his partner achieves orgasm, and he is instructed that his own orgasm is not of primary importance.

Farm men must not, therefore, view Farm women as sex objects. The idea of a woman as a sex object encourages macho aggressiveness and denies a woman's energy. Women, in turn, must not present themselves as adventuresses, prostitutes, or temptresses. Relations based on these role models are forbidden among the group. Promiscuity of any sort (for example, premarital sex or adultery) is believed to be based on these dangerous sex-role models and is therefore banned. No sexual relationship should exist that is not based on commitment—that is, permanent commitment—because that kind of responsibility is required to achieve a wholesome, nurturing relationship.

Stephen's followers innovate in the sphere of sexual relations by devaluing "macho" aggressiveness and by placing emphasis on the female orgasm, but in other respects the group sees itself as reasserting traditional mores of marital exclusiveness and premarital chastity—ideas provided by traditional American family models but not esteemed in contemporary mainstream society with its high rates of premarital sex and divorce. Stephen maintains that the ideas of traditional morality were wrongly abandoned. The Farm's models for sexual relationships thus combine traditional themes—such as the idea of differing sex attributes for men and women—with special attention to and innovative emphases on safeguarding the happiness of women, ensuring their orgasms, and protecting them from macho aggressiveness. In no other sphere of social relationships is this curious blending of traditional and innovative themes more apparent than in the group's sexual division of labor.

Husbands and Mothers: Sex Roles at the Farm

A woman's energy, according to Stephen, is a healing, beautiful vibration that can maintain the quality of the universe and nurture children. Stephen says that women can create a field around them that is "clean, pure, fresh and pretty, and that their *raison d'être* is childrearing:

> Ladies are supposed to take it upon themselves to create a field around them as far as their influence can reach that's nice and smells good and feels good and is clean and a good place for a baby to be. Any lady who wants to can just insist on it being that way as far as she can see. And men are supposed to be really chivalrous and really knightly and help them out to do that. How's that for a noble idea? [Gaskin 1974a:n.p.]

A woman's duty is to be a mother—to reproduce bounteously and to bring to the universe her beautiful life-power. A man's duty, in contrast, is to be a husband—a provider and a *manager* of the relationship such that a mother can be given every assistance she needs.

According to the group's publications and the reports of visitors and ex-Farm members, Farm women generally endorse enthusiastically the idea that women ought to be mothers and to be protected by their husbands. A visitor to the Farm notes that women "seemed euphoric, like they felt like their needs were taken care of.... 'The men respect us,' they said, 'we gets lots of strokes.... we have our place ... as mother, lover, homemaker.'" One of Stephen's wives, voicing this theme, said "I really enjoy taking care of my family. I consider it to be a holy duty to cook for them and keep them healthy and keep them clean and keep it sanitary and clean and together for my family" (quoted in ibid.). Ina May, another of Stephen's wives, concurred: "We think that what ladies are supposed to do is come on really strong with life force, and make there be enough for every-body" (quoted in ibid.).

Despite their apparent acquiescence to the Farm's sex-role ideology, it is nonetheless the case that Farm wives are occasionally mistreated by their husbands. It appears that so much stress is laid on a woman's role in creating a beautiful household that if anything goes wrong she is blamed. An ex-Farm member reports that "a guy hit his wife. She had been baking bread. But others stopped by—anyone can stop in to eat—and there wasn't enough for everyone. He smacked her quite hard on the head. She looked really hurt and sad. Nobody copped to it. Maybe nobody saw it but me." Wenner reports that

> only once did I hear a voice raised in anger, and that was in the middle of the night. One couple couldn't get their toddler to stop crying. They'd tried, as Stephen instructed, to "take him out of the juice"—to no avail. Their frustration mounted—less, it seemed, out of impatience with their son than from embarrassment at not being able to apply Stephen's principles properly. Suddenly, the husband blurted out to his wife, "Why can't you learn to do it right?" [Wenner 1977:82]

At least forty Farm wives appear to have been intimidated ver-bally or in other ways. At one Sunday morning service, Stephen asked:

> How many ladies here truly and honestly—and don't be afraid to put your hand up here, because if you're afraid to put your hand up here, what are you going to do at home—how many ladies here think they get intimidated by their husbands? How about that? We have twelve or fifteen ladies here with a severe enough case that they'll snitch their old man off here in the church. [Gaskin n.d.:114]

Despite his ridicule of the intimidated women for "snitching off" their husbands in church, Stephen stated that he sympathized with them: "It's funny, but the kinds of things that make me understand what it's like to be a lady in this country and this world are things like having been in the Marine Corps and the penitentiary. I've felt what it was like to be under somebody's hand" (ibid.:115). Neverthe-less, he suggests that acquiescence to intimidation is a flaw and that the intimidated women are responsible for their own continued in-timidation:

I'll bet none of these ladies that feel like they were intimidated live out of reach of somebody on the Farm to ask for assistance in that case. . . . If we didn't have any background radiation of a few husbands picking on their wives, we wouldn't have any intimidation on the Farm at all and nobody would be able to pull any off. Isn't that really where its at? . . . Well, intimidation on the Farm is really un-sane; un-sane because you have the most help and the best chance to get out from under it here; this is where you're going to find the most people dedicated to not being that way. [Ibid.:115–17]

Stephen called an "intimidated ladies meeting" later, and forty women showed up. Stephen lamented at the following week's Sunday service:

Now we say that the Farm is putting out this vibration of peace and love and good will into the world. We had forty ladies come to the intimidated ladies meeting; 4–0, not 1–4. Forty. Fourteen or so put their hands up in here last Sunday; the rest of them were apparently too intimidated to raise their hands at the meeting. And then we heard that besides forty that came to the meeting there were some who were too scared to come to the meeting because their husbands might get mad. Forty ladies, that's eighty people, plus all their kids, plus all the people that are associated close enough that it uses up most of their time to go through that stuff. So who's watching the store? Who is the backbone of good vibrations that's holding the Farm together and keeping our intelligence and integrity at a high enough level that we're going to make a difference in the world? . . . you haven't even gotten to the intimidated husbands, of which we have some. [Ibid.:124–25]

In Stephen's view the problem of "intimidated ladies" did not indict the Farm's system of social relationships, but rather its failure to live up to its goals. To surmount the problem of intimidation of women, Stephen suggested that Farm members take more seriously the Farm's several social institutions that offer protection and solace both to women and to men.

Women may appeal to Stephen for help. Since Farm members look to Stephen as not only the group's leader, but their personal counselor as well, any member can speak to Stephen directly. He has a telephone in his house. While Wenner was conducting her interview, the telephone rang, and Stephen spoke to a young woman who was having problems with her boyfriend. Stephen advised her, "You come from a traditional family don't ya? You'd be better off with an old man who'd take care of you" (Wenner 1977:83). Nevertheless, Stephen has lamented that some Farm members, fearing that they

would reveal themselves as unenlightened persons, are not completely honest with him when they bring their problems to him
(ibid.:n.p.). But it is possible for a woman to tell Stephen about any
intimidation that she experiences. If her husband is at fault, he may
be sent to live for a while with the single men. This institution is
called the "rock tumbler," since it knocks off a man's rough edges.

Furthermore, women at the Farm involve themselves in a specifically feminine world of social relationships that offers support and
solace. The men leave quite early in the morning for work in the
fields and shops, while most women stay behind to cook, clean, care
for infants, and tend to other domestic chores. Women's tasks are
done in work groups of several women. One such work crew is the
midwife team. The Farm delivers its own babies and has evolved a
birth-care system that incorporates Stephen's ideology. The midwife
crew is led by Ina May Gaskin, who trains the midwives and super-
vises births. Midwifery is presented in the group's literature as an
extremely holy institution; in the Farm's book on midwifery, a center foldout painting shows the midwives with pronounced halos (I.
M. Gaskin 1978). Giving birth and midwifery are highly esteemed
roles for women at the Farm, and the sentiment is strong that these
feminine roles are as prestigious and as spiritual as any role carried
on by a man.

The midwife crew is highly supportive of a woman during childbirth. Everything is done to ensure a comfortable and familiar setting for her. The midwives encourage the woman to feel relaxed and,
in the company of other sympathetic women, to let herself savor the
beauty and joy of the event. She is assured that she is with friends
who love her deeply. Anyone whose vibrations are deemed bad is
sent away, and this sometimes includes the husband. Usually, however, the woman's husband is there and plays a central role in
holding her and comforting her during the birth. The midwife crew
believes that their technique helps a woman to relax and to "open
up," resulting in a low rate of complications and of infant mortality
(I. M. Gaskin 1978:475).

Husbands who seek to abuse their wives must do so during rare
moments of privacy. The collapse of the four-marriage system did
not destroy the antiprivacy emphasis; the commune opted for complex households in which several married couples and single people
live. At a branch Farm in Wisconsin, couples' bedrooms are separated only by curtains (Kaplan 1978:381). Even toilets lack doors, so
that Farm members can work out, as they say, their "cultural shit-

shock" (Gaskin 1974a:n.p.). The lack of privacy is intended to maintain the group's communion, for it is feared that, if couples were to
escape the supervision of others, the old patterns of macho domination, submission, and individualism might reappear. Stephen points
out that "we'd rather be sane than highly individualistic" (ibid.).

Equality versus Identity

The Farm, in seeking to achieve its goals of *communitas,* euphoria, and beatitude without risk of chaos, has instituted a rigid
system of sex-role differentiation that, *ideally,* assigns equal prestige to men and to women. From the commune's perspective sexual
equality need not presuppose identity; that is, it is not necessary to
argue that men and women are exactly the same if one wants to
establish a social system in which men and women have equal statuses. In the view of Farm members, men's roles and women's roles
are accorded equivalent prestige: giving birth to a child is deemed
as holy as producing a bounteous harvest.

Yet it is an arguable point that, in seeking to institute a differentiated sex-role system, the Farm has inadvertently created sexual
inequality. While women's roles are highly esteemed, a woman's
responsibilities and decision-making power are restricted to the domestic sphere. Decisions about what to an outsider appear to be
larger matters—for example, allocation of the group's million-dollar
annual operating budget—are in the hands of a governing board
composed primarily of men. Furthermore, there appears to be some
sentiment that women ought not to emulate roles that are traditionally held by men.

According to an ex-Farm member, one woman tried with mixed
success to challenge the sexual allocation of work roles. She sought
a position driving a tractor, a job that normally is held only by men.
She was permitted to take the job over the objections of some men
and women, but did not hold it for long. Much of the opposition to
her carrying out this role stems from the belief, which is held very
strongly among Farm members, that a woman's reproductive potential is very important and very holy. A woman should marry, and
she should have as many children as possible. Indeed, one ex-Farm
member, while discussing the high pregnancy rate at the Farm,
remarked that the typical dress of women is maternity clothing.
Pregnant or lactating women should not, it is believed, emulate male
roles that might endanger their reproductive potential. Their re-

striction to a feminine and domestic sphere of social relationships thus appears to Farm members, male and female, as a prudent and spiritually valid course. If Farm women find themselves restricted to what appears to an outsider to be a powerless and degrading status, it should nonetheless be emphasized here that neither Farm men nor most Farm women commonly see the sex-role system that way. On the contrary, Farm members conceive themselves as having elevated women to a status equal to and in some respects surpassing that of men, but at the same time they assert fundamental differences between the two sexes.

In the view of mainstream society, the Farm's goals are contradictory. During the late Seventies, the American intelligentsia generally has come to believe that sexual differentiation entails sexual inequality, and most theorists in the field of communal studies have argued that no commune that, in the face of its egalitarian values, tried to maintain sex-role differentiation could long persist. Yet it is apparent that the Farm has been successful in its attempt to realize its goals. Although women have complained of abuse at the Farm, it is also true that its members were led to believe that the abuse did not result from the structure of Farm social relations. Stephen transformed the women's complaints of abuse so that the indictment pointed to the Farm's failure to meet its own, sacred objectives. Therefore these objectives—and ultimately the whole social system —derived even more sanctity from what might appear, on the surface, to be a minor rebellion. What we behold in the case of the Farm is the power of religion and ritual to define social relationships in mystical terms and therefore render them unassailable and sacrosanct. We are not likely to understand such a social system until we are prepared to grasp the meaning of its religious underpinnings.

ACKNOWLEDGMENTS

I should like to thank May Diaz and William Simmons, who read and commented on an earlier draft of this paper in 1972. More recently, Jon Wagner has made numerous helpful criticisms. Finally, I should like to thank the Farm visitors and ex-members who gave so willingly of their time in interviews. The opinions expressed in this paper are, however, mine alone. Fieldwork was undertaken in San Francisco in 1969 and 1970 during the latter phase of the Monday Night Class.

REFERENCES CITED

Anonymous
  1970   A 35-Year Old Guru Ministers to Hippies of Northern California.
         New York Times, 21 September, p. 48.
Cantwell, Mary, and Amy Gross
  1971   I Want Us to Get Real Good Understanding and Real Good Love
         and Peace and Brotherhood and Just Hang Around, Man: A Talk
         with Stephen Gaskin. Mademoiselle, March, pp. 142–47, 207–26.
Conover, Patrick
  1975   An Analysis of Communes and Intentional Communities with Par-
         ticular Attention to Sexual and General Relations. Family Coordi-
         nator 24:453–64.
Fiske, Edward B.
  1973   Marijuana Part of Religion at Commune in Tennessee. New York
         Times, 17 February, p. 33.
Gaskin, Ina May
  1978   Spiritual Midwifery. Summertown, TN: Book Publishing Co.
Gaskin, Stephen (author given as "Stephen" in some titles and various
editions)
  1970   Monday Night Class. San Francisco: Book Farm. Reprinted, n.d.,
         Summertown, TN: Book Publishing Co.
  1972   The Caravan. New York: Random House.
  1974a Hey Beatnik: This is the Farm Book. Summertown, TN: Book Pub-
         lishing Co.
  1974b Gaskin, Stephen, Defendant—Appellant. The Grass Case. Sum-
         mertown, TN: Book Publishing Co.
  1976   This Season's People: A Book of Spiritual Teachings. Summertown,
         TN: Book Publishing Co.
  1976   Volume One: Sunday Morning Services on The Farm. Summer-
         town, TN: Book Publishing Co. [ca. 177–78].
Kaplan, Robert E.
  1978   Maintaining Relationships Openly: Case Study of "Total Open-
         ness" in a Communal Organization. Human Relations 31:375–94.
Kanter, Rosabeth Moss
  1972   Commitment and Community: Communes and Utopias in Sociolog-
         ical Perspective. Cambridge, MA: Harvard Univ. Pr.
Link, Geoffrey
  1970   The Rainbow Maker. San Francisco 12(4).
Ramey, James W.
  1972   Emerging Patterns of Innovative Behavior in Marriage. Family
         Coordinator 21:435–56.
Robison, James
  1972   A Million-Dollar, Holes-in-the-Knee Society. Chicago Tribune Mag-
         azine, 2 October, pp. 18–19, 44, 46–48.
Turner, Victor
  1969   The Ritual Process: Structure and Anti-Structure. Chicago: Aldine.
  1974   Dramas, Fields, and Metaphors: Symbolic Action in Human Soci-
         ety. Ithaca, NY: Cornell Univ. Pr.
Wenner, Kate
  1977   How They Keep Them Down on the Farm. New York Times Maga-
         zine, 8 May, pp. 74, 80–81, 83.

-7- JON WAGNER

A Midwestern Patriarchy

Origins of the Haran Commune

"HARAN" IS A PSEUDONYM FOR a contemporary communal society located in the hilly woodlands of the Ohio River Valley. Founded in 1965 by a fundamentalist minister, it has since grown into a cohesive and stable commune of more than 100 members. Although the Haran commune has attracted the attention of a number of newspaper reporters, magazine writers, and television crews, its public image remains largely dependent on brief (and often distorted) media reports and on the statements of the members themselves. In 1972 I received the leader's permission to conduct ethnographic research in the community for my doctoral dissertation. I became a resident and full participant from June until December 1972 and continued to visit the community regularly until August 1973, during which time I collected data by means of interviews and participant-observation. Except where otherwise noted, the following description of the Haran commune refers to the period from 1972 through 1973.

The leader of the Haran commune, whom I shall call "Samuel," was born to a working-class family in the Midwest about 1918. He recalls having manifested certain extraordinary abilities and sensitivities as a child, including a capacity for extrasensory perception and an abiding interest in religious questions. By the time World War II broke out, Samuel had developed strong religious convictions which led him to become a conscientious objector to the war. Later, he continued to develop his leadership in ultrafundamentalist religious circles and to clarify and expound his own increasingly unique theology. By 1965 he had become the author of several radical, privately circulated religious tracts, a frequent disruptor of religious meetings, and the leader of a small but devoted fold.

It was in that year that, according to Samuel, the Lord directed him to the remote valley which the commune now occupies and made it clear to him that it was time to put his "revealed" beliefs into social practice. Samuel's entourage of about 25 persons occupied a ramshackle farmhouse and tried farming 86 acres of marginal land with only a mule and an old tractor. When interviewed by local newsmen in 1967, Samuel stated his intention to keep the commune simple and primitive, to eschew technology, to pursue economic self-sufficiency, and to avoid social and cultural corruption from the outside world. However, the communards soon became disillusioned about the viability of subsistence farming and concluded that, as Samuel's son and community business manager later said, "we were not rich enough to afford the luxury of being primitive."

During the first five years of its existence, the fledgling commune had to cope with troublemaking neighbors, uncooperative authorities, and the absence of physical facilities even as they were establishing their social order and developing a cash economy. It is a testimony to their endurance that by 1972 the communards had built a substantial log cabin village, won the grudging respect of their neighbors, and laid the foundations of what was to become a rapidly growing industrial economy. By 1972 the mainstay of Haran's economy was its hardwood logging and sawmill operation. Standing timber was bought and cut from property as far as sixty miles away, cut in the community-operated sawmill, and shipped to distant markets in the commune's own trucks. The operation was, even in 1972, run entirely by commune workers using communal equipment, and the gross income was measured in the hundreds of thousands of dollars. In addition to developing the cash economy, which since 1972 has expanded into composting and other commercial activities, the commune had revived and strengthened its subsistence activities including farming and meat production.

Life Is a School

During interviews with reporters and visitors, Samuel explains that one of the goals of the community is to lead a simple and healthy life. Such a life, he says, should entail the abolition of idleness and exploitation. "All work is honorable," Samuel tells visitors and prospective members, "but if any would not work, neither should he eat." Samuel also emphasizes the loving and peaceful character of social life in the commune, saying that the true communalist is one who loves the company of other people and who "will never let the sun set" on disagreements with others. Ultimately, Samuel explains, the purpose of communal living is to promote spiritual growth, and a commune such as Haran is best seen as a "school" for engendering such growth. Samuel does not usually volunteer much specific information on the commune's religious beliefs; in fact, he often denies that the commune holds any "particular religion." As for the relations of the sexes, Samuel acknowledges that "women's liberation," in the sense understood by the outside world, does not exist at Haran. Instead, he says, the women are completely fulfilled in their roles as "real women" and "true Eves."

Despite these reassurances from an apparently benign, serene, and fatherly personage, the rumors continue to fly. Samuel's community, they say, is the scene of unbridled brutalization of women, a place where everyone is under the hypnotic and exploitive control of a religious charlatan. The rumors are invariably distorted and, often as not, simply false. Yet their persistence points to the radically patriarchal and charismatic nature of the Haran commune.

One of the earliest features of Samuel's developing philosophy was an emphasis on the continuing struggle between the forces of "carnality" and those of "spiritual wisdom." Samuel's early writings contain repeated references to the Bible's most charismatic books: Daniel, Samuel, Revelations, and the epistles of Saint Paul. Like Paul, who said that "in my flesh dwelleth no good thing," Samuel sees the surrender to carnal impulses, emotions, and natural urges as the source of much human woe. This view, which Samuel shares with the radical Reformation and to some extent with medieval Christianity, sees the struggle for goodness—and for life itself—as the struggle against the flesh. For Samuel, the most ennobling experiences a human being can have are those of sacrificial love, divine "Wisdom," and the personal growth that allows one to transcend previous limitations. In these lie the meaning of life and the possibility of immortality in a very literal sense. Few, however, are able to experience love, Wisdom, or growth because they are, as Samuel might say, "encompassed in the mind of this world." The "mind of this world," the strictly "human" intelligence, however sophisticated it may become, is nothing more than the impulse to power and sexual gratification, ultimately motivated by the same greed and lust that gives rise to animal aggression. As evidence of the futility and self-destructiveness of this sort of "intelligence," Samuel points to capitalistic competition, warfare, injustice, disease, and death, each related to the others in a "web of carnality."

These evils are unnecessary, according to Samuel, but the means of overcoming them lies in those qualities of love, Wisdom, and growth which cannot be derived from the carnal mind. The sole source of the virtues which can overcome evil, Samuel argues, is divine revelation. Such revelation comes only to those whose discipline and devotion are strong; those who have forsaken their own "self" interests in favor of the divine. God makes His will known to such men, who in turn have the capacity to teach others how to overcome their carnal impulses. Moses, Jesus, and the other prophets were such men, and so is Samuel. Samuel teaches that history is a dialectic between the bearers of divine Wisdom and the forces of selfishness and social conservatism which degrade prophetic insights into churches and other "self-serving" institutions.[1] Thus Samuel views life as an opposition between a path which offers short-term satisfaction of carnal lusts leading to ultimate destruction, and that which demands short-term sacrifice but promises health, cosmic meaning, and immortality.

The path of the spiritual, which Haran calls "Wisdom," entails two principal elements. The first of these is "love of mankind." Even though Samuel and the Haran community do not consider themselves Christian in any affiliational sense, the notion of sacrificial love as taught by Jesus is a central tenet of their belief system. Samuel asks, "If you cannot love your fellow man whom you have seen, how can you love God whom you have not seen?" Love of humankind is not only a path to God, but is also an end in itself. Competition and hate, which stem from the carnal mind, always "reap" in kind, leading to violence, insanity, disease, and death (Samuel places little emphasis on the afterlife, but stresses instead the earthly consequences of carnality or Wisdom). But to love humankind is not merely to love those whom one finds attractive or lovable. Love which is conditional on some qualities of the person loved, or on some expected reward from that person, is really noth-

---

[1]Samuel's description of dialectic between "divine Wisdom" and "society" very closely resembles Weber's (1968) classic treatment of the opposition of "charisma" and "routinization." The similarity, one might suppose, results from two independent but converging analyses within the same cultural tradition.

ing more than love of self. Such "selfish love" includes romantic or sexual love, as well as the love of one's children (who are part of one's own "flesh"). In Haran it is thought that the person most "difficult" to love is the one on whom the most effort should be expended. If two men are inclined to dislike one another, they may be asked to work together. The ability to "bear with mankind," and especially its most "dislikable" elements, is the mark of divine Wisdom.

The other important element of Wisdom is the individual and communal quest for spiritual growth. Samuel teaches that "Life is a school," meaning that God's divine plan has purposefully structured the world so that every event or experience has something to teach us—provided, of course, we are willing to learn. Not all people are able to follow the path of learning, and indeed some are predestined to ignorance. But for those whom God has chosen (which includes all permanent members of Haran) every event is benign and potentially enlightening. The notion of divine will and the processual orientation to life gives rise to a doctrine of progress, or "evolvement." Human society as a whole "evolves," as does Haran and each individual within it. For the community and its participants, what matters is not the degree of perfection or imperfection that exists at any given time, but the *process* of improvement through Wisdom. As long as one can be assured that oneself and one's community are on the path of Wisdom, even "sins" and "mistakes" can be seen as inevitable, divinely predestined parts of the "evolutionary" process. It is under these conditions, and under these conditions only, that life is a school.

I have dwelt on these philosophical tenets because the philosophy, and Samuel's role as its spokesman and exemplar, are supremely important to the people of Haran. Even more cogent to the present discussion is the fact that Haran's sex roles cannot be understood unless one takes seriously the relation of sex symbolism to the philosophical and cognitive system.

No Woman Can Hear the Truth

Haran sometimes summarizes its purpose and philosophy with the directive "Come out of Her." For the outsider such a phrase probably has no meaning at all, much less any relation to the religious ideology or to sex roles. In Haran the statement expresses much of Samuel's inspired teachings. In one of Samuel's religious tracts written before the commune was founded, he recounts a seminal experience:

> Standing near the back of one of these man-made worship places and meditating over the undiscovered motive that had created these so-called holy places, the Lord said to me—"COME OUT OF HER." I then saw the complete intent and hidden design that had crept upon the degenerates of this day. The construction both interior and exterior was sex-symbolism it its rankest form. Right in the heart of the Christianites' worship, molded by brick and wood, was the secret parts of the male and female anatomy. The sleepy Christianites with their pretense against immorality, were secretly carrying on their Sabbath-breaking in the symbolical sex-organs. . . . Their worship was carried on with hidden symbolism, typifying the sex act. The ignorant Preach-Her while banging his Pull-pit trying to climax his message of love to Her, shouting against lewd glorification of sex immoralities, was practicing this very thing before all, and all were ready to give in to his line, seducing them into spiritual adulteries. To interrupt him before the climax was a crime to him and her. Let him who understandeth hear—. Every man walking down the aisle (navel) was heading for the womb again. The tall circumcised and uncircumcised towers, high and visible above all the surrounding dwellings was a constant reminder to women-hood and all Sodomites as a hidden persuader toward the male organ. . . . Other buildings were constructed as women laid down on their backs. Such demoralizing corruptions are unlawful to be uttered.

In the passage above Samuel equates "Her" with the church, but Samuel's sex symbolism can operate at an even more fundamental level. In Samuel's writings and in the informal "rap sessions" by which he communicates his theology, "the Woman Mind" is a frequently used synonym for the "mind of the world" or the "mind of the flesh." The all-important duality of carnal and spiritual is very often presented by Samuel in terms of female and male. On the most abstract level, the "Woman Mind" is the strictly natural intelligence, the glorified "mind of the beast." In this abstract sense, "Woman" refers not to a human gender, but to a way of thinking, the flesh, mother earth, the natural aspect of humankind, the material creation "which all men worship." To "Come out of Her" in this sense is to forsake the material realm for the spiritual.

The use of sex symbolism, however, does not end at the metaphysical level. At another level "Her" refers to the political state and to social institutions which are created and maintained by selfish human impulses. "The state, Self's daughter, owns earthly all," one of Samuel's revealed proverbs states. Samuel contends that the "Woman Mind" is behind the state and that states show their carnal and female essence by greedily attempting to annihilate one another:

> None of the leaders can get away from their Big Mama; they're all wantin' to please Big Mama, whether it's Mama Russia, Mama America, Mama England, or Mama France. Whatever it is, they're all affixed to their Mother and it's to us a decayed world. [Drake 1969]

Woman is literally as well as figuratively involved in the power of the state since, according to Samuel, women secretly control wealth, politicians, courts, laws, and all sources of secular power. Frequently cited examples range from women's extortionistic demand for alimony to the cultivation of patriotic ideologies which send sons off to war in order to "glorify their mothers." Haran believes that all other contemporary societies are "matriarchal," and refers to them in the feminine gender.

The "Woman Mind," as the force behind social institutions including churches, is held to be the main enemy of inspired religious teaching. Samuel states that all the prophets in history have been persecuted by an essentially matriarchal authority structure and that prophetic teachings are inevitably "castrated" to become the dogma ("Dog-ma") of female-controlled churches. For Samuel, the revolt against evil is a struggle of prophetic inspiration against the "great mother":

> I'm talking of a reorderized society. I'm talking of a universal true peace, not brought by fear, where death is destroyed, where divine wisdom is leadership, where men can live as brethren ... when they're awakened. I would say mankind is asleep, and this is an inner inspiration that comes on a man when he views the great Mama, the great castration of male. When he sees his friends and himself all bowed down and crippled under this great and bestial mother, without pity, without comfort. Then he begins to think perhaps for the first time, "Well, what's the inevitable result, where's it going to, where will this mathematics of carnality end up?" And at this point—I don't call it his supreme frustration, rather it's the point of beginning again. It's his day of awareness, his day of illumination. He gets his first taste then of a mind out of this world. Now you say, "Is it within a man?" It can be both. It can be either in a man or out of a man; I have experienced both. . . . It's a reservoir of Divine Wisdom. [Drake 1969]

Although sex-based terms are frequently applied in metaphysical contexts which have little to do with what Samuel calls "natural woman"—that is, female *Homo sapiens*—it should not be assumed that Haran is indifferent to the relations of male and female in the most literal sense. "Woman" and "Her" have multiple levels of meaning, ranging from the most abstract symbolism to obvious human reference. Samuel sees his own teachings as, among other things, a true and revolutionary view of the proper roles of men and women in society.

"When you examine the relationship between the normal woman and the normal animal," Samuel once said, "you've got the same thing, identical" (Drake 1969). In the same taped interview with Carlos C. Drake (ibid.), Samuel made the following comments:

> SAMUEL: Man alone is the thinker; he alone will bring peace out of the chaos.
> DRAKE: Do you think this is inherent in the nature of man; inherent in the nature of woman?
> SAMUEL: Yes. . . . Man is the head, woman is a heart. They are not alike mentally, emotionally, or physically. What is said, "marriage is fifty-fifty," this is ignorance, it's Pig Latin.
> [A few questions later:] What men can do, women can't do, but a man can do anything a woman can do except bear a baby.

Woman has a natural mind. Like nature itself she is not intrinsically bad, but when she is allowed to control human affairs the results are unfortunate. The "Woman Mind," being encompassed in carnal nature, is motivated by the desire to dominate and to compete. Such selfish thinking can lead only to violence, capitalism, and private property. Women's impulse is to "fight it out," but, being inferior in physical strength, they enlist men to do the fighting. Women, the "power behind the throne," are said to admire violent men and to instigate competition among them. If woman cannot dominate man, says Samuel, she will try to ruin him out of spite, for "what a woman can't rule she'll try to destroy." Thus equality between men and women is impossible to achieve and dangerous to attempt.

Women are thought to be more sexual than men, and they are said to use sex as a way of manipulating men and as a way of gratifying their bestial lust. Men, who do have a healthy need for some sexual activity, must beware of its potential as a tool for "feminine" domination, and the "ladies' man" or sexual adventurer is thought to be woman's lackey.

Men too can have a bestial or natural mind—they are, after all, reared by their mothers. Yet they are sometimes capable of transcending this aspect of themselves through divine inspiration. This is what separates men from women, for women are physically tied to their emotions and physiological "cycles" and cannot escape autonomously from the carnal realm. In some very important respects, men and women are in fundamentally the same situation: each participates in a "beast" or "carnal" nature which is good in its place, but evil when it is allowed to rule; and each is capable of moving in the direction of spiritual transcendence. The agenda for this process, however, is very different for the two sexes. For a man it involves throwing off the yoke of female dominance, seeking divine Wisdom through the tutelage of an inspired patriarch, and asserting his own rightful authority as a husband, father, and ultimately, perhaps, patriarchal prophet in his own right. For a woman the path of spiritual progress is quite different. She must forsake her lust for dominance—which like all lusts is contrary to ultimate self-interest —and place herself under the "headship," or the domination, of men. Once she has taken this step she will find the place in life which she has always unconsciously desired, and will be in a position to behave according to the principles of Wisdom. Wisdom will come slowly through constant tutelage from men, and, although it is questionable just how far a woman can go, it is certain that no woman can ever achieve enough Wisdom to exercise authority over any man.

Haran considers itself to be in the vanguard of human evolution because it leads the way in constructing a society free from the rule of the "Woman Mind." In contrast to the outside world of "Skag" or "Mama Skag," where women manipulate men toward violence and exploitive ends, the men and women of Haran are able to live harmoniously under the order of divine love, which the men freely learn from Samuel and impose on the women and children by the order of "law."

It might seem that such a recently formed society as Haran could not possess the complexity, coherence, or functional integration found in more traditional societies. In fact, the intensely creative efforts of charismatic leaders like Samuel may often lead to systems of thought and social behavior that rival or even surpass traditional societies in their functional cohesiveness. In this connection it is interesting to note that Samuel, during one of his 1973 "raps," gave an account of the creation which appropriately reinforces the commune's world view. In the beginning, he said, the earth did not turn. There were no days or nights, and therefore "no time as we know it." The sun shone directly onto a single continent, and only the edges of the land mass were cool enough to support human life. Under trance, some of the women of the commune have "regressed" to ancestral lives during this period, and their reports allow for a reasonably accurate picture of prehistoric social life. There were few women at that time, and they were of little importance to the men except insofar as they reproduced the species and satisfied men's sexual and other needs. There was no marriage, but only a communal sharing of women. Women had no influence of any sort, society being entirely dominated by the men who were remarkably wise and free from carnal influences. So intelligent were the men of this period that they could communicate either telepathically or by "seed words," which held complex thoughts. Disease, the result of worry which grows from greed and hate, was virtually absent; men lived for hundreds of years. It was a golden age. For some reason, however, women began to increase in numbers and influence, and society moved toward matriarchy. Men became carnal and diseased, and history developed into a lopsided struggle between woman-ruled "society" and a succession of divinely inspired "wise men," whose usual fate was martyrdom. Even the earth itself changed; the continents split apart and drifted and the earth commenced to rotate as historical time began. Samuel sees "continental drift" theories as one of science's reluctant concessions to "true history."

Even during his ministerial days, Samuel had suggested in his writings that the biblical account of the fall was a metaphor for man's "harkening" to female influence:

> All that is external in fallen Adam's world, lay dormant within Woman. When the first Adam saw and heard Eve's SELF express words foreign to what had come from the Cherubims, he was hearkening to his own flesh (within Woman). . . .
>
> He hearkened to a VOICE of expression coming from the lid-less ARK of his wife's beastly nature. Hearkening to HER and SELF or FLESH or KNOWLEDGE (unauthorized and forbidden by the God-Head), gave him an introduction to what is the beginning of all carnal creation—the TEN TRAITS WITHIN THE EXPOSED AND UNPROTECTED HEART of HIS WIFE, which traits were to be governed by ten commandments, added because of transgressions, our school master to bring us unto Christ.

Samuel is fond of pointing out the hidden connotations of words which, he says, are vestiges of a time when wise men packed their speech with meanings now hidden to ordinary men. "Woman," for example, means "whoa, man!" or "woe, man"; "evil" is the "ill," or sickness, of "Eve"; "together" means "to-get-her," or to conquer the woman; "drama" is "draw ma," a portrayal of life in the woman-ruled world; and so on. Even such words as "*herd*" and "*Materialism*" have hidden feminine connotations. The number of these inspired etymologies is countless and always increasing.

Haran also has inspired proverbs, some of which are preserved in written form, and many of which are used in everyday speech. Like most of Samuel's teachings, the proverbs were derived from voices and other direct revelations of the divine. Not all refer to women; one, for example, says that "man is caught in the trap he sets for his brother." Many, however, do make some reference to the male-female duality. Consider, for example, the following examples from a mimeographed list circulated by Samuel:

> No woman can hear or tell the truth.
> No two women can be friends.
> No man can be equal with a woman.
> No man can trust a woman and trust God.
> Women make lies their refuge and truth their prison.
> Self first, others second, man third, is woman's world.

Some of these, particularly the first two or three, often find their way into conversation. The proverbs are used within the community in literal reference to women, but they may also refer to the behavior of "woman-minded men" or to the abstract principle of carnality. The distinction is not a very important one to the members of the community, since all these levels of meaning are thought to be interdependent.

Daily Life in Haran

Describing Haran's ideology is one thing, but how does the ideology relate to the community's behavior? True to the community's self-image, the social behavior of Haran rests firmly in the context of the complex world view described (with unavoidable brevity) above.

If "Wisdom" is the key word that Haran would use in describing its intellectual outlook, the key word in describing the social order is "patriarchy." The term "patriarchy" refers to several different but related phenomena. To begin with, it means the rule of a community by a divinely inspired "father figure" whose moral, religious, and political authority is considered binding by the members of the community. It also refers to the more general principle of respect for age—or more accurately, respect for the divine Wisdom that, for some at least, comes with age. Patriarchy also refers to the rule of men over women and, by the application of these various principles, the rule of a husband-father over his wife and children. In each case the basis for "rule" or authority is not seen as brute power or as arbitrary ascription, but as the proper deference of a lower to a higher order of divine Wisdom. As the people of Haran say, "Wisdom is our leader."

It must be understood that in Haran "rule" and "authority" mean something different from what they mean in the outside world. They are seen as based not on the will to power (which is utterly renounced as a manifestation of carnality), but on love and responsibility. Although Samuel rules over the men, and the adults over the children, and the men over the women, such a system of rule is not acknowledged as a basis for brutality or exploitation. In fact, quite the contrary. Children, for example, are not evil in themselves, but they are certainly in possession of less Wisdom than adults. Therefore, if an adult cares for a child, the adult will make that child the object of responsibility and sacrificial love, but the adult will also recognize that it would not be in the best interests of the child or of the community to let the child rule the adult. A similar relationship is believed to exist between men and women. A man should care for a woman and not abandon, brutalize, exploit, or deceive her. He must, indeed, take special responsibilities for her that he might not expect to take for another male. But for the man to let the woman rule would be to destroy them both. Haran's theory of leadership is based not on power but on the notion of sacrificial love, as expressed in Haran's scripturally derived proverb "He who hath much, much is required; but he who hath little, little is required."

Samuel is conscientious in applying this concept of leadership to himself. He commands a disproportionately small share of living space or other material rewards, and he works longer and at a greater variety of jobs—including those an outsider would call "demeaning"—than anyone else in the commune. Although his authority in the community is virtually unlimited, he avoids direct use of power and encourages the men to do "as they wish." He encourages others, by his own example, to "rise above self."

"Law," says the Haran proverb, "is for self." The men of Haran would consider it an indignity to be "placed under law." Laws and rules are, as far as the men are concerned, part of the order of "society" by which selfish interests rule and spiritual development is suppressed. They therefore strive to avoid explicit rules of conduct and try to solve all problems by creative use of the principles of Wisdom and love. Each man considers himself to be on the path of progress and interprets his own apparent misconduct, as well as that of other men, as a "burning out" of the desire for sin or as providing some important lesson for oneself and others. Social control is highly internalized, and men are inclined to be overtly tolerant of others' faults as they move along the inexorable path of overcoming their own. The resulting system of social control, too complex to receive adequate treatment here, seems effective in encouraging the men to rise above their own vices, hang-ups, social pathologies, and poor self-images, and it appears to accomplish these ends with a minimum of inner agony and overt social conflict. A man entering the Haran commune may be encouraged to see his previous "failure" in society or his unsatisfactory relationships with women as evidence of his predestined place among God's elect. The sorts of behavior which are contrary to communal life (and likely to result in unsatisfactory human relations in any group), such as selfishness, impulsiveness, emotional immaturity, competitiveness, and violence, are labeled as "feminine" traits which he is now in a position to overcome while at the same time he establishes himself as a "real man" and a developing patriarch. The men of Haran, who come from diverse social backgrounds, seem to find satisfaction in this world view.

Women are in a somewhat different position. Another Haran proverb about "law" states that it is "for women and children." Samuel seems to believe that women are less able than men to achieve the sort of autonomous self-control and self-development that so effectively inspires the men. Women, like children, are supposedly much happier and much less a threat to the social order if they are kept gently under a set of rules and restraints. The man, for his own part, is expected to behave responsibly and generously toward women and children, and to rule them gently except when their own unruliness obliges the man to take sterner action.

Thus the code of morality is different for men and women. Men are expected to be sacrificial, but always autonomous, even in their loyalty to the communal patriarch. Women, on the other hand, are supposed to be obedient. It can be seen that this set of roles follows from the perceived nature of man and woman, but the difference is also related to divine purpose: women, as Saint Paul noted, are on earth to serve their men, just as men are on earth to serve God. Though woman as a ruler is the source of worldly misery, woman as an obedient helpmate is a source of beauty and joy to God and man, and in this role she is able to find ultimate fulfillment.

The ideal of feminine obedience and subordination is expressed in many facets of communal life in Haran. The economy in 1973 was organized as a business partnership which included the adult men but not the women. In fact, the system of bookkeeping actually debited a man for the support of his wife and children despite the fact that the women worked full time at various tasks in the community. This difference is more ideal than practical, since the bookkeeping system was adopted mainly as a way of dealing with the outside, and the real economy of Haran involved a roughly equitable sharing of labor and material benefits regardless of sex and other distinctions. Still, the economic contribution of the women was somewhat devalued. On the several occasions when Samuel enumerated for visitors the various "segments" of Haran's economy, he usually omitted all those activities in which women were principally engaged.

The division of labor at Haran follows the outlines of the traditional Euro-American system. The men work at logging, sawmilling, heavy-equipment operation, business management, and those domestic tasks (such as chopping wood and butchering) traditionally performed by men. Women cook, clean, launder, can food, care for small children, and perform other traditionally "feminine" tasks. This division of labor is no accident, for the men of Haran not only see these tasks as appropriate to the sexes, but also consider the men's tasks to be those which require a higher degree of intellectual or physical prowess, and the women's tasks as those involving direct service to the opposite sex. Aside from one urgent occasion when the men and women cooperated to put up hay, the only job both sexes performed in 1972–73 was harvesting vegetables from the garden.

Not surprisingly, women are expected to have no say in political decisions of the community. Although Haran is by its own assertion a patriarchy rather than a democracy, the men do participate informally in decisions. When Samuel, for example, suggested at a gathering that the commune "give up tobacco," he took the lack of enthusiastic response as an invitation to put the proposal aside. At that very time, however, the women of the community were under a male-imposed rule against the use of tobacco, even though their lack of enthusiasm for the rule was well known.

It is good etiquette in Haran for a woman to defer to a man. Women sit in silence when men speak. If men are talking together, the women sit at the periphery and avoid unnecessary talking or shuffling; on one rare occasion when some of the women forgot themselves, I saw Samuel silence them with a clap of his hands, as one might do with preschool children. Similar behavior toward men would have been unthinkable. Such "Skag" customs as holding the door for a woman are regarded as abominations, but their reverse may be practiced: during my stay in Haran it was not uncommon for a woman, even if carrying a child or other burden, to rush ahead of a man in order to open a door for him. Even in the very relaxed and informal atmosphere of the beer parties that were common at that time, the women were expected to fetch beer for the men without being asked.

Haran's general opposition to the exercise of authority by women became something of a problem when the community was ready to establish a school for the younger children. Schooling is important for any communal society, not only because it provides socialization and training in needed skills, but also because it saves the community from the potentially disruptive effects of an outside school. For Haran, with its image of itself as a "school" and of "Skag" as a bastion of ignorance, the necessity of sending the children to school in a nearby community was quite upsetting. Haran at the time had several certified teachers, some educated at the community's own expense. Although the various legal problems and the red-tape of establishing a school were gradually being overcome, Samuel remained troubled at the prospect of having the all-important function of education overseen entirely by women. He approached various educated men, including me, with the prospect of becoming "principal." Although I pointed out that I was utterly ignorant on the subject of elementary education, Samuel said that this did not matter, as the important thing was the establishment of male authority (the community eventually found a qualified male principal and now has a legally recognized grade school).

Samuel remarked that in an ideal community such as Haran the little girls would "quickly learn their limitations," but, when the first preschool and kindergarten classes began in 1973, the community had not yet developed any explicit methods for incorporating sex-role socialization into their formal educational program. All the same, Haran commune was acutely aware of the importance of bringing children up in a way that would suit them for adult life in the community. Little boys emulated the men and played at logging while the girls occasionally were allowed to help serve the men in the dining room. I overheard one girl of grade-school age recount to another an incident in which she had asked a woman to get her something, and the woman inquired sarcastically whether she was "a little boy or a little girl." On acknowledging that she was a girl, the youngster had been told, "Then get it yourself." Peer groups have some role in socialization also, as when one eleven-year-old boy sharply ordered a girl of the same age to leave her play and fetch him a banana from the bowl at his fingertips, and she complied sullenly without being thanked. It is also true, though, that children of both sexes are warmly indulged by the adults, and in most cases I could see little difference in the way adults usually interacted with the children of the two sexes.

Adults who wish to join or to visit the community are put to work in ordinary male or female work situations, where their socialization begins. The sole criterion of whether a person is admitted to the community is, in most cases, simply a matter of whether he or she chooses to stay after being introduced to the daily life and philosophy of the commune. Men who were in the process of such introduction told me that they saw nothing but "truth" in Haran's philosophy, and if they chose not to stay it was usually for reasons given as failure to "fit in socially." I never met a man, including those with college degrees, who admitted to having ever doubted Haran's sex-role concepts. The socialization of men to their new sex roles includes learning the behavior of dominance (such as not thanking women for favors), and this aspect of male role behavior is likely to be manifested in an exaggerated form among new men —a phenomenon which long-term residents, both male and female, see as a "passing phase." Men also learn that the expectations of the masculine role involve the avoidance of violent or selfish behavior as "feminine." Even though the process of behavioral change is never completed, the cognitive identification of generosity and gentleness with masculinity quickly becomes important in structuring the behavior of male recruits.

The process of socialization for females is more difficult to discuss because there were fewer female recruits, because I had fewer opportunities to speak with them, and because women in the community tend to say what they think the men want to hear. It is significant that a substantial number of women who come to the Haran community with husbands or lovers choose to leave them rather than live in the community. Seven of the men living in Haran during my study had split with their mates in this way, and I know of similar instances which befell earlier and later members as well. Some of the single women who left during my stay had also become disillusioned by the sex-role system. However, the reputation of Haran as a patriarchal community serves to exclude from the potential recruits most men and women strongly committed to sex equality. All the same, some of the women who stay in Haran have college degrees, and one was studying the community as part of her master's thesis research in anthropology when she became "converted" to the commune's philosophy.

During my study I spoke with many of the women regarding the community and its beliefs. Most were reticent about discussing or evaluating their position in the community. "Philosophy," one of them said, "is for men." The reticence did not seem to stem from doubt or disagreement, for without much pressing on the issue all of them agreed that Samuel's philosophy was completely correct and that it had brought great satisfaction into their lives to have found their "place." One woman explained that she was, as the Haran proverb said, incapable of hearing or speaking the truth, since she was "bound up" in her "emotions and cycles." "All women are like that most of the time," she added. When asked what they liked about the community, a few spoke of the sex roles as an attraction. "Here you find real men," one woman said. Some emphasized the ideological coherence, as in the case of a woman who confessed to having been "very confused about religion" until coming to Haran. Others, however, dwelt not on the sex roles or on religion, but on the security, the social rewards, and the material advantages of living in a community. One widow pointed out that she was not beaten at Haran as she had been before joining the community, that her children were well provided for, and that she had a moderate work load and a satisfying social life. As an afterthought she added that, if her children left the community, they might become corrupted with false ideas.

The men, with the exception of a few quiet individuals, showed enthusiastic involvement in the sex-role ideology. A favorite men's pastime was discussing Haran's philosophy with Samuel or among themselves, and most of this talk involved women, sex roles, or male-female symbolism. Among themselves the men earnestly discussed the implications of the "Woman Mind" and of "Coming out of Her." Social control and the settlement of disputes among the men took place in terms of the Haran ideology, and deviant male behavior of any sort was frequently linked to "femininity." Philosophical debate usually took the form of figuring out what Samuel had said, and disagreements on these points were referred to Samuel himself for resolution. The basic tenets of the belief system were taken for granted and never challenged either in public or, as far as I could see, in private conversation. Even men who had recently joined the community seemed eager to show that they too accepted the ideas, talking about the "Woman Mind" and the desirability of keeping women in their place, or attributing all the misery of their previous lives to "matriarchy."

Samuel conveys his theology through informal sessions at which mostly men (including visitors and new members) attend. He makes a special effort to direct his solicitous attention to new members, both male and female. Such attention continues for males who stay, but Samuel is less inclined to pay particular attention to the women. "I do not waste my time," Samuel once told a visitor, "talking to women."

Haran's attitude toward marriage and the nuclear family is somewhat ambivalent. On the one hand, Samuel teaches that premarital or extramarital sex is irresponsible and carnal and that sexual relations should take place only in the context of a total moral commitment, which in Haran's interpretation means marriage. On the other hand, it is believed that women use marriage as a means of manipulating and controlling men. The apparent tension between these aspects of the marriage relationship is partly resolved by distinguishing between "legal marriage" and marriage as practiced in Haran. Legal marriage, they say, is women's way of gaining control of men and children through the courts, and as such it has been eschewed by those couples not already married when the commune was formed. Haran's practice of marriage, though involving neither ceremonies nor legal contracts, is taken very seriously. Samuel lectures the men on their responsibility to control, teach, and care for their wives. The wives, for their part, are expected to render unquestioning obedience, support, and fidelity.

Some students of communal societies may be surprised to see a commune lend such moral support to the marriage relationship, since Kanter (1972:87) and others have hypothesized the need of a communal society to avoid the strongly divisive situation that can result when loyalties are directed to one's spouse or family rather than to the whole community. Kanter has even suggested that the reason for the frequent occurrence of either free love or celibacy among many successful nineteenth-century communes is the utility of such practices in discouraging coupling and familism. Indeed, many communards of the past and of the present have seen marriage and the family as exclusive, possessive institutions inimical to successful communalism.

Has Haran departed from the path of "de-familization" that characterizes many successful communes? From Haran's own perspective, the answer is that they have not. While Haran upholds the institution of marriage, it does not invest in it the same meanings and functions that it carries in "Skag." Marriage in Haran serves to eliminate promiscuity and to encourage responsibility. It also provides a microcosm for the establishment of patriarchy (a "husband," or "hussy-band," Samuel says, is supposed to "band," or bring under his control, the unruly woman, the "hussy"). At the same time, however, there are certain things which a marriage is *not* supposed to do. It is not, above all, to be an outlet for romantic love—at least, not for the man. While women are said to be "emotional" and attached to their men, it is considered demeaning for a man to fall under the sway of romantic love. A man should "love" his wife in the sense of being affectionate and responsible; but the sort of "love" touted in popular songs and in movies is regarded in Haran as idolatry. Such love is emotional, conditional, self-glorifying, carnal, and woman-directed. Furthermore, it is dangerous. The influence that a woman can exert on a man in love is potentially destructive of brotherhood and Wisdom. A man in love with his wife is one who "worships his flesh." At best, he is temporarily insane; at worst, he is personally doomed and socially dangerous. Attachment to a wife is frequently given as a cause for the departure of former members.

A similar attitude is taken toward children. Children are, of course, to be treated with affection and responsibility; that is their due as human beings and as members of the community. But to place a special emphasis on the love of one's own children at the expense of the community is, like romantic love, a worship of one's own flesh. Women (in their weakness) might be expected to manifest such selfish love, and the community is always on guard against the excesses of their "natural inclination." Men, however, are expected to keep their commitment to the community, or "the brotherhood," foremost.

Haran's system of childrearing is intermediate between a strictly private and a fully communal arrangement. Children live with their parents until adolescence, when they may take part in peer-group sleeping arrangements with others of their sex or take up residence in dormitories with the single adults. The influence of the family is counteracted by the notion of "Superma and Superpa"—that is, the responsibility of all adults for all children. The children are well behaved and rarely need any correction, but if the occasion arises it is considered appropriate for any adult to give admonitions (corporal punishment is rare), and the parent who objects is considered to be in the wrong. Children spend much of their time in peer groups, which are seen as integral to a child's social education; interference is avoided even when the behavior becomes somewhat violent.

Housing and spatial arrangements at Haran reflect the commune's feelings about sex roles and familism. For example, single women and men sleep in separate dormitories in order to eliminate the temptation of premarital sex. Married couples are housed in small rooms within larger communal dwellings, not only for practical reasons, but also because it is thought that in separate houses the women would exert such a strong influence over their husbands that the latter would become "woman-minded" and anticommunal. In 1973 there were communal dining tables, where the men ate earlier or later than the women—an arrangement which also was thought to minimize female and family influences. Indeed, Samuel once characterized separate family rooms as a concession to the women (Drake 1969).

Haran has retained the family, but its devaluation of "flesh" and "self" and its beliefs about the relationship of men and women serve to undercut familism. Renunciation of the family, which Kanter

(1972) sees as an outcome of either free love or celibacy, is accomplished here by other means.

In assessing the overall effect of the sex-role system at Haran, it should be mentioned that women and men differ very little from one another in the amount or variety of work they do or in the amount of leisure they enjoy. The sexes are equally well fed, clothed, and provided with medical care and other material needs. More women than men in 1973 were receiving college education at community expense. Men's work in the community is more dangerous and gives rise to more work-related medical problems, and sometimes involves longer hours, than does that of the women. In the external, observable features of everyday life, there is little or nothing to mark women as an exploited group in any material sense. Yet the commune of Haran attracts only half as many women as men, a fact which Samuel takes as evidence of woman's lack of commitment to communal life. Haran's critics have proposed other explanations.

Is Haran Sexist?

The issue of sexism at Haran is not so simple as it might appear, and it depends partly on one's definition of "sexism." Kinkade (1973:169), in discussing sex roles in the Twin Oaks commune, defined sexism as "the assumption that one's overall worth is measured in terms of one's desirability to the opposite sex." According to this definition, which links sexism with heterosexual attraction, Haran would probably be rated as an antisexist group: there can be little doubt that Haran plays down the ultimate value of heterosexual attractiveness in determining anyone's "overall worth." Other definitions of sexism are, of course, possible: for example, (1) sexism is the social ascription of arbitrary privileges and limitations on the basis of sex; (2) sexism is the belief that one sex is more valuable than the other; and (3) sexism is the unfair treatment of one sex by the other.

Without having given much thought to the matter of definitions, I occasionally mentioned to Samuel that I found some of his ideas sexist. Samuel was neither surprised nor shaken to encounter disagreement from an atheist upstart, but genuinely offended by the suggestion that his philosophy was sexist. Samuel and his followers would not consider themselves sexists by any of the definitions given above. From their point of view, the accusation of sexism is based on a misunderstanding of their ideas and of reality.

Samuel and other members of Haran say that many of their critics (of whom the nearby college town harbors many) fail to understand Haran's symbolic use of terms such as "her" and "woman." "People hear us say 'No woman can hear the truth,' " says Samuel, "and they think we mean natural woman." When I challenged Samuel's aphorisms and statements about "women," he usually defended them as abstractions that do not refer to "personal" women, but rather to the principle of carnality. If any person is an object for denunciation, Samuel points out, it is not the woman but the "woman-minded man."

People who criticize Haran's "sexism" are also, Samuel says, laboring under some illusions about natural reality. The "fact" is that men and women are fundamentally different in their abilities, limitations, needs, and aspirations. Those who claim to be defending women by treating them as equals of men actually pose the greatest imaginable threat to women's welfare. The role of women in Haran, Samuel says, is not an arbitrary cultural creation, but a recognition of immutable natural realities. Working within rather than against the natural order, Haran can provide both men and women with material fulfillment and thus pave the way for the higher development of women as well as of men.

In this way the people of Haran defend themselves against not only the accusation that they have placed arbitrary limits on the sexes, but also the accusation that they are unfair or unkind to women or that they consider women inferior to men. There is no question that they believe that both women and men can be happiest under their patriarchal system. Women serve men not simply because men want it so, but because such an arrangement is the only one capable of providing fulfillment for either sex. If anyone is unkind or unfair to women, they say, it is those who deny this simple "truth."

Samuel denies that he considers women inferior to men. Even though men and women at Haran are expected to behave differently, he says, that fact in no way implies a devaluation or dislike of women. "Woman is beautiful," says Samuel. "We are *for* women— the women here are very happy, because they have found their place." Woman is not evil as such; she has a proper place in which she can be happy and useful. Like the man, the child, or any other entity in the universe, woman is destructive only when she abandons her proper place and function in the order of things. That her place involves subordination should be recognized but not regretted, and it is not a reason for despising her.

After reading my doctoral dissertation on Haran (1975), Samuel explained to me that one ought to conceive of Haran's sex roles as "complementary equality." It is a misunderstanding, he said, to think that the sexes are unequal simply because man exercises the authority. The important thing, in his view, is that each sex has an indispensable role in the order of things and that each depends on the other.

Samuel is quick to point out that the women at Haran are there of their own accord because they find their life in the community satisfying. He also maintains that women in Haran, like the men, enjoy a high standard of living and that they reap the benefits of communal cooperation in domestic chores. He notes that Haran protects its women from dangerous and inappropriate situations (he uses the example of heavy-equipment operation), while "Skag" thinks so little of its women's health or welfare that it would strip them of this protection. In sum, Haran sees itself as exhibiting a superior understanding and concern for women and men.

Haran's defense deserves a hearing. It is true, for example, that many people are unaware of the abstract symbolism implied in the term "woman" and consider Haran's ideology as no more than a monomaniacal antifeminism. It is also true that Haran sincerely believes its system of sex roles to be rewarding for both sexes, not just for men. It does indeed view patriarchy as an expression of responsibility and sacrifice rather than of exploitation and power. Certainly, if one accepts Haran's assumptions about the natural characteristics of the sexes, the commune's sexual ethics make sense.

Haran's women seem to acquiesce in the beliefs and behavior surrounding Haran's sex-role system, affirming that they are fortunate to have found their place. Even the graffiti in the women's outhouse supports the ideology:

to be	don't believe a woman's word
loyal	trust man's words
to your	
master	women should be loyal to man
be your self	as man is to God
& not act as	
some-one else	

While certain women may in fact have a need to find their "place," it appears that some of the attraction of Haran is also practical. One woman told me that she had a pleasanter, more meaningful, and more secure life in Haran than she could achieve elsewhere. Her duties were not unreasonable and her children were well provided for—something which, as a single woman, she could not expect in "Skag." Childcare, cooking, cleaning, and other domestic operations are made less burdensome through communal cooperation. Medical care and other personal needs—including support in illness and in old age—are assured. The women I spoke with said that childbirth, which is overseen by Samuel and other members of the community, is much easier at Haran than in a hospital. Concerning female subservience and the sexual division of labor, one woman who had left the community said, "Sure, the men expected me to serve them, but they worked hard—harder than I could ever work—and I appreciated it. I was glad to serve them." Despite ideas about female servitude, the women do not work harder than the men, nor do they enjoy any less than men the material rewards of living in the community. And while the subject of servitude is at hand, it might be well to remember that Haran considers servitude to one's fellows as the mark of an enlightened person.

It would be a mistake to see Haran's women as the mindless pawns of male supremacy. They can and do set limits on the demands made on them. During my stay, for example, it happened more than once that new men in the commune who were excessively rude or demanding toward the women found themselves carefully ignored by the women serving meals. In these and similar instances of female resistance to excessive demands (usually from new men), the man's "power trip" was as much the object of disapproval as was the women's response.

The argument that Haran's sex-role system is complementary rather than unequal is similar to that used in defense of certain other communal sex-role systems, most notably in Mathieu's treatment of Shiloh Farm in this volume. It is a difficult argument to evaluate. Whereas the notion of complementarity has been used to "justify" not only sex roles but also caste systems and even slavery, the fact remains that "complementarity" is not incompatible with gross inequality or blatant exploitation. On the other hand, the question of just how much "complementary" difference *is* allowable within the context of "equality" remains open. Surely, equality does not have to mean identity.

Complementarity or no complementarity, it is difficult to imagine that any of the men I knew at Haran would wish to trade places with a woman. The list of qualities that a good person ought to avoid looks very much like the list of qualities women are thought to possess. Despite the complexity of meaning associated with "woman," the fact remains that "personal woman" is thought to have a "Woman Mind," and the many proverbs referring to women's ignorance or other disabilities *are* used in Haran with reference to "personal" women. Some of the members of the community, during the period of my study, even referred to the women of the commune collectively as "the whores" and "the bitches." Haran believes in an essential tension between the sexes that rules out the possibility of "brotherhood" between them and which can be successfully resolved only by male rule. This view stands in stark contrast to their idealization of universal brotherhood among the men. By defining "woman" as the harbinger of all those values that the commune opposes—and even using the phrase "the brothers" as synonymous with the community —Haran has created a situation in which women cannot participate in the spirit of the community in the same sense that men can. While men are freed from "law," women are placed under it, like children. The autonomous personal development which so greatly appeals to the men has as its female counterpart a degree of subordination which no man at Haran would ever accept.

It should be pointed out that the description and commentary given here concerning Haran's sex roles are in some respects unacceptable to the people of Haran. For one thing, they feel that their concepts are too subtle and too imbedded in their social life to lend themselves to this sort of abstract, intellectualized treatment. The people of Haran are also profoundly skeptical of the motives and the insights of conventional scholarship. Furthermore, they maintain that no nonbeliever, not even one who has lived in the community, can have more than a superficial and distorted view of their beliefs. For these same reasons they usually avoid any mention of their religious ideas or sex-role ideas in presenting themselves to the public. In some ways the contrast between my own views of Haran and those of its members reflect the classic dilemma of involvement versus distance, each of which carries its own advantages and biases. I was not surprised, then, to see that the community received my writings with mixed feelings and that, although they were hospitable to me in later visits, they declined to give permission for further research. They argued, rightly, that ethnographic work did little to serve their own interests. Indeed, they are to be commended for their tolerance of my study in the first place.

Since 1973 a number of things in Haran have changed. The commune itself has grown, and its logging industry has expanded rapidly. A large number of new children have been born, and the school has received attention in the local press as an "experimental" school. Samuel teaches that evolutionary change is the essence of all things, and in 1973 he remarked that the character of Haran would gradually be refined as the commune drew in more "intellectuals" and "philosophers." During my recent visit to the community, both Samuel and his daughter, who is working toward an advanced degree in educational psychology, maintained that the commune had indeed evolved, and they also hinted that a softening of the sex-role ideology might be part of the commune's evolutionary change. This is not inconceivable, for the statements Samuel made in early writings and in the 1969 and 1970 interviews with Professor Drake seemed harsher than those in the period of my study, and the commune's publicity tracts seem more determined than ever to avoid mention of sex roles and to play down the importance of religious ideologies or charismatic leadership. Nevertheless, Samuel's daughter did acknowledge that the male-female ratio in 1978 remained at the 1972 level of two to one, a fact which seems to reflect the community's continuing lack of appeal to women.

Haran's combination of male rule with communal equality seems such an unlikely one that it appeared at first to be the ethnographic phenomenon every fieldworker dreams of: a surprising and fundamentally unique society. The notion that successful communes simply must have sex equality is strongly reinforced by the contemporary writings of many communalists and sociologists, but, as the introduction to this volume has shown, many modern communes do favor inequality of the sexes. Both the nineteenth and the twentieth centuries have seen communes with sex roles ranging from liberal to conservative, but the contemporary communes, especially the religious communes of the 1970s, seem to present something unprecedented: communes which take the subordination of women as an explicit and central part of their program for human improvement. The modern communal movement, unlike that of preceding centuries, encounters a social milieu in which changing sex-role behavior (not just changing ideals) is a major cause of conflict for the average person, whether male or female. While some communes attribute the conflict to our excessively conservative, sexist ideas, others place the blame on our excessive tampering with the roles that God and nature ordained for the sexes. Those which take the first view may have the advantage of allegiance from the intellectual community, but their members must, like the people of Twin Oaks, struggle constantly with ethical issues and attitudinal changes whose resolutions cannot be simple. Hierarchal sex roles, like authoritarian answers of any kind, carry the advantage of unambiguous clarity, finality, and decisiveness. They might even allow some people a temporary or permanent respite from psychological distress. When the spokesman of the ideology manifests confidence and serenity, as Samuel does, people in "need of something to believe in," as one Haran man put it, "find it hard to think that any of it could be wrong."

Is Haran Successful?

Some writers have maintained that a commune cannot be "truly successful" or, as Kanter put it, "very communal" (1973:305) unless it recognizes equality of the sexes; according to such an argument, Haran must be an unsuccessful community. Haran, however, has a countertheory: since brotherhood and community are threatened by woman's power, "patriarchy" is a prerequisite for communal success. Haran explains the collapse of some earlier communes as the inevitable outcome of their "woman-rule," and for the same reason it doubts the viability of many modern communal ventures. If these two conflicting "theories" show nothing else, they point to the fragility of arguments about communal "success."

The terms "successful" and "unsuccessful" are frequently bantered about in almost all sociological discussions of communalism, despite the fact that judgments of this sort are almost entirely absent from other fields of sociology and anthropology. Perhaps the normative element can be justified by the fact that communes are "intentional" societies, and one is therefore entitled to ask whether the "intentions" have been fulfilled. By such reasoning, however, it follows that a commune ought to be evaluated only in terms of its goals and that the people best qualified to do the evaluating are the communalists themselves. Evaluating a commune in its own terms might raise some interesting questions; for example, if the com-

mune's stated goals include a short survival span (as in the case of
one "hippie" urban religious group whose leader I interviewed),
would the community then become "unsuccessful" by existing too
long? Haran's own goals are the acquisition of what they call "Wisdom" and the preparation for the Apocalypse. In their own terms
they are succeeding in both, but, if the Apocalypse fails to material-
ize, will the continued existence of the commune become "failure"?

Sociologists have attempted to apply various "objective" criteria
for success. Kanter, for example, in her salutory work on the sociology of communes, adopted the criterion of twenty-five years' existence as the mark of "success." But even if sociologists were all
agreed on the ultimate utility of that criterion, it will be some time
before anyone can apply it to modern communes, most of which have
been founded within the past ten or fifteen years. In the meantime
we might rely on size as a measure of success, but what of those
communes (including Haran) that have deliberately limited their
rate of growth? If size is the criterion, Haran and most religious
communes would on the whole be rated as more successful than the
majority of non-religious communes involving middle-class profes-
sionals, but the members of the latter groups are frequently very
successful in accomplishing their own goals. Similarly, one could
apply the criterion of social cohesiveness (whatever that might be),
but in so doing might load the argument in favor of authoritarian
groups for whom cohesion is a specialty. Haran is, by almost any
conceivable definition of social cohesiveness, a cohesive group.

If we define historical influence on mainstream society as a measure of success, we would do well to suspend judgment; but we could
note in passing that Haran has received its share of attention as a
commune and has turned more heads than any ordinary village of
similar size could have done. And what about utility to the mainstream society? The people of Haran claim to be happier and more
effective members of their social group than they could ever have
become in "Skag," and if they are correct Haran might be said to
perform some positive function as a therapeutic institution.

Personal growth is often cited both as a communal goal and as a
measure of success. If personal growth is to be measured either by
the community or by the individuals in it, the testimony of Haran
members concerning themselves and their fellows seems to indicate
a high success. But, if the evaluation comes from some other source,
what shall that source be?

Unless one begins with some carefully stated criteria (and possibly even then), the hidden agenda of most discussions of communal "success" is usually the evaluation of a commune in relation to the analyst's own "enlightened" concept of what a society ought to be. In that sense there is often less difference than one might suppose between utopian philosophy and the sociology of communes. While we are on the subject of "enlightened" preferences, let me state unequivocally that my own is for complete equality of the sexes; yet it must be recognized that Haran and many other communes are attracting members to a very different view. Local folklore and national press notwithstanding, the members of the Haran commune, at least, are not under "hypnosis." They have chosen what to them is a satisfying life, and they seem as aware of their choices as anyone else. Thus the notion that one's favorite liberal values are upheld and protected by some law of sociological necessity is a bit of complacency which, today of all times, we can scarcely afford.

ACKNOWLEDGMENTS

I am particularly grateful to "Samuel" and the people of "Haran" for their openness and tolerance toward my ethnographic work and for their critical reading of this and others of my writings; and to Carlos C. Drake for his comments on my initial field reports and for his sharing of interview data collected in 1969 and 1970.

REFERENCES CITED

Drake, Carlos C.
   1969   Taped interviews with "Samuel" and other members of "Haran."
          Unpublished.
   1970   Taped interviews with "Samuel" and other members of "Haran."
          Unpublished.
Kanter, Rosabeth Moss
   1972   Commitment and Community: Communes and Utopias in Sociological Perspective. Cambridge, MA: Harvard Univ. Pr.

Kanter, Rosabeth Moss
   1973   Family Organization and Sex Roles in American Communes. *In* Communes: Creating and Managing the Collective Life, ed. R. M. Kanter. New York: Harper and Row.
Kinkade, Kathleen
   1973   A Walden Two Experiment: The First Five Years of Twin Oaks Community. New York: Morrow.
Wagner, Jon
   1975   Haran: Charisma and Ideology in a Contemporary American Commune. Ph.D. diss., Indiana Univ.
Weber, Max
   1968   On Charisma and Institution Building. Selected Papers, ed. S. N. Eisenstadt. Chicago and London: Univ. of Chicago Pr.

About the Contributors

JON WAGNER is Associate Professor of Anthropology and Chairman of the Department of Sociology and Anthropology at Knox College. In addition to undertaking his 1972–73 fieldwork in the Haran Commune, he has visited other contemporary religious communes, has directed two historical archeological digs in the nineteenth-century Swedish commune of Bishop Hill, Illinois, and has lectured and written articles on both contemporary and historical communes and religious movements. In line with his broader interest, in religion and social change, he is a coauthor of the book *Politics and Change in the Middle East.* He was also one of the founders of the Society for Humanistic Anthropology and is former Associate Editor of the *Anthropology and Humanism Quarterly.*

HANS A. BAER is Assistant Professor of Anthropology in the Department of Sociology and Anthropology at the University of Southern Mississippi. He has taught at St. John's University, George Peabody College for Teachers, and Kearney State College. During the 1979–80 academic year, he was a post-doctoral fellow in the medical anthropology program at Michigan State University. In addition to his fieldwork among the Levites, he has conducted research on a Hutterite colony in South Dakota and was involved in an evaluation of a community health program designed for rural towns in Southern Utah. More recently, he has been involved in research on Black Spiritual churches and their complex of folk healers in various southern and northern cities as well as on the recent organizational growth of osteopathic medicine in the United States. He is the author of articles on the Hutterites, Levites, and the Black Spiritual movement in which he addresses such issues as culture change, religious conversion, revitalization movements, and the role of religion in the Black community.

ILSE MARTIN is a doctoral candidate in anthropology at the University of California, Los Angeles. Her doctoral dissertation, based on data collected during five months' resident fieldwork in the "New Age" commune described in this volume, focuses on the relationship between symbol systems and action and on the mechanisms employed for maintaining the community. She has also studied ethnicity in Guatamala, and her other interests include cognitive and psychological anthropology.

BARBARA MATHIEU is a doctoral candidate in anthropology at the University of California, Los Angeles. Her master's thesis was a comparative study based on 1977 fieldwork in two intentional communities: Shiloh Farms, described in this volume, and a group of five families in the process of establishing a community. She is now engaged in a doctoral field study on certain aspects of architectual esthetics in three communities, including a Hutterite village.

BRYAN PFAFFENBERGER teaches anthropology at Knox College. He first became interested in Stephen Gaskin's remarkable ministry while studying anthropology as an undergraduate at the University of California, Berkeley, where he received the Ph.D. degree in 1977. His field research (attendance at Gaskin's Monday Night Class meetings and interviews with Monday Night Class members) was undertaken during 1970 and 1971. His interest in Hinduism and Buddhism, which had played no small role in his interest in Gaskin's ministry, led eventually to field research among the Hindus of northern Sri Lanka (formerly Ceylon). His publications stress the role of religious beliefs and practices in human social life, and in particular the relationship between religion and forms of political authority.

MERRILL SINGER received the Ph.D. degree in anthropology in 1979 from the University of Utah. He currently teaches in the Department of Anthropology at The American University in Washington, D.C. His interest in communalism and new religious movements has led to research on several different sectarian groups, including the Lubavitcher Chassidim, Christian Scientists, and the Allredites, a polygynous Mormon schism in Utah. His wider interests include the relationship between religion and alcoholism, the political economy of medicine, and the class character of American society. He has published in several social science and psychology journals.